AP*
Q&A
WORLD HISTORY

600 QUESTIONS AND ANSWERS

Christina Giangrandi, M.A.

D1453248

BARRON'S

About the Author
Christina Gentile Giangrandi earned a Bachelor of Arts *cum laude* in History and Secondary Education from Hofstra University in 2003 and a Master of Arts from Stony Brook University in 2006. She has taught AP World History in the Smithtown Central School District in New York since 2004, in addition to the New York State Education Department Global History course and a Holocaust, Genocide, and Human Rights elective. She has served as an AP Reader for the College Board and attended numerous professional development courses and study tours in order to further her knowledge of World History.

Acknowledgments
The author would like to thank Jennifer Giammusso for her assistance in managing the editorial process and developing the manuscript. I am also grateful for the help given by Annie Bernberg regarding copyright information and permissions, and would like to extend my appreciation to those who developed the artwork and were involved in the production of the book.

This work would not have been possible without the support of my husband, Andrew, my children, Marco and Arianna, and the numerous family members that helped care for them while I spent many hours working on this book. I also am grateful for my students over the years, who have motivated me and provided insight into common struggles with this rigorous course.

All inquiries should be addressed to:
Barron's Educational Series, Inc.
250 Wireless Boulevard
Hauppauge, New York 11788
www.barronseduc.com

Library of Congress Control Number: 2017964142

ISBN: 978-1-4380-1125-7

PRINTED IN CANADA
9 8 7 6 5 4 3 2 1

Contents

Introduction

HOW TO USE THIS BOOK

Congratulations on taking the first step in preparing for this rigorous but rewarding course! This book can be used from the beginning of your AP World History course to prepare for quizzes and unit exams as well as to prepare for the AP Exam itself. It is organized by time period and key concept, and is designed to continue the development of historical thinking skills that you are learning in class, while providing exposure to AP-style questions, with both correct and incorrect answers explained to maximize your understanding of the content and concepts.

Each chapter begins with the key concept outline from the College Board that is the backbone of the course, along with a quick summary of the key concepts. Chapters 1–3 include multiple-choice questions (MCQs) and short-answer questions (SAQs), while Chapters 4–19 include MCQs, SAQs, and long essay questions (LEQs), and some include a document-based question (DBQ).

MULTIPLE-CHOICE QUESTIONS

Multiple-choice questions are based on a stimulus such as a primary source, secondary source, map, image, or graph, and appear in sets of 2–5 questions similar to the AP Exam. While the stimulus is generally from the time period and key concept that the chapter is focused on, some of the questions may ask you to draw from knowledge of earlier or later periods, or from different key concepts. If you come across a question on material you have not studied yet, skip it for now and you can return to it at a later time. Like the AP Exam, the questions are designed to test your application of historical reasoning skills and knowledge of key concepts rather than your ability to recall facts. You will likely encounter names, documents, and dates that you are not familiar with, but do not let that discourage you. If you study the key concept outline, complete the practice questions to hone your skills, and read the answers explained carefully, you will be successful on the exam. It should be noted that the multiple-choice section of the exam is not a reading comprehension test, nor can you ignore the stimulus. Instead, each question requires information that is not in the passage and application of a skill such as primary sources analysis, contextualization, comparison, causation, and change and continuity over time. It is suggested that you complete a question set before reading through the answers explained, as sometimes the explanation for one question may help you answer another in the set. If you are using this book for review for your class assessments as well as AP Exam review, it is suggested that you write down the answers on a separate piece of paper so you can use them for practice at a later time. Remember that if you complete the questions while studying the time period in class, the questions will seem easier than if you do them weeks or months later in preparation for the AP Exam.

SHORT-ANSWER QUESTIONS

In this book, short-answer questions may span more than one time period as they would on the exam, and align with the question types you would see for each time period. It is suggested that you use a separate piece of paper to write your responses before checking the answers explained. There are 35 SAQs in this book, and if you are limited on time you may want to focus on the ones from time periods 3–6 (Chapters 7–19) because three questions will be from that time frame, although a student has an option to choose a question from periods 1–3.

On the AP Exam there will be three short-answer questions. Question 1 will be based on a secondary source or two secondary sources from course content in periods 3–6, and will ask you to explain a historical interpretation, compare two interpretations, and/or explain how historical evidence backs a claim made in the source. Question 2 will be based on a primary or visual source from time periods 3–6, and you are expected to go beyond quoting from the source and provide specific evidence to answer the tasks. It will assess the historical reasoning skill of comparison or change and continuity over time. You will choose either question 3 from periods 1–3 or question 4 from periods 4–6. There will not be a stimulus and the question will require demonstration of the skill of either comparison or change and continuity over time. The skill assessed in question 3 will differ from the skill in question 2. In other words, if question 2 is comparative, then question 3 will be change and continuity over time and vice versa.

On the AP Exam, a response that would earn credit must be in complete sentences and should address all three tasks (parts a, b, and c) clearly. It is best to provide as much specific historical knowledge as you can, and it is a good idea to letter your responses so you are sure to address each distinct task. If it is based on a primary or secondary source, the source must be referred to but the response must go beyond quoting or paraphrasing the passage. If it is based on an image, it must be specifically referred to in the response but the response must go beyond merely describing the image.

LONG ESSAY QUESTIONS

The long essay question assesses the skills of causation, comparison, and change and continuity over time. Even though you probably do not want to write more essays than what is required in your class, the key to success is practice! If you can set a timer and attempt to plan and write a response in about 40 minutes, you will be much more comfortable with it on the exam. There are 32 LEQ questions in this book, however, so you may want to focus on writing full essays for the time period you feel most comfortable with and planning the others because you will have a choice of questions on the exam. If you are using this book for exam review and are limited in time, then practice thesis writing and outlining the essay. Although it may be tempting to just read the answer explanation, it is better if you attempt to answer the question from memory first to determine which key concepts and time periods you should focus on when reviewing.

On the exam, you will have a choice of three questions, all addressing the same historical reasoning skill and theme. One option will be from periods 1–2, one will be from periods 3–4, and one will be from periods 5–6. A strong response on the LEQ must have a thesis that makes a historically defensible claim, which should be stated in the introduction, but can receive credit in the conclusion. Often when writing in a limited time frame, the thesis may be like a draft in the introduction, but you may be able to make a more definitive claim with specific evidence once you have written the essay. It must also explain how relevant historical context relates to the topic of the question by specifically discussing broader events or historical processes that occurred before, during, or after the time frame of the question (known as contextualization). You must also show how stated evidence links back to your thesis or claim, and demonstrate analysis. Analysis varies depending on the type of essay you are writing, but generally explains why changes, continuities, similarities, differences, causes, or effects occurred. Finally, the essay must show an understanding of historical complexity, which can be done in a variety of ways. For more information, please see the explanation of the rubric below. You will not receive the rubric with the point values on the exam itself, so familiarize yourself with the points on the rubric so that you do not forget anything on exam day.

LONG ESSAY QUESTION RUBRIC
(6 points possible)

Rubric Requirement	How to Earn the Point	Additional Information
Thesis/Claim 1 point	The thesis must respond directly to the question with a claim that is historically accurate and addresses a reasoning skill (comparison, continuity and change over time, causation)	Should be 1–2 sentences that directly responds to the question, and must be located in the introduction or conclusion. Always attempt your thesis in the introduction, and try to make it more specific in your conclusion.
Contextualization 1 point	The essay must describe a broader historical context that relates to the question.	Should have at least 2–3 detailed sentences that discusses how the topic of the question relates to broader events or processes of the time period. Ideally should be located in the introduction before your thesis.
Evidence 1 point	The essay must give detailed examples of evidence that relates to the question.	Should provide evidence from one or more societies relating to the question.
Use of Evidence to Support an Argument 1 point	The evidence must be used to prove the argument stated in the thesis.	Specific evidence should be used to substantiate your claim or thesis. It differs from the previous point in that it explains fully how the evidence relates to the changes/continuities, similarities/differences, or causes/effects stated in the thesis.

Historical Reasoning 1 point	The essay must use a reasoning skill that addresses the question to organize the argument.	Depending on the question, the reasoning skill may be comparison, change and continuity over time, or causation. Rather than simply providing evidence, the essay must use it to show changes/continuities, similarities/differences, or causes/effects.
Historical Complexity 1 point	The essay must show a complex understanding of the main topic of the question by introducing evidence that shows other sides of the argument or addresses nuances of an issue.	This understanding should be demonstrated as part of the argument, not simply in a sentence or two to address the point. The best way to approach it is to examine similarities if the question asks for differences, continuities if it asks for changes, and effects if it asks for causes. You may also explain how the argument relates to other periods (synthesis), modifying the argument by examining exceptions to it, or by examining different themes related to the argument (for example, economic issues if the question is politically focused).

DOCUMENT-BASED QUESTIONS

In this book, document-based questions generally focus on the key concept of the chapter they appear in, but may include content from other concepts or time periods. It is strongly suggested that you spend about 15 minutes reading and annotating the documents and practice writing the essay in about 45 minutes. There are 8 within this book, and the more full essays you can write, the better! Otherwise, planning the essays and practicing document analysis is helpful. As with the long essay question, it is best to attempt analysis yourself before reading the explanation provided.

On the exam, the DBQ essay will have seven documents from time periods 3–6 and will assess your ability to develop an argument that is backed with analysis of historical evidence. The documents can include written materials or visuals, such as charts, images, or data. A good response on the DBQ essay must make a claim that responds directly to the question. Similar to the long essay, it must also explain how relevant historical context relates to the topic of the question by specifically discussing broader events or historical processes that occurred before, during, or after the time frame of the question (known as contextualization). You must also show how evidence from at least six of the documents supports your thesis or claim, and go beyond just describing the document. Describing a document is explaining what happened, while analyzing a document is explaining why it matters and how it relates to your claim or argument. For three of the documents, you must explain how the purpose, point of view, audience, and/or historical situation is relevant to the argument. One piece of evidence outside of what is presented in the documents must be included, but it must support the argument, and it cannot be information used to earn another point. For example, information used to explain the broader historical context cannot also be used to earn the point for evidence beyond the documents. For more information about the components being scored, please see the detailed rubric that follows this section.

DOCUMENT-BASED QUESTION RUBRIC
(7 points possible)

Rubric Requirement	How to Earn the Point	Additional Information
Thesis/Claim 1 point	The thesis must respond directly to the question with a claim that is historically accurate and addresses a reasoning skill (comparison, continuity and change over time, causation).	Should be 1–2 sentences that directly responds to the question, and must be located in the introduction or conclusion. Always attempt your thesis in the introduction, and try to make it more specific in your conclusion.
Contextualization 1 point	The essay must describe a broader historical context that relates to the question.	Should have at least 2–3 detailed sentences that should discuss how the topic of the question relates to broader events or processes of the time period. Ideally should be located in the introduction before your thesis.
Use of the Documents to Support an Argument 2 points	The essay must give detailed examples of evidence that relates to the question. One point is earned for using three documents, and two points are earned for using six documents to support the stated argument.	To earn one point, the essay must describe, not quote, three documents. To earn two points, the essay must use six documents as evidence for the argument, rather than merely summarizing them.
Evidence Beyond the Documents 1 point	One piece of concrete evidence must be provided that supports the argument.	The "outside" evidence must add to the argument, and cannot be the same evidence used for contextualization or sourcing. It should add to the stated argument and must be more than a passing mention.
Analysis/Sourcing of the Documents 1 point	For three of the documents, an analysis of the significance of the historical situation, audience, point of view, and/or purpose must be explained.	Analysis must go beyond attribution, or simply identifying. The significance, or reason why the source is important in understanding the document, must be explained. A stronger analysis may use more than one element, such as purpose and audience.
Historical Complexity 1 point	The essay must show a complex understanding of the main topic of the question by introducing evidence that shows other sides of the argument or addresses nuances of an issue.	This understanding should be demonstrated as part of the argument, not simply in a sentence or two to address the point. This could include comparing documents in order to support your argument, examining change over time in the set of documents, explaining the reason why a document may represent an exception to your argument, or examining causes of the event that the question focuses on. You may also explain how the argument relates to other periods (synthesis), modifying the argument by examining exceptions to it, or by examining different themes related to the argument (for example, economic issues if the question is politically focused).

FORMAT OF THE AP EXAM

There are two sections of the exam, with two parts within each section. Between the sections of the exam you are given a ten-minute break.

Section	Number of Questions	Time Allotted	Percentage of Score
I, Part A: Multiple-choice questions	55	55 minutes	40%
I, Part B: Short-answer questions	3	40 minutes	20%
II, Part A: Document-based question	1	60 minutes, including a 15-minute reading period	25%
II, Part B: Long essay question	Choose 1 of 3 questions	40 minutes	15%

SCORING OF THE AP EXAM

Individual parts of the exam are weighted, and scores are calculated based on a complicated formula that is converted to scores from 1 to 5. Scores are set each year based on the result of the group of students who took that particular exam, and are aligned with the performance of students enrolled in courses at the college level.

You will not see your scores on individual sections. Scores are generally interpreted as:

5: Extremely well qualified. Equivalent to an A in a college course, and accepted by many institutions for credit or some kind of benefit, such as course substitution.

4: Well qualified. Equivalent to an A–, B+, or B in a college course, and accepted by many higher-level institutions for credit or benefit.

3: Qualified. Equivalent to B–, C+, or C in a college course, and may be accepted for credit or benefit.

2: Possibly qualified, and rarely accepted for credit or benefit.

1: No recommendation. Not accepted by institutions.

Course Periodization

The course is divided into 6 historical periods, as shown on the next page. Major developments have been listed, but be aware that your teacher may have used different names, as historians do.

Period	Dates	Weight
Period 1: Technological and Environmental Transformations - Paleolithic Age and Early Humans - The Neolithic Revolution - River Valley and other Early Civilizations	up to c. 600 B.C.E.	5%
Period 2: Organization and Reorganization of Human Societies - The Development of Major Belief Systems - The Rise and Fall of Classical Empires - The Beginnings of Interregional Trade	c. 600 B.C.E. to c. 600 C.E.	15%
Period 3: Regional and Transregional Interactions - Post-Classical States - Intensification of Interregional Trade - New Forms of Labor	c. 600 to c. 1450 C.E.	20%
Period 4: Global Interactions - European Age of Exploration - Rise of Truly Global Trade - Centralization of Imperial Rule - Expansion of Labor Systems	c. 1450 to c. 1750 C.E.	20%
Period 5: Industrialization and Global Integration - The Rise of Industrialization - European Imperialism - The Decline of Land-Based Empires - Global Migrations	c. 1750 to c. 1900 C.E.	20%
Period 6: Accelerating Global Change and Realignments - Global Conflict and Global Capitalism - Decolonization - Technological Innovations and Rise of Nation States - Globalization	c. 1900 to the present	20%

Note: Full Answers Explained with detailed explanations why the incorrect answers are wrong can be found at *www.barronsbooks.com/ap/docs/h72bdc/QA1125.pdf* or by using the QR code below.

PERIOD 1
(UP TO C. 600 B.C.E.)
The Period of Technological and Environmental Transformations

The Peopling of the Earth and the Paleolithic Age

Answers for Chapter 1 are on pages 311–312.

 Key Concept 1.1—Throughout the Paleolithic era, humans developed sophisticated technologies and adapted to different geographical environments as they migrated from Africa to Eurasia, Australia, and the Americas.

I. Archaeological evidence indicates that during the Paleolithic era, hunting-forager bands of humans gradually migrated from their origin in East Africa to Eurasia, Australia, and the Americas, adapting their technology and cultures to new climate regions.

   A. Humans developed increasingly diverse and sophisticated tools—including multiple uses of fire—as they adapted to new environments.

   B. People lived in small groups that structured social, economic, and political activity. These bands exchanged people, ideas, and goods.

In the Paleolithic era, or Old Stone Age, early humans gradually populated the globe. These groups were nomadic due to the need to follow animal herds, worked together to secure food through hunting and foraging, and had to adapt to the local climate and landscape.

Questions 1–4 refer to the map below.

EARLY HUMAN MIGRATION

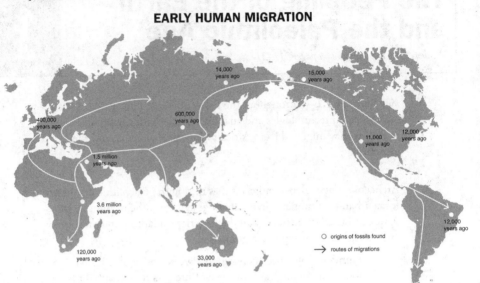

1. **Which of the following conclusions can be supported by the map?**

   (A) Humans failed to migrate into areas of North America until after the end of the Ice Age.

   (B) Human migration occurred gradually from Africa to Eurasia and then to the Americas.

   (C) Migrations occurred relatively rapidly due to the need to find additional resources.

   (D) Early humans originated in Eastern Asia and moved eastward into the Americas.

2. **Which of the following most directly contributed to the movement of people as reflected on the map?**

   (A) Early humans domesticated draft animals, which allowed for many of the early migrations.

   (B) The adoption of agriculture led to the growth and movement of early human populations.

   (C) Early humans responded to strains on local resources, which may have precipitated migration.

   (D) The end of the last Ice Age allowed early humans to move more easily from one region to another.

3. Which of the following was most likely a direct result of the patterns reflected on the map?

   (A) The establishment of sedentary communities organized through a rigid system of social hierarchy

   (B) The development of new technologies that allowed for adaptations to a wide range of environments

   (C) The development of long-distance interregional trade networks

   (D) The creation of advanced navigational technologies that led to increased communication and economic exchange among regions

4. Which of the following characterizes the nature of early human societies in the era depicted on the map?

   (A) Civilizations developed among foragers due to the need for militaries to protect settlements.

   (B) Small groups of foragers lived in isolation, with very little contact with other groups.

   (C) Settlements characterized by monumental architecture and large militaries formed.

   (D) Small nomadic clans traveled seasonally to procure food.

Questions 5–7 refer to the following two images.

Image 1

DRAWINGS OF PALEOLITHIC ERA ARTIFACTS

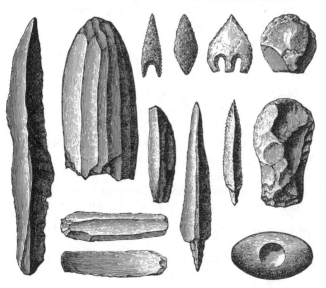

Image 2

CAVE PAINTINGS FROM THE MAGURA CAVE IN BULGARIA, EASTERN EUROPE, CIRCA 8000 B.C.E.

5. The objects in Image 1 best support which of the following conclusions about life in the Paleolithic Age?

   (A) Humans developed a variety of stone tools to adapt to their surroundings.
   (B) Metallurgy enabled early humans to develop more sophisticated tools.
   (C) Tools were primarily developed to control draft animals.
   (D) Technologies were mainly developed independently, with very little diffusion from one group to another.

6. The drawings shown in Image 2 best illustrate which of the following about early humans?

   (A) The centralized nature of government was reflected in artistic traditions.
   (B) Systems of written symbols were used to record knowledge of animal herds.
   (C) Monotheistic belief systems with icon paintings were common.
   (D) Art reflected interactions between humans and animals.

7. When taken together, the two images best support which of the following conclusions?

   (A) Early humans adapted their technology and cultures to new regions as they migrated.
   (B) Early humans lacked the intellectual ability to adapt to the environment effectively.
   (C) Early humans mainly lived in regions in which caves were accessible.
   (D) Early humans primarily gathered small plants to sustain themselves.

Questions 8–10 refer to the passage below.

"Lower and Middle Paleolithic hominins [humans] were capable of at least some innovation, of solving novel adaptive problems by altering their behavior. They learned to cope successfully with a wide range of environments, particularly after 800,000 years ago when they began to establish populations in the northern temperate zones. They also were able to exploit stones with very different working properties to produce tools, and to maintain a supply of tools and raw materials even when suitable stone was scarce. The proposition that early humans could maintain highly conservative traditions over such long spans of time and over such a large area implies a very high level of fidelity in cultural transmission."

L. S. Premo and Steven Kuhn, anthropologists, 2010

 Tip: Look at the questions before reading a passage to help guide you as to what to look for.

8. Based on Premo and Kuhn's argument, why were humans of the Paleolithic Age able to produce stone tools consistently?

   (A) Conservative attitudes led to a lack of innovation.
   (B) Stone was widely available in the various environments where humans settled.
   (C) Groups were able to transfer knowledge due to contact with one another.
   (D) Knowledge of stonemaking was developed by individual clans.

9. The migrations described in the passage were most likely due to which of the following?

   (A) The need for land for cultivation as populations grew
   (B) The need for resources to sustain their populations
   (C) The desire to escape control of an authoritarian government
   (D) The development of specialized jobs leading to more opportunities

10. Human behavior described in the passage best supports which of the following conclusions about the Paleolithic era?

   (A) People of the Paleolithic era had limited capacity to modify their environments effectively.
   (B) Groups exploited one another due to the demand for a large workforce.
   (C) Large groups adopted sedentary lifestyles due to their adaptations to the environment.
   (D) Early humans were creative in adapting to different geographic settings from savanna to tundra.

Questions 11–12 refer to the image below.

**STONE SCULPTURE NAMED VENUS OF WILLENDORF,
C. 24,000–22,000 B.C.E.**

11. The sculpture is best seen as evidence of which of the following?

    (A) The political dominance of women in Paleolithic society
    (B) The use of art to glorify rulers
    (C) The development of tools to manipulate available resources
    (D) The availability of ample leisure time in the Paleolithic era

12. A historian would most likely use the image as support for which of the
    following assertions?

    (A) Women played a prominent role in cultural life of the Paleolithic era.
    (B) Paleolithic society was matriarchal in nature.
    (C) Women did not play a role in securing resources in the Paleolithic era.
    (D) Gender roles were strictly defined as patriarchal societies developed.

Questions 13–15 refer to the passage below.

"Nomadic tribes ventured across the landscape, driven neither by the
spirit of adventure nor the pursuit of profit nor the desire to accumulate property, but merely in hope of survival. Traditions, habits,
and customs were almost reverently passed on from one generation
to the next because, primitive and unimaginative as these behavioral
guidelines might appear today, they were considered to be proven

means of keeping small groups of people alive. Relative isolation reduced possibilities for advances in technological know how or what institutionalists call the community of knowledge.

In this pre-scientific era, superstition and ceremonialism held an enormous influence over the thought patterns people possessed. Superstition was rampant as primitive humans sought to understand that which they could not explain in practical terms. Various gods were invented to account for the inexplicable; the sun god, for example, was somewhat logically worshipped as the source of life. Wind, water, and thunder were similarly judged to possess divine attributes. In place of critical or scientific reasoning, prehistoric humans often resorted to imaginary explanation and false belief rooted in lack of understanding (or, put more bluntly, ignorance)."

Joseph E. Pluta, economist, "Technology vs. Institutions in Prehistory," *Journal of Economic Issues* (*http://www.informaworld.com*), Taylor and Francis Ltd., 2014

Tip: Underline or highlight the main ideas of longer passages to save time rereading the excerpt. On the AP Exam, your pacing should be approximately 1 minute per question!

13. **Based on Pluta's argument, why did habits and rituals guide early humans?**

 (A) The people lacked the capacity to use logic to understand the environment.
 (B) These practices ensured the preservation of early humans.
 (C) The development of organized belief systems promoted these rituals.
 (D) These practices were encouraged by the political system.

14. **The beliefs about divine forces as discussed in the passage is best understood in the context of which of the following?**

 (A) The development of organized belief systems that provided an ethical code by which to live
 (B) The rise of large settlements dependent on favorable conditions for agriculture
 (C) The necessity of natural forces in ensuring successful crop harvests
 (D) The precarious relationship between foragers and the environment

15. Based on the passage and on your knowledge of world history, which of the following could be best inferred about the lifestyle of early humans?

    (A) The sedentary nature of Paleolithic era humans caused a strong belief in nature gods.
    (B) The superstitions and customs of early humans were rooted in scientific understanding.
    (C) The nomadic lifestyles of early humans prevented the formation of organized belief systems.
    (D) The rise of monotheistic belief systems centered on a sun god arose in the Paleolithic era.

    (Answers on pages 311–312.)

The Neolithic Revolution and Early Agricultural Societies

CHAPTER 2

Answers for Chapter 2 are on pages 312–313.

Key Concept 1.2—Beginning about 10,000 years ago, some human communities adopted sedentism and agriculture, while others pursued hunter-forager or pastoralist lifestyles—different pathways that had significant social and demographic ramifications.

I.   The Neolithic Revolution led to the development of more complex economic and social systems.

    A.   Possibly as a response to climatic change, permanent agricultural villages emerged first in the lands of the eastern Mediterranean. Agriculture emerged independently in Mesopotamia, the Nile River Valley, sub-Saharan Africa, the Indus River Valley, the Yellow River (or Huang He) Valley, Papua New Guinea, Mesoamerica, and the Andes.

    B.   People in each region domesticated locally available plants and animals.

    C.   Pastoralism developed in Afro-Eurasian grasslands, affecting the environment in a variety of ways.

    D.   Agricultural communities had to work cooperatively to clear land and create the water control systems needed for crop production, drastically affecting environmental diversity.

II. Agriculture and pastoralism began to transform human societies.

    A.   Pastoralism and agriculture led to more reliable and abundant food supplies, which increased the population and led to the specialization of labor, including new classes of artisans and warriors and the development of elites.

    B.   Technological innovations led to improvements in agricultural production, trade, and transportation.

    C.   Patriarchal forms of social organization developed in both pastoralist and agrarian societies.

At the end of the last Ice Age, around 8000 B.C.E., warmer temperatures and more land availability contributed to the rise of agriculture. Cultivation arose in a variety of regions independently, and the domestication of animals led to the rise of pastoral societies. Sedentary lifestyles arose as farmers needed to remain with their land, crops, and animals. Pastoral groups were nomadic in order to remain with their herds. As a result of these new lifestyles and more reliable food sources, population growth and job specialization occurred. In order to adapt to local environments and improve efficiency, new technologies developed, such as pottery and wheels. Gender inequalities arose as methods of securing food became more labor intensive, and property rights and inheritance were reflected in legal codes.

Questions 16–19 refer to the map below.

THE NEOLITHIC REVOLUTION, C. 10,000 B.C.E. TO C. 2000 B.C.E.

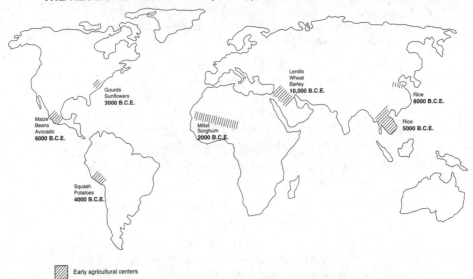

Early agricultural centers

16. Which of the following most likely contributed to the adoption of agriculture throughout the world as depicted on the map?

    (A) Increasing contacts throughout the period between the Americas and Afro-Eurasia
    (B) Development of new agricultural tools, such as the heavy plow
    (C) Climatic changes that allowed for agricultural production and created a need to find alternate food sources
    (D) Increases in public works provided by the state, including irrigation

17. Cultivation of crops depicted on the map had all of the following effects EXCEPT

    (A) decreased reliance on cooperation among community members
    (B) technological innovations, such as the plow and pottery
    (C) patriarchal societies developing as gender roles changed
    (D) increased population density and the rise of early villages

18. Which of the following conclusions is best supported by the information on the map?

(A) Knowledge of agriculture spread mainly as a result of interregional contacts.

(B) People in each region domesticated what was locally available in their environments.

(C) The vast majority of the world's population adopted agriculture by 6000 B.C.E.

(D) Agriculture was first adopted in Southeast Asia.

19. Based on your knowledge of world history, which of the following best describes the lifestyle of human communities in the areas on the map that did not adopt agriculture?

(A) Sedentary cultivators settled in mountainous areas.

(B) Foraging clans settled in river valleys.

(C) Sedentary herders occupied the plains of Europe.

(D) Pastoralism developed on the Eurasian steppe.

 Tip: A key to answering question set 16–19 correctly is knowing the different characteristics of foraging, pastoral, and cultivating societies, as well as the different names that could be substituted for each of these societies.

Questions 20–22 refer to the following two images.

Image 1

ARCHAEOLOGICAL SITE AT CATALHÖYÜK, TURKEY, CIRCA 7500 B.C.E.

The image shows a Neolithic settlement featuring several homes of varying sizes clustered together with roof access into the buildings.

Image 2

RE-CREATION OF A TYPICAL HOME OF CATALHÖYÜK, TURKEY, CIRCA 7000 B.C.

20. Which of the following contributed most directly to the rise of Neolithic settlements as shown in the images?

    (A) Surpluses of grain and domesticated animals
    (B) Development of iron metallurgy
    (C) A diminished reliance on the natural environment
    (D) The growth of specialized labor

21. The architectural style depicted in Image 1 best supports which of the following conclusions?

    (A) Early cities were constructed communally by a strong central government.
    (B) Cities of the Neolithic era reflected the egalitarian nature of society.
    (C) Job specialization led to social stratification.
    (D) Technologies, such as sewers and running water, were common in early cities.

22. The objects in Image 2 best illustrate which of the following developments in the period before 600 B.C.E.?

    (A) Agriculture led to more reliable and abundant food supplies.
    (B) Agricultural communities worked cooperatively to create water control systems.
    (C) Technological innovations led to improvements in agricultural production and trade.
    (D) Clearing of land for agriculture drastically affected environmental diversity.

Questions 23–25 refer to the passage below.

"The agriculture practiced by these first women farmers and their children, producing enough food for subsistence only, must be distinguished from that agriculture which developed out of subsistence farming and which produced surpluses and fed nonfarming populations in towns. The first type is commonly called horticulture and is carried out with hand tools only. The second is agriculture proper, and involves intensive cultivation with the use of the plow and (where necessary) irrigation. In areas like the hilly flanks of the fertile crescent in the Middle East, horticulture moved fairly rapidly into agriculture as it spread to the fertile plains. As we shall see, trading centers grew into towns and cities needing food from the countryside. Women and children could not unaided produce the necessary surpluses, and by the time the digging stick had turned into an animal-drawn plow, they were no longer the primary workers of the fields.

The simpler form of farming continued in areas where the soil was less fertile, and particularly in the tropical forest areas of Africa. Here soils were quickly exhausted, and each year the village women would enlist the men in helping clear the fields which were then burned over in the slash-and-burn pattern which helped reconstitute the soils for planting again.... Where the simple horticultural methods continued to be used, women continued as the primary farmers, always with their children as helpers. In a few of these societies women continued also in the positions of power; these are usually the tribes labeled by ethnologists as matrilocal."

Elise Boulding, historian, *The Underside of History:*
A View of Women Through Time, 1976

23. **Based on Boulding's argument, the rise of patriarchal societies were most clearly influenced by which of the following?**

    (A) The religious beliefs regarding the role of women in Mesopotamia
    (B) The characteristics of the physical environment in which the societies developed
    (C) The type of political system that dominated the region
    (D) The rise of strong militaries that were male dominated

24. The agricultural methods of tropical areas described in the passage best illustrate which of the following continuities in world history?

    (A) The negative impact of human activity on the environment
    (B) The persistence of patriarchy through the twentieth century
    (C) The primitive technologies used for cultivation in tropical climates
    (D) The negative effects of overpopulation on the environment

25. Based on the passage, it can be inferred that patriarchal societies were more likely to develop in which of the following?

    (A) Berber nomads of the Sahara region
    (B) Pastoralists on the Eurasian steppe
    (C) Foragers of sub-Saharan Africa
    (D) Sedentary cultivators of East Asia

 Tip: To grow your vocabulary, circle any word you are unsure of, look it up, and keep a list that you can review before the exam.

Questions 26–28 refer to the excerpt below.

"Hail to thee, O Nile! Who manifests thyself over this land, and comes to give life to Egypt! Mysterious is thy issuing forth from the darkness, on this day whereon it is celebrated! Watering the orchards created by Re, to cause all the cattle to live, you give the earth to drink, inexhaustible one! Path that descends from the sky, loving the bread of Seb and the first-fruits of Nepera, You cause the workshops of Ptah to prosper!

Lord of the fish, during the inundation, no bird alights on the crops. You create the grain, you bring forth the barley, assuring perpetuity to the temples. If you cease your toil and your work, then all that exists is in anguish. If the gods suffer in heaven, then the faces of men waste away."

Excerpt from *Hymn to the Nile*, c. 2100 B.C.E.

26. The power of the deities described in the passage most strongly supports which of the following statements about the Nile River civilization?

    (A) The inhabitants mainly practiced monotheism.
    (B) The religious beliefs were closely tied to agriculture.
    (C) The inhabitants viewed gods as punitive rather than beneficial.
    (D) Government had a role in overseeing cultivation.

27. **A historian would most likely use this passage to illustrate which of the following?**

    (A) The emergence of social hierarchies based on wealth
    (B) The negative effect of flooding on bird populations
    (C) The precarious nature of early civilizations' relationship to their physical environment
    (D) The rise of record keeping in early civilizations

28. **Which of the following was an important similarity between agricultural communities, such as those along the Nile, and pastoral societies in this era?**

    (A) The populations grew due to more reliable food sources.
    (B) Centralized governments formed bureaucracies.
    (C) Specialization of labor led to more egalitarian societies.
    (D) Poor sanitation in urban areas led to disease.

Questions 29–30 refer to the passage below.

"In Mesopotamia, the flood was the enemy. The Mesopotamian deities who ruled the waters, Nin-Gursu and Tiamat, were feared. The forces of nature were often evil. Life was a struggle. In Egypt, on the other hand, life was viewed as a cooperation with nature. Even the Egyptian god of the flood, Hapi, was a helpful deity, who provided the people's daily bread. Egyptian priests and priestesses were much more at ease with their world than were their Mesopotamia counterparts. And, partly because of their different experiences with the rivers, the Meso-potamians developed a civilization based on cities, while the Egyptians did not. From the first Sumerian city-states on the lower Euphrates to the later northern Mesopotamian capital of Babylon, civilization was the product and expression of city life. Egyptian civilization, in contrast, was the creation of the pharaoh's court rather than of cities. Beyond the court, which was moved from one location to another, Egypt remained a country of peasant villages."

Kevin Reilly, world historian, *The West and the World:
A History of Civilization*, 1989

29. **Based on Reilly's argument, belief systems of Mesopotamia and Egypt were most clearly influenced by which of the following?**

    (A) The differing levels of urbanization in the two civilizations
    (B) The emergence of social hierarchies in both due to unequal distribution of surplus food
    (C) Dependence on agriculture for survival that led to a view of gods as malevolent in both civilizations
    (D) Environmental factors that determined the relationship with deities in their respective civilizations

30. **The passage best illustrates which of the following processes in the period before 600 B.C.E.?**

    (A) The development of pastoral societies on the Eurasian steppe as animals were domesticated
    (B) The rise of long-distance trade networks as agricultural settlements producing a variety of goods
    (C) Agricultural communities working cooperatively to clear land
    (D) Rulers of early states often claiming divine connections to power

    (Answers on pages 312–313.)

The Rise and Interactions of Early Agricultural, Pastoral, and Urban Societies

CHAPTER 3

Answers for Chapter 3 are on pages 313–315.

Key Concept 1.3—The appearance of the first urban societies 5,000 years ago laid the foundations for the development of complex civilizations; these civilizations shared several significant social, political, and economic characteristics.

I. Core and foundational civilizations developed in a variety of geographical and environmental settings where agriculture flourished.

   • Mesopotamia in the Tigris and Euphrates River Valleys

   • Egypt in the Nile River Valley

   • Mohenjo-Daro and Harappa in the Indus River Valley

   • Shang in the Yellow River (Huang He) Valley

   • Olmec in Mesoamerica

   • Chavin in Andean South America

II. The first states emerged within core civilizations in Mesopotamia and the Nile River Valley.

   A. States were powerful new systems of rule that mobilized surplus labor and resources over large areas. Rulers of early states often claimed divine connections to power. Rulers also relied on the support of the military, religious, or aristocratic elites.

   B. As states grew and competed for land and resources, the more favorably situated had greater access to resources, produced more surplus food, and experienced growing populations, enabling them to undertake territorial expansion and conquer surrounding states.

   C. Pastoralists were often the developers and disseminators of new weapons and modes of transportation that transformed warfare in agrarian civilizations.

III. Culture played a significant role in unifying states through laws, language, literature, religion, myths, and monumental art.

   A. Early civilizations developed monumental architecture and urban planning.

B. Systems of record keeping arose independently in all early civilizations and writing and record keeping subsequently spread.

C. States developed legal codes that reflected existing hierarchies and facilitated the rule of governments over people.

D. New religious beliefs that developed in this period—including the Vedic religion, Hebrew monotheism, and Zoroastrianism—continued to have strong influences in later periods.

E. Interregional cultural and technological exchanges grew as a result of expanding trade networks and large-scale population movements, such as the Indo-European and Bantu migrations.

F. Social hierarchies, including patriarchy, intensified as states expanded and cities multiplied.

In the centuries following the Neolithic Revolution, villages and cities developed, inevitably leading to the emergence of complex civilizations around the world. Surplus food, favorable locations for resources, and larger populations were all factors that contributed to the dominance of certain states over others. Interactions with pastoral groups often led to the spread of military technologies, such as bows and iron weapons, and to the spread of new methods of transportation, such as chariots. These early civilizations were often characterized by monumental architecture, record keeping, social hierarchies, organized governments, and belief systems that were often tied to natural surroundings. Interregional trade and regional migrations connected some of these civilizations, allowing for the transfer of knowledge.

Questions 31–33 refer to the passage below.

195. Anyone assaulting his father shall suffer the loss of his hands.

196. Anyone destroying the eye of another shall suffer the loss of an eye as punishment therefor.

197. If anyone fractures the bones of another, the guilty one, upon conviction, shall have his bones fractured in punishment therefor.

198. If anyone destroys the eye of a freedman or fractures the bones of a freedman, he, upon conviction thereof, is to pay 1 mina of silver.

199. If anyone destroys the eye or fractures the bones of anyone's slave, he, upon conviction thereof, is to pay half of his value [to the owner of the slave].

200. If anyone knocks out the teeth of one, his equal [in rank], his teeth are to be knocked out, upon conviction of the offence.

201. If he has knocked out the teeth of a freedman, he is to pay one-third of a mina of silver.

202. If anyone commits assault and battery upon the person of another one of higher rank than himself, he is publicly to receive 60 lashes with the oxhide [upon conviction of the offence]."

Hammurabi's Code, Babylonian legal code, 18th century B.C.E.

31. **The consequences imposed by Hammurabi's Code most strongly illustrates which of the following about Babylonian society?**

   (A)   The social hierarchy was marked by inequalities.
   (B)   Society was relatively egalitarian in nature.
   (C)   Slavery was the most common form of labor.
   (D)   The society was patriarchal.

 Tip: If two answers are complete opposites, such as choices (A) and (B) in this question, one of them is usually the answer!

32. **A historian would most likely use this passage to illustrate which of the following?**

   (A)   The relatively high literacy rates of ancient Mesopotamians due to the need to interpret the laws
   (B)   The development of legal codes that reflected existing hierarchies
   (C)   The authoritarian nature of early governments due to the control of all surplus food
   (D)   The development of monetary systems in early civilizations due to the rise of law codes

33. **In addition to establishing systems of rules as demonstrated in the passage, most rulers of early civilization used which of the following as a source of political legitimacy?**

   (A)   The separation of religion and government
   (B)   The protection of conquered groups
   (C)   The establishment of republican political institutions
   (D)   The claim of links to divine power

Questions 34–36 are based on the following two images.

Image 1

STONE RELIEF SHOWING A PROCESSION OF PALACE OFFICIALS OF THE HITTITE PERIOD, 8TH CENTURY B.C.E.

Image 2

STONE CARVING SHOWING ASSYRIAN CHARIOTS, MESOPOTAMIA, CIRCA 4000 B.C.E.

34. The carving in Image 1 best illustrates which of the following continuities in world history?

(A) The use of art by governments to foster nationalism among their populations

(B) The power of states based on the use of violence by rulers

(C) The use of art and ceremony to glorify rulers

(D) The dependence of artists on royal patronage for their livelihoods

35. The carving in <u>Image 2</u> best illustrates which of the following characteristics of early Mesopotamian civilization?

   (A) Rulers of early states often claimed divine connections to power.
   (B) Governments relied on the support of a large priestly class.
   (C) New forms of transportation, often spread by pastoralists, transformed warfare.
   (D) Monumental architecture unified the population.

36. When taken together, the two images best support which of the following conclusions?

   (A) Mesopotamian society used technological innovations and strong rule to help the civilization thrive.
   (B) Mesopotamian society was highly militaristic and conquered much of Eurasia.
   (C) Mesopotamians developed a monotheistic belief system with rulers who claimed connections to the divine.
   (D) Mesopotamians benefited from contact with East Asia due to the diffusion of technology.

Questions 37–40 refer to the passage below.

August is Wên the king;

Oh, to be reverenced in his glittering light!

Mighty the mandate that Heaven gave him.

The grandsons and sons of the Shang,

Shang's grandsons and sons,

Their hosts were innumerable.

But God on high gave His command,

And by Zhou they were subdued.

By Zhou they were subdued;

Heaven's charge is not forever.

The knights of Yin, big and little,

Made libations and offerings at the capitol

What they did was to make libations

Dressed in skirted robe and close cap.

O chosen servants of the king,

May you never thus shame your ancestors!

   The Ode to King Wên, c. 600 B.C.E., Zhou dynasty, China

Tip: If there is vocabulary in a passage that you are unsure of, try to infer whether the word is positive or negative based on context. If that does not help, focus on what you know. You do not need to understand every single word in order to answer the question.

37. Which of the following conclusions about the Zhou dynasty is most directly supported by the passage?

   (A) Belief systems had little influence on the development of states during the period.
   (B) The establishment of monarchies created stability by reducing the likelihood of rebellion.
   (C) A lack of central government resulted in political upheaval.
   (D) Rulers legitimized their power by claiming connections to divine power.

38. Rulers of states similar to those described in the passage often depended on which of the following in the period before 600 B.C.E.?

   (A) The support of the elite merchant class to sustain the state financially
   (B) The support of the military to maintain power and authority
   (C) The support of pastoralists to protect imperial borders
   (D) The support of the peasantry to build monumental architecture

39. Based on the passage, which of the following could be best inferred about the Shang and the Zhou dynasties?

   (A) The Shang were more stable than the Zhou because they had the support of the priestly class.
   (B) The Zhou ruled more effectively than the Shang through a centralized bureaucracy.
   (C) The Zhou had greater access to resources, allowing them to overthrow the Shang.
   (D) The Shang placed more emphasis on ancestor veneration than did the Zhou.

40. Ideas similar to those expressed in the passage have directly contributed to the development of which of the following aspects of later Chinese imperial history?

   (A) The overthrow of rulers perceived to be ineffective due to the concept of the dynastic cycle
   (B) The selection of bureaucrats based on results of the civil service examination system
   (C) The elimination of the threat of rebellion against established imperial families
   (D) The idea that emperors are subject to a different set of ethical standards than the rest of the population

Questions 41–42 refer to the map below.

LONG-DISTANCE MIGRATIONS, C. 4000 B.C.E. TO C. 600 B.C.E.

⟶ Indo-Europeans

·--› Bantu

41. Which of the following factors contributed most to movement of Indo-European and Bantu populations as shown on the map?

(A) More reliable food sources led to population growth and demand for more land.

(B) Innovations in agriculture, such as the heavy plow and crop rotation, led to population growth.

(C) New military technologies enabled both groups to conquer and establish empires.

(D) Maritime innovations, such as the lateen sail, enabled these groups to travel longer distances.

42. Based on the map and on your knowledge of world history, which of the following best describes the effect of the Bantu and Indo-European migrations?

(A) The disappearance of previously established trade networks

(B) The spread of language and technologies to regions beyond their origins

(C) The creation of the first trade links between Europe and Asia

(D) The expansion of maritime trade due to navigational innovations

Questions 43–45 are based on the images below.

Image 1

PYRAMIDS AT GIZA, EGYPT, CONSTRUCTED CIRCA 2500 B.C.E.

Image 2

REMAINS OF THE ZIGGURAT OF WARKA, PRESENT-DAY IRAQ, ORIGINALLY BUILT CIRCA 4500 B.C.E.

43. The object in Image 1 best illustrates which of the following characteristics of early civilizations?

    (A) Interregional trade networks allowed for the diffusion of knowledge of engineering.

    (B) Availability of leisure time enabled peasants to develop monumental architecture.

    (C) Large-scale building projects were carried out by a large urban working class.

    (D) Monumental architecture often reflected religious beliefs.

44. The object in Image 2 best illustrates which of the following continuities in world history?

    (A) Religious buildings were often constructed by a large priestly class.
    (B) States often used monumental architecture to demonstrate their power.
    (C) Belief systems often reflected the architectural styles of the civilization.
    (D) Architects were influenced by Mesoamerican building styles.

45. When taken together, the two images best support which of the following conclusions?

    (A) Egyptian and Mesopotamian societies mobilized surplus labor and resources.
    (B) Egypt and Mesopotamia had similar belief systems as reflected in their monumental architecture.
    (C) Egyptian and Mesopotamian governments used record keeping to facilitate public works projects.
    (D) Egypt and Mesopotamia benefited from pastoral nomadic technologies.

 Tip: Often with these types of questions, two choices correctly describe the societies. However, only one answer is linked back to the images. You must always consider what the images are showing and draw conclusions from them. See the answers explained for this question.

Short-Answer Questions

Answer all parts of the question that follows.

46. a) Identify ONE change in economic activity that occurred as a result of the Neolithic Revolution.

    b) Explain ONE reason why the Neolithic Revolution changed economic patterns.

    c) Explain ONE continuity in lifestyles from the Paleolithic era through circa 3000 B.C.E.

Answer all parts of the question that follows.

47. a) Identify ONE way pastoral and agricultural societies interacted in the period 8000–600 B.C.E.

    b) Explain ONE similarity between pastoral and agricultural societies in the period 8000–600 B.C.E.

    c) Explain ONE difference between pastoral and agricultural societies in the period before 600 B.C.E.

Answer all parts of the question that follows.

48. a) Identify ONE change that occurred following the Neolithic Revolution that led to the rise of complex civilizations.

b) Explain ONE reason why complex civilizations developed in river valleys following the Neolithic Revolution.

c) Explain ONE continuity that occurred in the period c. 8000–600 B.C.E.

(Answers on pages 313–315.)

PERIOD 2
(c. 600 B.C.E.–600 C.E.)
Organization and Reorganization of Human Societies

The Development and Codification of Religious Traditions

CHAPTER

4

Answers for Chapter 4 are on pages 316–320.

Key Concept 2.1—As states and empires increased in size and contacts between regions intensified, human communities transformed their religious and ideological beliefs and practices.

I. Codifications and further developments of existing religious traditions provided a bond among people and an ethical code to live by.

    A. The association of monotheism with Judaism further developed with the codification of the Hebrew Scriptures, which also reflected the influence of Mesopotamian cultural and legal traditions. The Assyrian, Babylonian, and Roman Empires conquered various Jewish states at different points in time. These conquests contributed to the growth of Jewish diasporic communities around the Mediterranean and Middle East.

    B. The core beliefs outlined in the Sanskrit scriptures formed the basis of the Vedic religions—developing later into what was known as Hinduism, a monistic belief system. These beliefs included the importance of multiple manifestations of brahman and teachings about dharma and reincarnation, and they contributed to the development of the social and political roles of a caste system.

II. New belief systems and cultural traditions emerged and spread, often asserting universal truths.

    A. The core beliefs preached by the historic Buddha and collected by his followers in sutras and other scriptures were, in part, a reaction to the Vedic beliefs and rituals dominant in South Asia. Buddhism branched into many schools and changed over time as it spread throughout Asia—first through the support of the Mauryan emperor Ashoka, and then through the efforts of missionaries and merchants and the establishment of educational institutions to promote Buddhism's core teachings.

    B. Confucianism's core beliefs and writings originated in the writings and lessons of Confucius. They were elaborated by key disciples, including rulers such as Wudi, who sought to promote social harmony by outlining proper rituals and social relationships for all people in China.

    C. In major Daoist writings, the core belief of balance between humans and nature assumed that the Chinese political system would be altered indirectly. Daoism also influenced the development of Chinese culture.

    D. Core beliefs of Christianity were based on the teachings of Jesus of Nazareth as recorded by his disciples and their belief in his divinity. Christianity drew on Judaism as well as Roman and Hellenistic influences. Despite initial Roman imperial hostility, Christianity spread through the efforts of missionaries, merchants, and early martyrs through many parts of Afro-Eurasia and eventually gained Roman imperial support by the time of Emperor Constantine.

    E. Greco-Roman religious and philosophical traditions offered diverse perspectives on the study of the natural world, the connection to the divine, and the nature of political power and hierarchy. Some of these perspectives emphasized logic, empirical observation, and scientific investigation.

    F. Art and architecture reflected the values of religions and belief systems.

III. Belief systems generally reinforced existing social structures while also offering new roles and status to some men and women.

    A. Confucianism emphasized filial piety.

    B. Some Buddhists and Christians practiced a monastic life.

IV. Other religious and cultural traditions continued and in some places were incorporated into major religious traditions.

    A. Shamanism, animism, and ancestor veneration continued in their traditional forms in some instances, and in others were incorporated into other religious traditions.

As states grew and empires developed, organized belief systems and religions formed that offered universal truths to believers. These belief systems and religions united populations and provided a moral code to guide daily living. Belief systems were often embraced by governments seeking to enhance their own power and usually reflected existing social hierarchies and economic systems. These religions shaped cultural traditions throughout history. These cultural traditions continue to shape the world today.

Questions 49–52 refer to the passage below.

"I say: Promote the worthy and the capable without waiting for them
to rise through the ranks. Dismiss the unfit and incapable without
waiting for even a single moment... Transform the ordinary people
without waiting for government controls. If social divisions are not
yet set, then take control of illuminating the proper bonds. Even the
sons and grandsons of kings, dukes, gentry, and grand ministers, if
they cannot submit to ritual and *yi*, should be assigned the status
of commoners. Even the sons and grandsons of commoners, if they
accumulate culture and learning, correct their person and conduct,
and can submit to ritual and *yi*, should be assigned the status of prime
minister, gentry, or grand ministers. And so, for those engaging in
vile teachings, vile doctrines, vile works, and vile skills, and for those
among the common people who are rebellious and perverse, give them
each an occupation and teach them, and take a while to wait for them."

Xunzi, Chinese philosopher, circa 250 B.C.E.

49. According to the passage, Xunzi supported an approach to government
    that most clearly reflected the principles of

    (A) Confucianism
    (B) Legalism
    (C) Daoism
    (D) Buddhism

50. Ideas similar to those in the passage have directly contributed to the
    implementation of which of the following by the Han dynasty?

    (A) The practice of foot binding
    (B) A strict social hierarchy
    (C) An imperial examination system
    (D) Military conscription

51. A historian would most likely use this passage to illustrate which of the
    following?

    (A) The brutality of imperial rule in China
    (B) The emergence of patriarchal values during the Han dynasty
    (C) The diffusion of ideas from South Asia to East Asia
    (D) The concerns regarding proper behavior in China

52. Xunzi's idealized vision of Chinese society as described in the passage <u>differs</u> most strongly from the values of which of the following belief systems?

(A) Christianity
(B) Hinduism
(C) Buddhism
(D) Islam

Questions 53–55 refer to the excerpts below.

[Excerpt 1] "Beloved-of-the-Gods, King Piyadasi [Ashoka], speaks thus: To do good is difficult. One who does good first does something hard to do. I have done many good deeds, and, if my sons, grandsons and their descendants up to the end of the world act in like manner, they too will do much good. But whoever amongst them neglects this, they will do evil. Truly, it is easy to do evil . . . ."

[Excerpt 2] "Beloved-of-the-Gods, King Piyadasi, desires that all religions should reside everywhere, for all of them desire self-control and purity of heart. But people have various desires and various passions, and they may practice all of what they should or only a part of it. But one who receives great gifts yet is lacking in self-control, purity of heart, gratitude and firm devotion, such a person is mean."

Excerpts from *Edicts of Mauryan Emperor Ashoka*
(reigned 269 B.C.E. to 232 B.C.E.)

 Fun Fact: Ashoka inscribed his edicts on large rock pillars, which were scattered throughout the empire for all of his subjects to see.

53. The discussion of good deeds referred to in the <u>first excerpt</u> was most likely influenced by which of the following developments in the period before 600 B.C.E.?

(A) The Hindu concept of karma
(B) The Confucian idea of filial piety
(C) The Zoroastrian concept of dualism
(D) The Buddhist concept of reincarnation

54. The practice of religion as described in the <u>second excerpt</u> is best understood in the context of which of the following?

(A) The conversion of merchants in South Asia to Islam
(B) The large Hindu population of the Mauryan Empire
(C) Ashoka's goal of promoting religious uniformity
(D) The arrival of Christian missionaries

55. The edicts issued by Ashoka most clearly reflect which of the following patterns in world history?

    (A) The influence of religion on social hierarchies

    (B) The role that religious leaders have played in government systems

    (C) The influence of belief systems on legal systems

    (D) The impact of laws on the formation of new religions

Questions 56–58 are based on the images below.

Image 1

**YUANTONG BUDDHIST TEMPLE, CHINA,
BUILT CIRCA 9TH CENTURY C.E.**

Image 2

**STATUE NEAR MAHABODHI TEMPLE, INDIA, ORIGINALLY
COMMISSIONED BY EMPEROR ASHOKA IN THE 3RD CENTURY B.C.E.**

56. The building in <u>Image 1</u> best illustrates which of the following processes in world history?

    (A) The spread of Chinese values throughout Asia
    (B) The diffusion of architectural styles as religions spread
    (C) The influence of Indian political systems on neighboring societies
    (D) The diffusion of religion due to contacts through trade networks

57. The object in <u>Image 2</u> best illustrates which of the following patterns in world history?

    (A) The power of states was based on the ability of rulers to control religion.
    (B) Rulers used art to glorify themselves.
    (C) Rulers used religious imagery to enhance their political standing.
    (D) Governments used art and architecture as propaganda.

58. When taken together, the two images best support which of the following continuities in world history?

    (A) Belief systems contributed little to artistic expression of societies.
    (B) Art and architecture reflected the values of religions and belief systems.
    (C) Belief systems rarely spread outside of their place of origin.
    (D) Religious practices remained consistent as belief systems spread.

Questions 59–61 are based on the excerpt below.

"I approached Ekron and slew the governors and nobles who had rebelled, and hung their bodies on stakes around the city. The inhabitants who rebelled and treated [Assyria] lightly I counted as spoil. The rest of them, who were not guilty of rebellion and contempt, for whom there was no punishment, I declared their pardon. Padi, their king, I brought out to Jerusalem, set him on the royal throne over them, and imposed upon him my royal tribute. As for Hezekiah the Judahite, who did not submit to my yoke: forty-six of his strong, walled cities, as well as the small towns in their area, which were without number, by levelling with battering-rams and by bringing up siege-engines, and by attacking and storming on foot, by mines, tunnels, and breeches, I besieged and took them. 200,150 people, great and small, male and female, horses, mules, asses, camels, cattle, and sheep without number ..."

Excerpt from *The Sennacherib Prism*, an Assyrian
account of their siege of Jerusalem, circa 701 B.C.E.

59. **A historian would most likely use this excerpt to illustrate which of the following about the period before 600 B.C.E.?**
    - (A) Warfare in this period combined military force with diplomacy.
    - (B) Military technology failed to facilitate the expansion of an empire.
    - (C) States of this period lacked military organization and strategy.
    - (D) The expansion of states led to competition among groups for resources.

60. **Based on the excerpt, which of the following can be inferred about Assyrian military policies?**
    - (A) Diplomacy could be used to avoid conquest.
    - (B) Surrender to the Assyrians led to complete loss of local control by existing states.
    - (C) Those who cooperated with the Assyrians were more likely to avoid harsh treatment.
    - (D) The Assyrians established tributary relationships with all of the groups they conquered.

61. **Which of the following best describes an important long-term effect of the expansion of the Assyrian Empire?**
    - (A) The diffusion of navigational technologies throughout the Mediterranean basin
    - (B) The creation of the first written law code to unify the region
    - (C) The establishment of Jewish diasporic communities as a result of Assyrian military conquest
    - (D) The transmission of polytheistic religious beliefs to Western Europe

Questions 62–65 refer to the passage below.

"The self embodied in the body of every being is indestructible;
you have no cause to grieve for all these creatures, Arjuna!
Look to your own duty; do not tremble before it;
Nothing is better for a warrior than a battle of sacred duty.
The doors of heaven open for warriors who rejoice
to have a battle like this thrust on them by chance.
If you fail to wage this war of sacred duty,
you will abandon your own duty and fame only to gain evil.
People will tell of your undying shame,
and for a man of honor, shame is worse than death."

Bhagavad Gita, ancient Indian text, circa 4th century B.C.E.

62. Ideas expressed in the passage formed the basis of which of the following belief systems?

    (A) Zoroastrianism
    (B) Hinduism
    (C) Sikhism
    (D) Animism

63. Which of the following conclusions about Indian society during the period before 600 B.C.E. is most directly supported by the passage?

    (A) The founding of new religious traditions challenged existing customs.
    (B) The concepts of dharma and reincarnation were reflected in written traditions.
    (C) Religious traditions were influenced by cross-cultural interactions.
    (D) Cultural traditions influenced military strategies.

64. The ideas expressed in the passage contributed to the development of which of the following?

    (A) The Hindu belief in reincarnation
    (B) The rise of patriarchal cultural practices, such as *sati*
    (C) The Buddhist principle of nirvana
    (D) The concept of *moksha*

65. Compared to the actions described in the passage, Buddhist teachings <u>differed</u> in that they

    (A) rejected the belief in reincarnation
    (B) advocated monasticism for all followers
    (C) promoted the concept of dharma
    (D) rejected the caste system

Questions 66–68 refer to the map below.

THE SPREAD OF EARLY CHRISTIANITY AND BUDDHISM

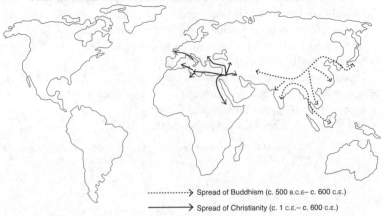

·············▷ Spread of Buddhism (c. 500 B.C.E.– c. 600 C.E.)

──────▷ Spread of Christianity (c. 1 C.E.– c. 600 C.E.)

66. The paths of Christianity and Buddhism as shown on the map best reflect which of the following?

    (A) Merchants actively spread religion in order to enhance their political standing.
    (B) Missionaries often had the support of the empires in which they lived.
    (C) Trade networks facilitated the spread of belief systems.
    (D) Geographic features prevented the spread of religions beyond their places of origin.

67. Which of the following factors contributed most to the spread of Christianity as depicted on the map?

    (A) Missionaries and saints spread teachings of the religion despite initial imperial Roman hostility.
    (B) Support of the imperial Roman government facilitated the spread of Christianity throughout the empire.
    (C) Merchants used trade contacts to establish religious schools throughout the Mediterranean.
    (D) Jesus of Nazareth traveled throughout the Roman Empire and diffused its core beliefs.

68. Which of the following best describes how the spread of Buddhism affected its core beliefs?

    (A) The teachings of the historic Buddha were relatively unchanged as they spread.
    (B) Syncretism occurred as the basic beliefs were adapted by followers in various regions.
    (C) The beliefs of reincarnation and karma changed to suit the ideals of those adopting these beliefs.
    (D) The religion was drastically altered as it spread to East Asia.

Questions 69–71 refer to the following passage.

"God spoke, and these were his words: I am the Lord your God who brought you out of Egypt, out of the land of slavery.
—You shall have no other god to set against me. You shall not make a carved image for yourself nor the likeness of anything in the heavens above, or on the earth below, or in the waters under the earth.
—You shall not bow down to them or worship them; for I, the Lord your God, am a jealous god. I punish the children for the sins of the fathers to the third and fourth generations of those who hate me. But I keep faith with thousands, with those who love me and keep my commandments.
—You shall not make wrong use of the name of the Lord your God; the Lord will not leave unpunished the man who misuses his name.

—Remember to keep the Sabbath day holy. You have six days to labor
and do all your work. But the seventh day is a Sabbath of the Lord
your God; that day you shall not do any work, you, your son or
your daughter, your slave or your slave-girl, your cattle or the alien
within your gates; for in six days the Lord made heaven and earth,
the sea, and all that is in them, and on the seventh day he rested.
Therefore the Lord blessed the Sabbath day and declared it holy.

—Honor your father and your mother, that you may live long in the
land which the Lord your God is giving you.

—You shall not commit murder.

—You shall not commit adultery.

—You shall not steal.

—You shall not give false evidence against your neighbor.

—You shall not covet your neighbor's house; you shall not covet your
neighbor's wife, his slave, his slave-girl, his ox, his [donkey], or
anything that belongs to him."

"Ten Commandments," Old Testament of the Bible, Exodus 20:1–17

69. The guidelines described in the passage are best understood in the context
of which of the following?

(A) Christianity drew upon the earlier teachings of Judaism.
(B) Judaism based its teachings on Christian core beliefs.
(C) Christianity was influenced by Persian legal traditions.
(D) Judaism and Christianity were inspired by Roman legal codes.

70. The passage best illustrates which of the following patterns in the period
600 B.C.E.–600 C.E.?

(A) As states increased in size and contacts intensified, technological
diffusion occurred.
(B) The founding and spread of all the world's major belief systems
(C) Codification of religious traditions provided a bond among people
and an ethical code by which to live.
(D) Belief systems often reinforced patriarchal gender systems.

71. Ideas similar to those expressed in the passage directly contributed to which
of the following in the period 600–1450 C.E.?

(A) The development of Islam in the Arabian Peninsula
(B) The implementation of Justinian's Code in the Byzantine Empire
(C) The establishment of the Twelve Tables of Roman law
(D) The rise of Protestantism in Western Europe

 **Tip: If dates are underlined in a question, it usually means that
the question is asking about a period that is different from the
source provided. So be sure to take note of the underlined dates.**

Questions 72–74 are based on the sources below.

Source 1

DAOIST TEMPLE, NORTHERN CHINA

Source 2

Quotes from the *Daodejing*, attributed to Laozi, founder of Daoism

"When the Master governs, the people are hardly aware that he exists.
Next best is a leader who is loved.
Next, one who is feared.
The worst is one who is despised."

"Cultivate virtue in yourself, and it will be true.
Cultivate virtue in the family, and it will be overflowing.
Cultivate virtue in the town, and it will be lasting.
Cultivate virtue in the country, and it will be abundant.
Cultivate virtue in the world, and it will be universal."

"When the government is quite unobtrusive,
People are indeed pure.
When the government is quite prying,
People are indeed conniving."

72. **A historian would most likely use the image in** Source 1 **as support for which of the following assertions?**

   (A) Daoism was supported by Chinese imperial rulers.
   (B) Daoist beliefs influenced much of Asia.
   (C) Daoist temples often served as monasteries.
   (D) Daoism influenced Chinese architectural styles.

73. <u>Source 2</u> indicates that Daoism influenced all of the following aspects of Chinese culture EXCEPT

(A) ideas about proper behavior
(B) centralized bureaucratic rule
(C) the relationship between humans and nature
(D) the role of leaders and government

Tip: Be very careful with questions that contain "EXCEPT." It is very tempting to misread the question and pick the first choice that answers the root of the question. Remember that in these types of questions, there will be three choices that are correct about the topic. The test is looking for the one answer choice that is incorrect.

74. Based on the sources and your knowledge of world history, which of the following best describes the influence of Chinese belief systems in the period <u>600–1450 C.E.</u>?

(A) Tributary relationships led to the complete adoption of Daoism by people from Southeast Asia.
(B) Cross-cultural contacts led to the diffusion of Daoist beliefs to South Asia.
(C) Principles of Daoism and Confucianism influenced the development of Japanese cultural traditions.
(D) Mongol conquest led to the abolition of Daoist beliefs.

Questions 75–78 refer to the following passage.

"Trade and external alliances enabled local rulers to organize states on a larger scale than ever before in Southeast Asia. The first of these well represented in historical sources—though by no means the only early state in Southeast Asia—was Funan, founded along the Mekong River in the first century C.E. Through its main port, Oc Eo, Funan carried on trade with China, Malaya, Indonesia, India, Persia, and indirectly with Mediterranean lands. By the end of the second century, similar trading states had appeared in the Malay peninsula and Champa (southern Vietnam).

Indian influence ran so deep in these states that they and their successors for a millennium or more are commonly referred to as the 'Indianized states of southeast Asia.' Indian traditions manifested their influence in many different ways. In a land previously governed by charismatic individuals of great personal influence, for example, rulers adopted Indian notions of divine kingship. They associated themselves with the cults of Siva, Visnu, or the Buddha, and they claimed both foreign and divine authority to legitimize their rule. They built walled cities with temples at the center, and they introduced Indian music and ceremonies into court rituals. They brought in Hindu and Buddhist advisers, who reinforced the sense of divinely sanctioned rule ...

By no means did indigenous cultures fade away or disappear. During the early years after their arrival in Southeast Asia, Indian traditions worked their influence mostly at the courts of ruling elites, and not much beyond. Over a longer term, however, Indian and native traditions combined to fashion syncretic cultural configurations and to bring about social conversion on a large scale."

Jerry Bentley, world historian, *Old World Encounters*, 1993

 Tip: Even if you feel pressed for time on the exam, be sure to read the entire passage. Some students are intimidated by longer passages. However, the questions are designed to assess your knowledge of world history, comprehension of the stimulus, and application of a historical thinking skill.

75. Based on Bentley's argument, the influence of Indian ideas in Southeast Asia best illustrates which of the following patterns in world history?

    (A) The blending of existing cultural norms with ideas diffused through cross-cultural contacts
    (B) The complete preservation of indigenous beliefs despite the introduction of new ideas
    (C) The link between rulers and the divine due to the founding of monotheistic belief systems
    (D) The complete adoption of new belief systems by a large segment of the population

76. Bentley's argument best illustrates which of the following characteristics of many early states?

    (A) The impact of trade on technological innovation
    (B) The use of monumental architecture to glorify rulers
    (C) The impact of trade on the spread of language
    (D) The use of religion to justify the authority of rulers

77. Which of the following would support the author's assertion that Indian traditions did not extend far beyond the elites of Southeast Asia?

    (A) The adoption of Buddhism by kings
    (B) The practice of Animism by nomadic tribes
    (C) The worshipping of Hindu gods by cultivators
    (D) The practice of Zoroastrianism by local merchants

78. Based on your knowledge of world history, which of the following most likely contributed to the spread of Indian ideas to Southeast Asia?

    (A) The development of the Eurasian Silk Routes
    (B) The intensification of Indian Ocean basin trade
    (C) The expansion of Mediterranean basin trade
    (D) The use of trans-Saharan caravan routes

Short-Answer Questions

Answer all parts of the question that follows.

79. a) Identify ONE way in which Hinduism influenced the development of Buddhism in the period 600 B.C.E.–600 C.E.

    b) Explain ONE similarity in the core beliefs of Hinduism and Buddhism.

    c) Explain ONE difference in the core beliefs of Hinduism and Buddhism.

Answer all parts of the question that follows.

80. a) Identify ONE cultural change that occurred as Confucianism spread throughout China.

    b) Explain ONE political change that occurred as Confucianism spread throughout China.

    c) Explain ONE cultural continuity in China through 600 C.E.

Long Essay Questions

81. In the period 600 B.C.E.–600 C.E., as states and empires increased in size and contact among regions intensified, human communities transformed their religious beliefs and practices.

    Develop an argument that evaluates how the rise of belief systems changed one or more political systems in this period.

82. In the period 600 B.C.E.–600 C.E., as states and empires increased in size and contact among regions intensified, human communities transformed their religious beliefs and practices.

    Develop an argument that evaluates the similarities in the core beliefs of two or more religious traditions that developed before 600 C.E.

(Answers on pages 316–320.)

The Development of States and Empires

Answers for Chapter 5 are on pages 320–324.

Key Concept 2.2—As the early states and empires grew in number, size, and population, they frequently competed for resources and came into conflict with one another.

I. The number and size of key states and empires grew dramatically as rulers imposed political unity on areas where previously there had been competing states.

    A. Key states and empires that grew included:

       • Southwest Asia: Persian Empires

       • East Asia: Qin and Han Empires

       • South Asia: Mauryan and Gupta Empires

       • Mediterranean region: Phoenicia and its colonies, Greek city-states and colonies, and Hellenistic and Roman Empires

       • Mesoamerica: Teotihuacan, Maya city-states

       • Andean South America: Moche

       • North America: Chaco and Cahokia

    Note: *Students should know the location and names of the key states/ empires.*

II. States and empires developed new techniques of imperial administration based, in part, on the success of earlier political forms.

    A. In order to organize their subjects, in many regions imperial rulers created administrative institutions, including central-ized governments, as well as elaborate legal systems and bureaucracies.

    B. Imperial governments promoted trade and projected mil-itary power over larger areas using a variety of techniques, including issuing currencies; diplomacy; developing supply lines; building fortifications, defensive walls, and roads; and drawing new groups of military officers and soldiers from the location populations or conquered populations.

III. Unique social and economic dimensions developed in imperial societies in Afro-Eurasia and the Americas.

A. Imperial cities served as centers of trade, public performance of religious rituals, and political administration for states and empires.

B. The social structures of empires displayed hierarchies that included cultivators, laborers, slaves, artisans, merchants, elites, or caste groups.

C. Imperial societies relied on a range of methods to maintain the production of food and provide rewards for the loyalty of the elites.

D. Patriarchy continued to shape gender and family relations in all imperial societies of this period.

IV. The Roman, Han, Persian, Mauryan, and Gupta Empires encountered political, cultural, and administrative difficulties that they could not manage, which eventually led to their decline, collapse, and transformation into successor or states or empires.

A. Through excessive mobilization of resources, erosion of established political institutions, and economic changes, imperial governments generated social tensions and created economic difficulties by concentrating too much wealth in the hands of elites.

B. Security issues along their frontiers, including the threat of invasions, challenged imperial authority.

In this period, states developed and expanded quickly into empires that built strong militaries and administrations to manage their diverse populations. These empires are often referred to by historians as *classical* because they provided the foundations for later governments. Some of these early empires were tolerant of conquered groups, while others excluded ethnic or cultural groups that were conquered. Eventually, most of these empires grew too large too quickly. They had difficulty managing political and economic affairs, leading to discontent. These issues led to a period of decline. Many of these empires eventually fell to nomadic groups living on their borders.

Questions 83–86 refer to the following passage.

"The three kinds of government, monarchy, aristocracy, and democracy, were all found united in the commonwealth of Rome. For if they turned their view upon the power of the consuls, the government appeared to be purely monarchial and regal. If, again, the authority of the senate was considered, it then seemed to wear the form of aristocracy. And if regard was to be had to the share which the people possessed in the administration of affairs, it could then scarcely fail to be denominated a popular state.

The consuls, when they remain in Rome, before they lead out the armies into the field, are the masters of all public affairs. For all other magistrates, the tribunes alone excepted, are subject to them, and bound to obey their commands. They introduce ambassadors into the senate. They propose also to the senate the subjects of debates; and direct all forms that are observed in making the decrees. Nor is it less a part of their office likewise, to attend to those affairs that are transacted by the people; to call together general assemblies; to report to them the resolutions of the senate; and to ratify whatever is determined by the greater number. In all the preparations that are made for war, as well as in the whole administration in the field, they possess an almost absolute authority."

> Polybius, Greek historian of the Hellenistic period,
> "An Analysis of Roman Government," circa 150 B.C.E.

83. **The role of Roman consuls described in the passage most strongly supports which of the following statements about the Roman Empire?**

    (A) The senate was dominated by the aristocratic class.
    (B) The republic was characterized by shared power between landholding elites and consuls.
    (C) The government was centralized under rulers who had political and military power.
    (D) The democratic government allowed for the participation of all citizens in decision making.

84. **A historian would most likely use this passage to illustrate which of the following about empires in the period 600 B.C.E.–600 C.E.?**

    (A) Imperial rulers created administrative institutions in order to organize their subjects.
    (B) Imperial rulers controlled most aspects of the government, economy, and religion.
    (C) Imperial rulers shared power with the wealthy elites and priestly class.
    (D) Imperial rulers developed elaborate bureaucracies to manage long-distance trade.

85. Polybius's description of the role of the consuls is similar to which of the following in the period 1450–1750 C.E.?

    (A) Samurai in the Tokugawa Shogunate
    (B) Janissaries in the Ottoman Empire
    (C) Eunuchs in imperial China
    (D) Monarchs in European kingdoms

86. Which of the following was a long-term effect of the expansion of the Roman Empire?

    (A) Expansion led to rebellions as ethnic minorities challenged intolerant policies.
    (B) Military expansion involved the excessive mobilization of resources that created economic difficulties.
    (C) Conquest of the Mediterranean basin enabled merchants to control the Silk Road.
    (D) Control of the Middle East provided access to oil reserves.

Questions 87–89 refer to the sources that follow.

Source 1

GREAT WALL OF CHINA, FIRST BUILT AROUND 220 B.C.E. AND EXTENDED BY SUCCESSIVE DYNASTIES

Source 2

HAN DYNASTY MAP

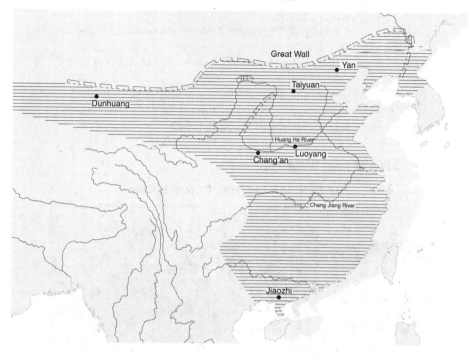

87. A historian would most likely use the image in Source 1 as support for which of the following?

(A) Defensive walls were successful in preventing borderland nomads from conquering the Han dynasty.

(B) The Han government built fortifications to protect the Silk Road.

(C) Monumental architecture served both a religious and a military purpose in the Qin and Han dynasties.

(D) Fortifications were built to project military power and defend against invasions.

88. Which of the following best explains the extent of the Han dynasty as shown in Source 2?

(A) The Han dynasty faced few geographical challenges, which allowed for rapid expansion.

(B) The Han dynasty established cities as centers for religious rituals and sacrificial ceremonies.

(C) The Han dynasty imposed political unity where there had previously been competing states.

(D) The Han dynasty failed to expand borders of previous Chinese dynasties.

89. **Based on your knowledge of world history, which of the following contributed most directly to the Han dynasty's ability to maintain imperial rule?**

   (A) Han rulers developed the imperial examination system to recruit capable bureaucrats.
   (B) Han rulers chose bureaucrats from landowning families who demonstrated loyalty.
   (C) The Han government used tax revenues to fund regional military rulers.
   (D) The Han chose eunuchs to serve as bureaucrats due to the eunuchs' inability to have children.

Questions 90–92 refer to the map below.

THE PERSIAN EMPIRE, C. 500 B.C.E.

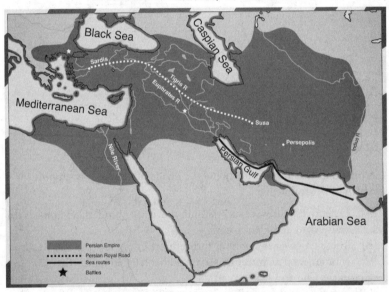

90. **The map supports which of the following assertions about empires in the period 600 B.C.E.–600 C.E.?**

   (A) Few challenges were encountered when conquering neighboring groups.
   (B) Empires used road networks and new administrative techniques to manage their territories.
   (C) Access to an extensive network of maritime trade was necessary to expand the military.
   (D) Empires often imposed a single language and religion on conquered groups.

91. Based on your knowledge of world history, which of the following factors contributed to the success of the Persian Empire?

    (A) The conquest of diverse populations contributed to cultural unity.
    (B) The enslavement of conquered populations ensured a reliable labor force.
    (C) An elaborate bureaucracy managed the expansive territory.
    (D) The implementation of a single state religion integrated all inhabitants.

92. Based on the map and your knowledge of world history, which of the following could be inferred about the cities identified on the map?

    (A) They often provided crops and metals to the surrounding countryside.
    (B) They were controlled by dictators with complete military authority.
    (C) They served as centers of trade and political administration.
    (D) They had Muslim diasporic merchant communities.

Questions 93–95 refer to the table below.

ROMAN CITIZENS OF MILITARY AGE, 338 B.C.E. TO 47 C.E.

Year	Number of Citizens
338 B.C.E.	165,000
293 B.C.E.	262,322
251 B.C.E.	279,797
220 B.C.E.	270,213
204 B.C.E.	214,000
164 B.C.E.	327,022
115 B.C.E.	394,336
70 B.C.E.	900,000
27 B.C.E.	4,063,000
8 B.C.E.	4,233,000
13 C.E.	4,937,000
47 C.E.	6,944,000

93. Which of the following best explains the overall population trend shown in the table?

    (A) Longer life expectancy due to medical innovations, such as vaccines
    (B) The extension of legal rights to all who lived within the empire
    (C) Access to new food crops, such as fast-ripening rice
    (D) The integration of conquered populations into the Roman political system

94. **Which of the following best describes an impact of the population trend shown in the table?**

    (A) Military expansion created economic difficulties by concentrating too much wealth in the hands of elites.

    (B) Extension of citizenship to conquered groups generated resentment among Roman peasants, leading to protests.

    (C) Enslavement of all conquered groups led to large-scale rebellions that threatened the unity of the empire.

    (D) Incorporation of new territories led to a weaker military due to a lack of foreigners for conscription.

95. **The trend represented by the table is most similar to which of the following?**

    (A) Spanish imperialism in the Americas

    (B) Ottoman expansion in the Mediterranean

    (C) British control of Hong Kong

    (D) Russian rule over Siberia

Questions 96–99 refer to the following passage.

"In the midst of the houses of the people of all the four castes and to the north from the centre of the ground inside the fort, the king's palace, facing either the north or the east shall, as described elsewhere, be constructed occupying one-ninth of the whole site inside the fort.

On the eastern side, merchants trading in scents, garlands, grains, and liquids, together with expert artisans and the people of Kshatriya caste shall have their habitations.

To the south, the superintendents of the city, of commerce, of manufactories, and of the army as well as those who trade in cooked rice, liquor, and flesh, besides prostitutes, musicians, and the people of Vaisya caste shall live.

To the west, artisans manufacturing worsted threads, cotton threads, bamboo-mats, skins, armors, weapons, and gloves as well as the people of Súdra caste shall have their dwellings.

To the north, the royal tutelary deity of the city, ironsmiths, artisans working on precious stones, as well as Bráhmans shall reside."

"Wives who belong to Sudra, Vaisya, Kshatriya or Brahman caste, and who have not given birth to children should wait as long as a year for their husbands who have gone abroad for a short time; ... If the husband is a Bráhman, studying abroad, his wife who has no issue should wait for him for ten years; but if she has given birth to children, she should wait for twelve years. If the husband is of Kshatriya caste, his wife should wait for him till her death."

Arthashastra, a legal and political treatise produced for
Chandragupta Maurya of India, circa 300 B.C.E.

96. Compared to the regulations in the passage, Buddhist practices concerning social status in the period 600 B.C.E.–600 C.E. differed in that they

(A) banned marriage as an institution
(B) discouraged social mobility
(C) rejected the caste system
(D) encouraged monasticism for all

97. Which of the following conclusions about the period 600 B.C.E.–600 C.E. is most directly supported by the passage?

(A) The emergence of new religious traditions often challenged existing social norms.
(B) The codification of religion diminished the role of women in imperial societies.
(C) The rise of powerful imperial states led to the beginning of the caste system.
(D) Patriarchy continued to shape gender and family relations in imperial societies.

98. The passage is best used as evidence of which of the following in Mauryan society?

(A) Caste significantly influenced one's place of residence and relationships.
(B) Cities primarily served as centers of religious ritual.
(C) The government established elaborate regulations concerning commerce.
(D) Rulers lived in isolation from most of the population.

 Tip: Often one word can make a choice incorrect, so read every choice carefully.

99. Which of the following changes to Mauryan religious policy occurred under Chandragupta's grandson, Emperor Ashoka?

(A) The promotion of Buddhist ideals as reflected by the laws
(B) The emergence of a syncretic faith that merged Hindu and Buddhist values
(C) The establishment of Islam as the official religion of the kingdom
(D) The separation of religious and political affairs

Tip: Be sure not only to underline or highlight the passages but also to underline key words in the question. Remember to eliminate answers you know or are pretty sure are wrong by crossing them out. Do not look at those choices again! If you can get down to two choices, you'll have a 50% chance of answering the question correctly.

Questions 100–102 refer to the images below.

Image 1

CARVING OF MAYAN KING PAKAL, PALENQUE, MEXICO, CIRCA 600 C.E.

Image 2

MAYAN TEMPLE OF THE INSCRIPTIONS, PALENQUE, MEXICO

100. The object in Image 1 best supports which of the following conclusions about imperial governments in the Americas?

    (A) They relied on a large slave class to create art to glorify themselves.
    (B) They used a variety of techniques to project power over large areas.
    (C) They developed a written alphabet to unite their populations.
    (D) They created elaborate legal systems and bureaucracies.

Tip: Often the wording of the key concepts is used in the choices, so be sure to familiarize yourself with the key concepts.

101. The object in Image 2 best supports which of the following conclusions?

    (A) Imperial cities were solely used for religious rituals.
    (B) Imperial cities were often disconnected from the surrounding countryside.
    (C) Imperial cities served as centers of trade, religious rituals, and political administration.
    (D) Imperial cities were located in remote areas to prevent wide-scale looting.

102. This city was abandoned around the 9th century C.E. Which of the following can be inferred about Mayan civilization at that time?

    (A) Mayan merchants may have advocated for new centers of trade.
    (B) Mayan religious beliefs may have evolved, rendering temples obsolete.
    (C) Mayan cities may have been conquered by Aztec warriors.
    (D) Mayan rulers may have encountered difficulties that they could not manage.

Questions 103–105 are based on the map below.

INVASIONS IN THE ROMAN EMPIRE, C. 300 TO C. 500 C.E.

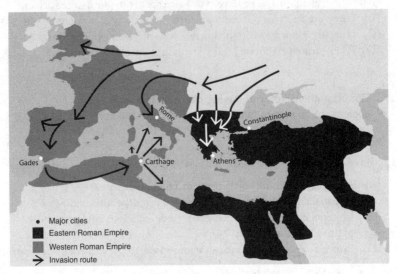

103. **Which of the following may explain the patterns on the map?**

    (A) Invaders fled Northern Europe due to cooler temperatures of the Little
        Ice Age.
    (B) Invaders sought to build new settlements on the Mediterranean coastline.
    (C) Invaders targeted cities for the opportunity to gain wealth and resources.
    (D) Invaders attacked religious centers to prevent the spread of Christianity.

104. **Which of the following factors contributed most to the success of the
    invaders shown on the map?**

    (A) Roman political institutions eroded as tensions arose due to unequal
        distribution of resources.
    (B) Roman slaves revolted, leading to the sudden collapse of the central
        government.
    (C) Roman merchants traded weapons with the bordering tribes, enabling
        them to conquer Rome.
    (D) Roman priests refused to support the divinity of Roman emperors.

105. **Which of the following was a long-term effect of the movements shown on
    the map?**

    (A) Western Europe became centralized under German rule.
    (B) Nomadic invaders adopted Roman legal systems.
    (C) Feudalism arose in Western Europe.
    (D) Christianity became the official religion of the Roman Empire.

Questions 106–109 refer to the passage below.

"If slave labor was indeed more common in the Roman world than in early imperial China, what were the reasons? With respect to agriculture, modern scholarship on early China tends to emphasize the generous supply of landless free labor from which landowners could cheaply draw tenants and hired or indentured workers. This, however, was probably also true of much of the Roman world. Real slave prices—expressed in grain equivalent—were very broadly similar in both societies. Patchy fields were common both in the Mediterranean and in China. In Italy under the Roman Republic, conscription and growing urbanization 'thinned' labor markets by increasing worker mobility and creating stronger incentives for the purchase of slaves by an elite that benefited from the spoils of empire in the form of growing personal wealth and access to large numbers of war captives and other slave imports. Yet the Warring States period likewise witnessed massive dislocations and mounting pressure on labor resources driven by heavy military and civilian conscription.

Rome's greater reliance on slave labor can be traced to two factors, the relative paucity of slaves on the Chinese market and the less privileged position of Chinese wealth elites. In the Warring States period, war captives were turned into forced laborers or drafted into the military instead of being sold off to private bidders as they were in Rome (even though some may have been distributed to members of the military). Whereas Roman elites effectively owned the state and sought to maximize their benefits from it, in the centuries leading up to the completion of the Qin conquests the most successful Chinese states worked hard to contain elite privilege, and Western Han rulers (and then especially Wang Mang) strove to maintain this practice at least up to a point. Both of these processes served to restrict private slave use."

Walter Scheidel, historian, "Slavery and Forced Labor in Early China and the Roman World," 2013

106. **Based on Scheidel's argument, what accounts for the differences in the use of slave labor in the Han dynasty and Roman Empire?**

   (A) Han China had a larger group of wealthy elites to purchase slaves than did the Romans.

   (B) Romans sold conquered peoples as slaves, while the Han incorporated them into the military.

   (C) China had a large supply of cheap labor for agriculture, while Rome did not.

   (D) Romans drafted slaves into the military, while the Han forced conquered groups to work for the state.

107. Which of the following conclusions about the period 600 B.C.E.–600 C.E. is most directly supported by the passage?

    (A) Patriarchy continued to shape gender and family relations in imperial societies.
    (B) Imperial cities served as centers of trade and political administration for empires.
    (C) In order to organize their subjects, imperial rulers created administrative institutions.
    (D) Imperial societies relied on a variety of methods to maintain the production of food.

108. The labor system described in the passage is most similar to which of the following labor systems of the period 1450–1750 C.E.?

    (A) The plantation system
    (B) Indentured servitude
    (C) Serfdom
    (D) The *mit'a* system

109. Based on your knowledge of world history, which of the following practices of the Han dynasty supports the author's claim about the restriction of elite privilege?

    (A) The practice of recruiting peasants to serve as tax collectors
    (B) The use of the Mandate of Heaven to justify imperial rule
    (C) The recruitment of bureaucrats using the imperial examination system
    (D) The Confucian belief that education can improve one's status

Questions 110–112 refer to the passage below.

"Most revered and serene of all emperors, although in your most felicitous times all other persons enjoy an untroubled and calm existence, since all wickedness and oppression have ceased, we, alone experiencing a fortune most alien to these most fortunate times, present this supplication to you. We are unreasonably oppressed and we suffer extortion by those persons whose duty it is to maintain the public welfare. For although we live remotely and are without military protection, we suffer afflictions alien to your most felicitous times. Generals and soldiers and lordlings of prominent offices in the city and your Caesarians, coming to us, traversing the Appian district, leaving the highway, taking us from our tasks, requisition-ing our plowing oxen, make exactions that are by no means their due. And it happens thus that we are wronged by extortions. Our possessions are spent on them, and our fields are stripped and laid waste...."

> Petition of the Araguenians to the Emperor Philip on
> Official & Military Extortion, 246 C.E.

110. The circumstances described in the passage are best understood in the context of which of the following?

(A) The Roman practice of recruiting bureaucrats based on civil service examinations

(B) The adoption of Christianity by rulers of the late Roman Empire

(C) The expansion of the Roman Empire and erosion of political institutions

(D) The nomadic invasions on the borders of the Roman Empire

111. Which of the following conclusions about the period 600 B.C.E.–600 C.E. is most directly supported by the passage?

(A) Imperial societies relied on a range of methods to maintain the production of food and to reward loyal elites.

(B) In many regions, imperial rulers created administrative institutions, including centralized governments.

(C) Imperial governments projected military power over larger areas using roads and defensive walls.

(D) Rulers imposed political unity on areas where previously there had been competing states.

 Tip: All of the choices for this question are directly taken from the key concepts and are true about the time period. However, only one relates directly to the passage, so understanding the main idea is crucial.

112. The actions of Roman officials described in the passage most directly contributed to which of the following?

(A) Resentment of bureaucratic elites contributed to rebellions.

(B) Invaders threatened the security of the empire.

(C) Emperors eliminated bureaucratic institutions due to corruption.

(D) The Roman military expanded to protect villages on the borders.

Short-Answer Questions

Answer all parts of the question that follows.

113. a) Identify ONE new technique that empires used to administer their territories 600 B.C.E.–600 C.E.

b) Explain ONE similarity in the political administration or military power of two empires in the period 600 B.C.E.–600 C.E.

c) Explain ONE difference in the political administration or military power of two empires in the period 600 B.C.E.–600 C.E.

Answer all parts of the question that follows.

114. a) Identify ONE change that contributed to the decline of imperial authority in the period 600 B.C.E.–600 C.E.

b) Explain ONE reason for the decline of imperial authority in the period 600 B.C.E.–600 C.E.

c) Explain ONE continuity in the social structure or cultural values in imperial states throughout the period 600 B.C.E.–600 C.E.

Long Essay Questions

115. In the period 600 B.C.E.–600 C.E., states and empires developed new techniques of imperial administration based, in part, on the success of earlier political forms.

Develop an argument that evaluates how one or more expanding states or empires governed their empires.

116. In the period 600 B.C.E.–600 C.E., empires encountered political, cultural, and administrative difficulties that they could not manage. These difficulties eventually led to the empires' decline, collapse, and transformation into successor or states or empires.

Develop an argument that evaluates how political, cultural, and/or administrative difficulties led to the decline and collapse of one or more empires in this time period.

(Answers on pages 320–324.)

Emergence of Interregional Networks of Communication and Exchange

CHAPTER 6

Answers for Chapter 6 are on pages 324–327.

 Key Concept 2.3—With the organization of large-scale empires, transregional trade intensified, leading to the creation of extensive networks of commercial and cultural exchange.

I. Land and water routes became the basis for interregional trade, communication, and exchange networks in the Eastern Hemisphere.

    A. Many factors, including the climate and location of the routes, the typical trade goods, and the ethnicity of people involved, shaped the distinctive features of a variety of trade routes, including Eurasian Silk Roads, trans-Saharan caravan routes, Indian Ocean sea lanes, and Mediterranean sea lanes.

II. New technologies facilitated long-distance communication and exchange.

    A. New technologies permitted the use of domesticated pack animals to transport goods across longer routes.

    B. Innovations in maritime technologies, as well as advanced knowledge of the monsoon winds, stimulated exchanges along maritime routes from East Africa to East Asia.

III. Alongside the trade in goods, the exchange of people, technology, religious and cultural beliefs, food crops, domesticated animals, and disease pathogens developed across extensive networks of communication and exchange.

    A. The spread of crops, including rice and cotton from South Asia to the Middle East, encouraged changes in farming and irrigation techniques.

    B. The spread of disease pathogens diminished urban populations and contributed to the decline of some empires, including the Roman and Han.

    C. Religious and cultural traditions—including Christianity, Hinduism, and Buddhism—were transformed as they spread partly as a result of syncretism.

As empires grew in area and wealth, the amount of goods exchanged on trade networks expanded. New technologies facilitated long-distance trade, which developed over sea and land, including the Eurasian Silk Roads, trans-Saharan routes, Indian Ocean sea lanes, and Mediterranean sea lanes. As trade led to new contacts among merchants, ideas, religions, and disease spread along with the physical goods that were exchanged.

Questions 117–119 refer to the map below.

TRANS-SAHARAN TRADE ROUTES, CIRCA 100 C.E.

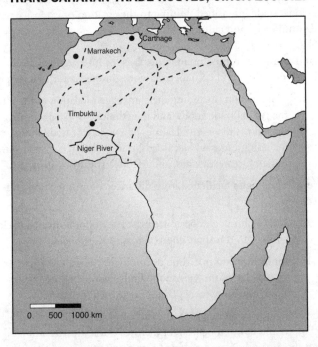

117. Which of the following factors most directly contributed to the development of the trade routes depicted on the map?

(A) Maritime technologies, such as the compass, enabled merchants to travel longer distances.

(B) The rise of sub-Saharan empires led to the accumulation of wealth and the demand for luxury goods.

(C) The domestication of pack animals, such as camels, allowed for the transport of goods across longer distances.

(D) The adoption of Islam by West African merchants improved commercial relationships.

118. The map supports which of the following assertions about the period 600 B.C.E.–600 C.E.?

    (A) Increased contact between the Mediterranean and sub-Saharan Africa was due to the rise of new empires in each region.
    (B) Transregional trade intensified, leading to the creation of extensive networks of exchange.
    (C) The spread of religious and cultural traditions, such as Islam, led to syncretism.
    (D) The diffusion of pathogens along trade routes led to population decline in sub-Saharan Africa.

119. Based on the map and on your knowledge of world history, which of the following best describes a cultural impact of this trade route in the period 600–1450 C.E.?

    (A) The spread of Islam to sub-Saharan Africa
    (B) The adoption of Animist beliefs by Berber merchants
    (C) The conquest of much of sub-Saharan Africa by the Mali Empire
    (D) The diffusion of Bantu languages throughout sub-Saharan Africa

Tip: Examine the language of the question carefully. A key word in this question is "cultural," so look for choices about language, religion, customs, food, and other cultural elements.

Questions 120–122 refer to the images that follow.

Image 1

INTERIOR OF A *QANAT*, UNDERGROUND CANALS OF ANCIENT PERSIA, FOUND IN IRAN

Qanats *took advantage of aquifers to bring water to the surface using gently sloping canals.*

Image 2

A *NORIA*, OR WATER WHEEL, BUILT CIRCA 450 C.E., HAMA, SYRIA

Norias *used water power to bring water into aqueducts.*

120. The development of the object in <u>Image 1</u> is most likely due to which of the following?

   (A) The climatic conditions created a need for underground cultivation of crops.
   (B) The decline in population led to the need for labor-saving devices.
   (C) The growth of urban areas reduced the availability of arable land.
   (D) Cotton and rice crops were introduced to the Middle East from South Asia.

121. <u>Image 2</u> best illustrates which of the following continuities in world history?

   (A) The need for humans to adapt to their environments
   (B) The production of cash crops on plantations
   (C) The use of slave labor for cultivation
   (D) The use of technology to project military power

122. When taken together, the images support which of the following conclusions?

   (A) The spread of pathogens via trade routes led to a smaller labor force.
   (B) The diffusion of irrigation techniques from China led to population growth.
   (C) The spread of crops encouraged changes in irrigation techniques.
   (D) The trade in luxury goods allowed for the development of public works projects by merchants.

Questions 123–126 are based on the map below.

EURASIAN TRADE ROUTES, CIRCA 100 C.E.

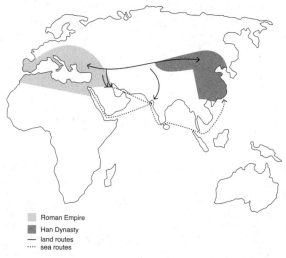

Roman Empire
Han Dynasty
— land routes
···· sea routes

123. **Which of the following factors contributed most to the ability of merchants to travel along the routes depicted on the map?**

  (A) The use of imperial armies and navies to protect trade routes
  (B) The sponsorship of maritime expeditions by imperial governments
  (C) The development of new technologies for long-distance travel
  (D) The adoption of a common language for merchants throughout Eurasia

124. **Based on your knowledge of world history, which of the following was an effect of the trade routes depicted on the map?**

  (A) The diffusion of Roman engineering techniques throughout Eurasia
  (B) The spread of pathogens contributing to the decline of the Roman and Han Empires
  (C) The integration of Chinese religious traditions into Roman society
  (D) The restriction of trade by the imperial government of the Han dynasty

125. **Which of the following contributed to changes in the volume of trade conducted on the routes depicted on the map in the period 200–600 C.E.?**

  (A) The volume decreased as the Roman and Han Empires declined.
  (B) The volume increased as merchants developed syncretic faiths to improve relationships.
  (C) The volume decreased due to changes in climate that made it more difficult to travel.
  (D) The volume increased due to the growing wealth of Roman and Han elites.

126. Which of the following conclusions about the period 600 B.C.E.–600 C.E. is supported by the map?

(A) Trade networks provided all resources necessary for imperial expansion.
(B) Maritime and overland trade indirectly linked imperial states.
(C) Trade routes led to the diffusion of Islam throughout the Indian Ocean basin.
(D) Maritime and overland trade relied on the domestication of pack animals.

Questions 127–129 are based on the images below.

Image 1

MOGAO CAVE COMPLEX, DUNHUANG, CHINA, BUILT CIRCA 350 C.E.

Image 2

BUDDHA STATUE, LEI YINSI TEMPLE, DUNHUANG, CHINA

127. **Image 1 best illustrates which of the following continuities in world history?**

  (A) Architectural styles of civilizations tend to remain consistent over time.
  (B) Cities are often constructed in remote areas to avoid conquest.
  (C) Natural shelters, such as caves, are often used for construction.
  (D) Environmental factors have influenced local architectural styles.

128. **Image 2 best reflects which of the following processes in world history?**

  (A) Buddhism spread rapidly throughout all of Eurasia.
  (B) Religious beliefs rarely changed as they were adopted by new groups.
  (C) The core beliefs and practices of Buddhism remained consistent among its followers.
  (D) Religious traditions transformed as they spread to regions beyond their origins.

129. **Dunhuang was located on the Silk Road. Which of the following can be inferred about the city based on your knowledge of world history?**

  (A) The city was frequently visited by merchants of the Roman Empire.
  (B) The Chinese government strongly regulated merchant activity in the city.
  (C) The city was home to Christian diasporic merchant communities.
  (D) The Buddhist community lived in isolation from other religious groups.

Questions 130–132 refer to the map below.

MEDITERRANEAN TRADE, CIRCA 200 C.E.

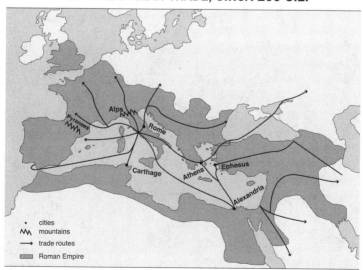

130. Which of the following factors contributed most to the ability of merchants to conduct trade as depicted on the map?

    (A) Access to ports and a variety of manufactured and luxury goods
    (B) Advanced knowledge of monsoon winds
    (C) Roman economic policies that controlled production of all goods
    (D) The absence of physical barriers to trade

131. Which of the following best describes a long-term effect of trade in the Mediterranean basin through 600 C.E.?

    (A) The diffusion of epidemic disease, such as the Black Death
    (B) The spread of Christian religious traditions beyond their place of origin
    (C) The adoption of a universal Mediterranean culture and language
    (D) The decline and fall of the Roman Empire

132. Based on the map and on your knowledge of world history, which of the following best describes trade in the Eastern Hemisphere in the period 600 B.C.E.–600 C.E.?

    (A) Little interregional trade occurred due to a lack of innovations.
    (B) Mainly sea routes were used to conduct long-distance trade.
    (C) Land and water routes linked civilizations of Afro-Eurasia.
    (D) Trade was mainly conducted within large empires.

Questions 133–136 refer to the map below.

INDIAN OCEAN TRADE, CIRCA 100 C.E.

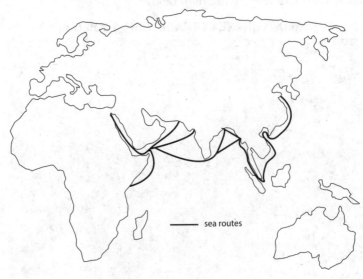

133. Which of the following factors contributed to the ability of traders to undertake the voyages shown on the map?

    (A) Advanced knowledge of monsoon wind patterns
    (B) New ship designs, such as caravels and lateen sails
    (C) The domestication of pack animals, such as camels
    (D) New tools, such as the compass and back staff

134. Which of the following was an effect of the routes depicted on the map in the period before 600 C.E.?

    (A) The spread of Islam to Southeast Asia
    (B) The spread of Hinduism to East Asia
    (C) The spread of Christianity to South Asia
    (D) The spread of Hinduism and Buddhism to Southeast Asia

135. Which of the following can be inferred about the merchants who traveled the routes depicted on the map?

    (A) They forced their religious beliefs on the cities to which they traveled.
    (B) They had little interaction with locals beyond commercial transactions.
    (C) They introduced their own traditions to the local cultures.
    (D) They fully adopted the cultural practices of the cities to which they traveled.

136. Which of the following events led to the intensification of the trade shown on the map in the period <u>600–1450 C.E.</u>?

    (A) Advancements in existing transportation and commercial technologies
    (B) The expansion of land-based caravan trade in Central Asia
    (C) The establishment of the first trans-Saharan trade routes
    (D) The control of East African ports by the Caliphates

Questions 137–140 refer to the graph below.

POPULATION OF THE ROMAN AND HAN EMPIRES FROM THE BEGINNING OF THE MILLENNIUM THROUGH 600 C.E.

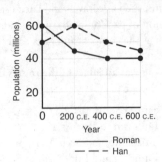

137. Which of the following best explains the overall trend shown on the graph?

    (A) Migrations to areas of Central Asia for resettlement
    (B) The spread of pathogens across the Silk Road
    (C) Invasions by Mongol tribes
    (D) Large-scale famine due to crop failures

138. Which of the following best explains the changes in the population of the Han dynasty between the beginning of the millennium and 200 C.E.?

    (A) Government efforts to promote large families
    (B) The availability of crops and political stability
    (C) An influx of immigrants from Japan and Korea
    (D) The importation of slaves from Southeast Asia

139. Which of the following best explains the changes in the population of the Roman Empire between 200 and 400 C.E.?

    (A) Migrations to urban centers in the Mediterranean
    (B) Conflict with the Caliphate in the Middle East
    (C) Invasions by Germanic and Central Asian tribes
    (D) Mutiny by the Roman military forces

140. Which of the following best explains an effect of the trend shown on the graph?

    (A) Population decline contributed to labor shortages that weakened the Roman and Han Empires.
    (B) Population growth in the Han dynasty initially led to famine and war, which contributed to population decline.
    (C) The Roman population stabilized due to political stability and economic recovery.
    (D) The Han and Roman Empires grew stronger as the population stabilized around 600 C.E.

Questions 141–143 refer to the passage below.

"Long-distance trade served as a conduit for the spread of virulent diseases as well as for the distribution of goods and the dissemination of religious and cultural traditions. During the second and third centuries, population declined precipitously in the Mediterranean and China, and probably other parts of Eurasia as well. Epidemics of measles, smallpox, and bubonic plague took ferocious human tolls on peoples previously unexposed to their pathogens. Demographic collapse aggravated social and economic difficulties, which resulted in a shrinking of the markets that long-distance trade depended on. Combined with increasing instability and insecurity along the trade routes, this weakening of the international markets led to a sharp cutback in the volume of long-distance trade. Long-distance travel did not come to a complete halt, but it became far less common than during the era of the ancient silk roads. Eventually, too, the Roman and Han empires, twin anchors of the Eurasian networks of cross-cultural exchange, both succumbed to nomadic invaders."

Jerry H. Bentley, world historian, *Old World Encounters*, 1993

141. **According to Bentley, which of the following factors contributed to the decline of the Roman and Han dynasties?**

(A) Diseases led to fewer job opportunities.
(B) Less demand for luxury goods decreased trade.
(C) Lower populations exacerbated existing issues.
(D) Decline in long-distance trade weakened the economies.

142. **Which of the following best describes an effect of the spread of diseases as described in the passage?**

(A) Peasant rebellions against the government
(B) An increased demand for luxury goods
(C) A rise in public health measures
(D) A decline in urban populations

143. **Which of the following led to a revival of the trade described in the passage in the period 600–1450 c.e.?**

(A) The eradication of epidemic diseases
(B) The expansion of the Mongol Empire
(C) The reunification of the Roman Empire
(D) The development of technologies for navigation

Questions 144–146 refer to the passage below.

"After travelling for seventeen days, a distance we may calculate of about 1500 *li*, (the pilgrims) reached the kingdom of Shen-shen, a country rugged and hilly, with a thin and barren soil. The clothes of the common people are coarse, and like those worn in our land of Han, some wearing felt and others coarse serge or cloth of hair; this was the only difference seen among them. The king professed (our) Law, and there might be in the country more than four thousand monks, who were all students of the Hinayana [Theravada]. The common people of this and other kingdoms (in that region), as well as the sramans [monks], all practice the rules of India, only that the latter do so more exactly, and the former more loosely. So (the travelers) found it in all the kingdoms through which they went on their way from this to the west, only that each had its own peculiar barbarous speech. (The monks), however, who had (given up the worldly life) and quitted their families, were all students of Indian books and the Indian language."

> Faxian (Fa-Hsien), Chinese Buddhist monk,
> account of his trip to India via Central Asia, c. 399–414 C.E.

144. **A historian would most likely use the passage to illustrate which of the following?**
    (A) The sponsorship of expeditions by the Chinese government
    (B) The impact of Indian government systems on Central Asia
    (C) The emergence of religious syncretism as Buddhism spread
    (D) The nature of tributary relationships between China and Central Asia

145. **Based on the passage, which of the following best describes the practice of Buddhism throughout Asia?**
    (A) The religion branched into many schools and changed as it spread.
    (B) Monks adapted their practices to the local customs.
    (C) Religious practices remained consistent over time.
    (D) Followers of the religion devoted themselves fully to the practice of the faith.

146. **Which of the following most likely facilitated Faxian's travels through Central Asia?**
    (A) The financial backing of the Han government
    (B) The knowledge of foreign customs, such as clothing and language
    (C) The diplomatic relationship between the Han and local kings
    (D) The use of routes typically traveled by merchants

Short-Answer Questions

Answer all parts of the question that follows.

147. a) Identify ONE cultural impact of interregional trade between 600 B.C.E. and 600 C.E.

   b) Explain ONE similarity in the factors that facilitated Silk Road and Indian Ocean trade between 600 B.C.E. and 600 C.E.

   c) Explain ONE difference in the impact of Silk Road and Indian Ocean trade in the period 600 B.C.E.–600 C.E.

Answer all parts of the question that follows.

148. a) Identify ONE change that occurred to interregional trade networks between 600 B.C.E. and 600 C.E.

   b) Explain ONE way increased trade impacted imperial economies between 600 B.C.E. and 600 C.E.

   c) Explain ONE continuity in the social structure or cultural values in imperial states throughout the period 600 B.C.E.–600 C.E.

Long Essay Questions

149. In the period 600 B.C.E.–600 C.E., new technologies facilitated long-distance communication and exchange.

   Develop an argument that evaluates how new technologies changed trade networks in the period before 600 C.E.

150. In the period 600 B.C.E.–600 C.E., the organization of large-scale empires led to the intensification of transregional trade and the creation of extensive networks of commercial and cultural exchange.

   Develop an argument that evaluates how the development of empires affected Eurasian trade in this period.

(Answers on pages 324–327.)

PERIOD 3 (c. 600–1450 c.e.)
Regional and Transregional Interactions

Expansion and Intensification of Communication and Exchange Networks

CHAPTER 7

Answers for Chapter 7 are on pages 327–332.

 Key Concept 3.1— A deepening and widening of networks of human interaction within and across regions contributed to cultural, technological, and biological diffusion within and between various societies.

I.   Improved transportation technologies and commercial practices led to an increased volume of trade and expanded the geographical range of existing and newly active trade networks.

   A.   Existing trade routes—including the Silk Road, the Mediterranean Sea, the trans-Saharan routes, and the Indian Ocean basin—flourished and promoted the growth of powerful new trading cities.

   B.   Communication and exchange networks developed in the Americas.

   C.   The growth of interregional trade in luxury goods was encouraged by significant innovations in previously existing transportation and commercial technologies—including the caravanserai, compass use, the astrolabe, and larger ship designs in sea travel—and new forms of credit and the development of money economies.

   D.   Commercial growth was also facilitated by state practices, including the Inca road system; trading organizations, such as the Hanseatic League; and state-sponsored commercial infrastructures, such as the Grand Canal in China.

   E.   The expansion of empires—including China, the Byzantine Empire, various Muslim states, and the Mongols—facilitated Afro-Eurasian trade and communication as new peoples were drawn into their conquerors' economies and trade networks.

II.   The movement of peoples caused environmental and linguistic effects.

   A.   The expansion and intensification of long-distance trade routes often depended on environmental knowledge and technological adaptations to the environment.

B. Some migrations had a significant environmental impact, including migration of Bantu-speaking peoples who facilitated transmission of iron technologies and agricultural techniques in sub-Saharan Africa, as well as the maritime migrations of the Polynesian peoples who cultivated transplanted foods and domesticated animals as they moved to new islands.

C. Some migrations and commercial contacts led to the diffusion of languages throughout a new region or the emergence of new languages.

III. Cross-cultural exchanges were fostered by the intensification of existing, or the creation of new, networks of trade and communication.

A. Islam, based on the revelations of the prophet Muhammad, developed in the Arabian Peninsula. The beliefs and practices of Islam reflected interactions among Jews, Christians, and Zoroastrians with the local Arabian peoples. Muslim rule expanded to many parts of Afro-Eurasia due to military expansion, and Islam subsequently expanded through the activities of merchants, missionaries, and Sufis.

B. In key places along important trade routes, merchants set up diasporic communities where they introduced their own cultural traditions into the indigenous culture.

C. As exchange networks intensified, an increased number of travelers within Afro-Eurasia wrote about their travels.

D. Increased cross-cultural interactions resulted in the diffusion of literary, artistic, and cultural traditions, as well as scientific and technological innovations.

IV. There was continued diffusion of crops and pathogens, including epidemic diseases like the bubonic plague, along the trade routes.

Trade routes that were previously established increased in volume, and trade networks expanded in their reach and level of interaction. This occurred due to new technologies, economic policies promoting commerce, and expansion of new empires. Increased cross-cultural interactions led to environmental changes, the spread of Islam, and the continued diffusion of religion, disease, and language.

Questions 151–155 refer to the maps below.

Map 1

EURASIAN TRADE NETWORKS, CIRCA 500 C.E.

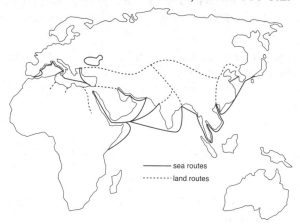

```
——— sea routes
------- land routes
```

Map 2

EURASIAN TRADE NETWORKS, CIRCA 1450 C.E.

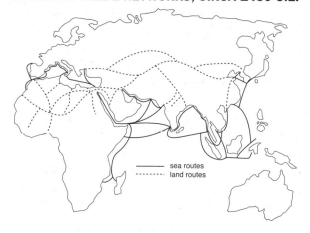

```
——— sea routes
------- land routes
```

151. **Which of the following best explains the changes in the trade routes depicted on the maps between 600 and 1450 C.E.?**

   (A) The collapse of the Gupta Empire that led to greater opportunities for Arab merchants

   (B) The availability of new forms of credit and the development of money economies

   (C) The increased influence of Buddhism, which rejected the accumulation of luxury goods

   (D) The domestication of camels and horses that facilitated exchange on overland trade routes

Tip: Knowing your time periods is essential to answering this question correctly.

152. Which of the following factors contributed most to the ability of traders in the Indian Ocean basin to undertake voyages in the period 600–1450 C.E.?

    (A) Innovations in navigational technologies, such as the compass and astrolabe, and larger ships
    (B) The financial support of voyages by empires in India and the Middle East
    (C) Superior shipbuilding techniques of the Chinese diffusing throughout the region
    (D) Innovations in agriculture helping supply food for larger crews aboard ships

153. Which of the following best illustrates a continuity in Eurasian trade between 500 B.C.E. and 1450 C.E.?

    (A) The role of Western European empires in promoting interregional trade
    (B) The spread of Islam through merchants and missionaries
    (C) The diffusion of crops and pathogens along trade routes
    (D) The dominance of Chinese merchants in trading cities

Tip: Read the dates in the question carefully and check them against the dates on the maps.

154. Which of the following best describes an effect of trade in the period 600–1450 C.E.?

    (A) The Swahili language diffused to areas of Southeast Asia.
    (B) The caste system took root in areas of the Middle East.
    (C) Hinduism was adopted by cultivators throughout sub-Saharan Africa.
    (D) Muslim merchant diasporic communities were established.

155. Which of the following best describes an effect of increased interactions in the period 600–1450 C.E.?

    (A) The widespread adoption of Islam throughout Afro-Eurasia
    (B) The diffusion of scientific and technological innovations
    (C) The spread of Christianity to eastern Asia
    (D) The universal acceptance of Chinese philosophies

Questions 156–158 refer to the passage below.

"We then reached Jerusalem (may God ennoble her!), third in
excellence after the two holy shrines of Mecca and Medina and the
place whence the Prophet was caught up into heaven. . . . The sacred
mosque is a most beautiful building, and is said to be the largest
mosque in the world. . . . The entire mosque is an open court and
unroofed, except the mosque al-Aqsa, which has a roof of most
excellent workmanship, embellished with gold and brilliant colours.
Some other parts of the mosque are roofed as well. The Dome of the
Rock is a building of extraordinary beauty, solidity, elegance, and
singularity of shape. It stands on an elevation in the centre of the
mosque and is reached by a flight of marble steps. It has four doors.
The space round it is also paved with marble, excellently done, and
the interior likewise. Both outside and inside the decoration is so
magnificent and the workmanship so surpassing as to defy description.
The greater part is covered with gold so that the eyes of one who gazes
on its beauties are dazzled by its brilliance, now glowing like a mass of
light, now flashing like lightning.

The Christian holy places
Among the grace-bestowing sanctuaries of Jerusalem is a building,
situated on the farther side of the valley called the valley of Jahannam
[Gehenna] to the east of the town, on a high hill. This building is said
to mark the place whence Jesus ascended to heaven. In the bottom
of the same valley is a church venerated by the Christians, who say
that it contains the grave of Mary. In the same place there is another
church which the Christians venerate and to which they come on
pilgrimage. This is the church of which they are falsely persuaded
to believe that it contains the grave of Jesus [Church of the Holy
Sepulcher]. All who come on pilgrimage to visit it pay a stipulated tax
to the Muslims, and suffer very unwillingly various humiliations."

Ibn Battuta, *Travels in Asia and Africa*, 1325–1354

156. The description of interactions in Jerusalem in the second paragraph reflects
which of the following?

(A) The attitudes of Christians toward Islamic holy sites
(B) The common features of mosques throughout the Islamic world
(C) The tensions between Christians and Muslims as a result of the
Crusades
(D) The varying architectural styles of Christian and Muslim holy sites

157. The passage best illustrates which of the following patterns in world history?

    (A) Holy sites visited by religious pilgrims are often located in major trading cities.
    (B) Rulers often claimed a connection to the divine.
    (C) Governments often supported the construction of religious buildings.
    (D) Architecture reflected the values of religions and belief systems.

158. The passage best illustrates which of the following patterns in the period 600–1450 c.e.?

    (A) As exchange networks intensified, travelers within Afro-Eurasia wrote about their journeys.
    (B) Religious pilgrims often fought one another at holy sites.
    (C) As trade networks extended, missionary activity decreased due to government policies.
    (D) Urbanization occurred due to the construction of monumental architecture.

Questions 159–162 refer to the image below.

View of the Grand Canal, Zhouzhuang, Southern China

159. The construction of the canal shown in the image best illustrates which of the following patterns of the period 600–1450 c.e.?

    (A) Commercial growth was facilitated by state-sponsored commercial infrastructures.
    (B) The diffusion of industrial technologies from Europe enabled the construction of public works.
    (C) Confiscation of privately owned land often occurred to benefit political leaders.
    (D) Daoist ideas supported the construction of natural waterways.

160. **The economic impact of the Grand Canal in China is most similar to the economic impact of which of the following?**

    (A) The spread of bubonic plague in Western Europe
    (B) The establishment of the Incan road system in South America
    (C) The construction of the ziggurats in Mesopotamia
    (D) The creation of aqueducts in the Roman Empire

161. **Based on the image and on your knowledge of world history, which of the following could be best inferred about the city of Zhouzhuang in the period 600–1450 C.E.?**

    (A) It was weakened by constant flooding and subsequently abandoned.
    (B) It benefited from access to European technologies.
    (C) It declined as a result of increased susceptibility to invasion.
    (D) It flourished due to the availability of resources from beyond the local area.

162. **Which of the following best describes the long-term impact of the Grand Canal on China?**

    (A) The region became more economically and politically integrated.
    (B) The cost of building the canal led to an economic depression.
    (C) The rise of an elite merchant class led to social upheaval and rebellion.
    (D) The northern capital region became increasingly disconnected with the south.

Questions 163–166 refer to the map below.

AFRICAN TRADE ROUTES AND MIGRATIONS, CIRCA 600 TO 1450 C.E.

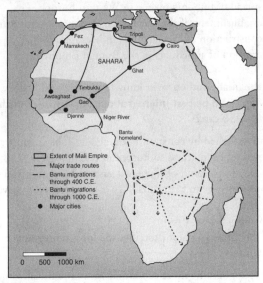

163. Which of the following best describes an effect of the migrations shown on the map?

    (A) The widespread conversion of commoners to Islam
    (B) The diffusion of language and foraging techniques
    (C) The spread of iron technologies and agricultural techniques
    (D) The dissemination of Greco-Roman culture

164. The impact of the migrations shown on the map is most <u>similar to</u> which of the following?

    (A) The voyages of merchants in the Indian Ocean basin
    (B) The movements of nomads on the Eurasian steppe
    (C) The migrations of Polynesian peoples in Oceania
    (D) The travels of Vikings in Northern Europe

165. Which of the following factors contributed to the extension of trade routes between North and West Africa?

    (A) Kingdoms in West Africa, such as Mali, increased their demand for gold and slaves.
    (B) New kingdoms in West Africa, such as Mali, conquered the Berbers of North Africa.
    (C) The expansion of the Caliphates to West Africa led to the protection of trade routes.
    (D) Knowledge of the environment grew and adaptations were made to the environment, such as camel caravans.

166. Which of the following best explains the reason for the spread of Islam to areas in West Africa?

(A) Increased interactions between merchants and local peoples led to conversions.

(B) Many tribal leaders adopted the religion and forced their people to convert.

(C) Islamic beliefs about nature gods appealed to cultivators who depended on reliable harvests.

(D) Arab missionaries from the Middle East spread their beliefs through all of sub-Saharan Africa.

Questions 167–169 refer to the excerpt below.

"The German envoys came to Novgorod the Great . . . and concluded an agreement with the Novgorod posadnik Boris Iur'evich, and with the Novgorod tysiatskii Feodor Iakovlevich, and with the merchant elders, for all of Novgorod, to the effect that German merchants shall have free passage to come to Novgorod the Great and to leave, by water and by land, in accordance with the old oaths sworn upon the cross, and in accordance with this treaty and by this agreement, without any deceit. Likewise did the German envoys . . . conclude an agreement with the Novgorod posadnik Boris Iur'evich, and with the Novgorod tysiatskii Feodor Iakovlevich, and with the merchant elders Aleksandr and Efrem, and all the merchants' sons, and all of Novgorod the Great, for all the seventy-three towns and for all the merchantry, to the effect that the people of Novgorod should have free passage to travel to the German land and to the German towns, by land and by water, to come and go with their goods, in accordance with the old treaties and in accordance with the old oaths sworn upon the cross, and in accordance with this treaty and by this agreement, without any deceit. And the German merchants shall trade with the merchants of Novgorod in Novgorod the Great or on the Neva, in accordance with the old oaths sworn upon the cross and in accordance with this treaty and by this agreement, without any deceit. The people of Novgorod shall give legal protection to the Germans as to their brother Novgorodians, and the Germans shall give legal protection to the people of Novgorod as to their brother Germans."

Excerpt from a treaty between Novgorod and Hanseatic towns, 1436

Tip: It is pretty likely that the passages and excerpts on the exam will be ones you have not seen and about places you may not have heard of. Don't panic! The exam is testing your knowledge of the key concepts and your skills as a historian, not your recall of facts.

167. Which of the following best explains the terms of the treaty that were proposed in the excerpt?

    (A) The leaders of Novgorod wanted to protect their merchants from competition.
    (B) The German merchants wanted to establish a monopoly over trade with Novgorod.
    (C) Each party wanted to ensure that they would benefit from the proposal.
    (D) Merchants from both cities wanted to avoid government taxation.

168. The activities of the German merchants described in the excerpt resulted in which of the following?

    (A) Commercial growth occurred as the trading organization they represented expanded.
    (B) Wage-based economies developed in Germany due to capitalist practices.
    (C) Economic collapse occurred in Novgorod as Hanseatic cities flourished.
    (D) Migration to German cities increased as peasants sought industrial employment.

169. Interactions described in the excerpt most directly contributed to which of the following?

    (A) The outbreak of war between Germany and Novgorod
    (B) The diffusion of literary, artistic, and cultural traditions
    (C) The consolidation of power by rulers in Germany and Novgorod
    (D) The rise of German as a global trade language

Questions 170–173 refer to the map below.

MAJOR EMPIRES, CIRCA 1000 C.E.

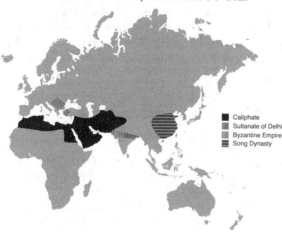

Caliphate
Sultanate of Delhi
Byzantine Empire
Song Dynasty

170. Which of the following factors contributed to the growth of trade in the era depicted on the map?

   (A) Nomadic control of the entire length of the Silk Road decreased risks for merchants.
   (B) Expansion of empires led to the incorporation of conquered groups into trade networks.
   (C) The universal adoption of Islam by merchants throughout Eurasia improved trade relations.
   (D) The migrations of Chinese-speaking peoples to Central and Southwest Asia enhanced trade.

171. Which of the following best explains the extent of Muslim-ruled empires as shown on the map?

   (A) The prophet Muhammad led military expeditions as far as Central Asia.
   (B) Muslim missionaries used diplomacy to extend political control of the Caliphate.
   (C) The Caliphate developed gunpowder weapons to conquer large areas.
   (D) Muslim rule expanded due to military conquests and the spread of Islam through missionaries.

172. Which of the following developments increased the interregional exchange of luxury goods in the areas shown on the map between 600–1450?

   (A) Slave labor contributing to lower prices for cotton, sugar, and tobacco
   (B) The development of industrial technology to mass produce these goods
   (C) Improvement of transportation, including caravanserai and the compass
   (D) Increased incomes for commoners due to political reforms

173. Which of the following was an effect of increased contact among political entities shown on the map?

   (A) The spread of crops and pathogens along trade routes
   (B) The diffusion of Confucian principles to the Caliphates
   (C) The outbreak of wars among these empires, leading to their decline
   (D) The transfer of Western European scientific principles to the Delhi Sultanate

Questions 174-176 refer to the passage below.

"We Genoese and Venetians bear the responsibility for revealing the judgments of God. Alas, once our ships had brought us to port we went to our homes. And because we had been delayed by tragic events, and because among us there were scarcely ten survivors from a thousand sailors, relations, kinsmen, and neighbors flocked to us from all sides. But, to our anguish, we were carrying the darts of death. While they hugged and kissed us we were spreading poison from our lips even as we spoke.

When they returned to their own folk, these people speedily poisoned the whole family, and within three days the afflicted family would succumb to the dart of death. Mass funerals had to be held and there was not enough room to bury the growing numbers of dead."

Gabriele de' Mussis, Italian lawyer, c. 1348

174. The deaths described in the passage were most likely due to which of the following?

   (A) New military technologies were introduced by Genoese and Venetian merchants.
   (B) Poisons acquired by overseas trade inadvertently spread to family members.
   (C) The diffusion of epidemic diseases spread as a result of trade contacts.
   (D) Influenza and cholera spread due to unsanitary conditions in urban areas.

175. A historian would most likely use this passage to illustrate which of the following?

   (A) Political responses to the spread of pathogens
   (B) Burial practices of the early Renaissance era
   (C) The link between religious beliefs and epidemics
   (D) Family relationships in Italian port cities

176. **Which of the following was a direct effect of the situation described in the passage?**

(A) The Catholic Church grew more powerful.
(B) Overseas trade between Europe and Asia was created.
(C) Antibiotics were developed to counter epidemics.
(D) Labor shortages weakened serfdom.

Questions 177–180 refer to the passage below.

"The vigorous expansion of nomadic peoples and their establishment of large empires between the eleventh and fourteenth centuries ensured that cross-cultural encounters would take place on a systematic basis throughout central Asia and east Asia. The experiences of steppe peoples such as the Khitans and Mongols differed considerably, though, from those of Turks in the more southern and western regions. Turkish conquerors attacked the established religious and cultural order in India, and in Anatolia they used their newly acquired Islamic faith even more explicitly as an ideological weapon. The Turks' commitment to Islam provided them with a rationale and justification for a spirited attack on the Hindu and Christian cultural establishments that they encountered. This cultural dimension of their expansion naturally complemented their political and military campaigns. It also helped to secure the establishment of Islamic faith and institutions in new lands.

In central and east Asia, nomadic peoples did not undertake the sort of cultural campaign that Turkish conquerors did in India and Anatolia. They naturally took their beliefs and values with them on their imperial campaigns, but they did not attempt to displace existing cultural establishments or to impose foreign values on the peoples they conquered."

Jerry H. Bentley, historian, *Old World Encounters*, 1993

177. **According to Bentley's argument, which of the following best describes a difference between nomadic conquest in South Asia and in East Asia?**

(A) Nomads in Central and East Asia were more tolerant of existing beliefs.
(B) Nomads in South and West Asia were more tolerant of existing beliefs.
(C) Nomads in India and Anatolia often incorporated existing beliefs into their empires.
(D) Nomads in China discouraged the practices of Buddhism and Daoism.

178. Which of the following was the most direct effect of the cross-cultural interactions described in the passage?

    (A) The start of a civil war between Hindus and Muslims in India
    (B) The adoption of Mongol spiritual practices by the Chinese
    (C) The spread of the Turkish language to Anatolia
    (D) The conversion to Islam by Chinese peasants

179. Which of the following empires arose as a result of nomadic conquests described in the passage?

    (A) The Gupta Empire
    (B) The Russian Empire
    (C) The Ming dynasty
    (D) The Ottoman Empire

180. New contacts between nomads and sedentary populations described in the passage resulted in which of the following?

    (A) The adoption of pastoralism by cultivators in Central and East Asia
    (B) An intensification of Eurasian trade as new people were drawn into trade networks
    (C) The collapse of bureaucratic institutions in India and Anatolia
    (D) A decline in Eurasian trade due to warfare among nomadic tribes

Short-Answer Questions

Use the passage below to answer all parts of the question that follows.

"Southernization was well under way in Southern Asia by the fifth century c.e., during the reign of India's Gupta kings (320–535 c.e.). It was by that time already spreading to China. In the eighth century various elements characteristic of southernization began spreading through the lands of the Muslim caliphates. Both in China and in the lands of the caliphate, the process led to dramatic changes, and by the year 1200 it was beginning to have an impact on the Christian Mediterranean. One could argue that within the Northern Hemisphere, by this time, the process of southernization had created an eastern hemisphere characterized by a rich south and a north that was poor in comparison. And one might even go so far as to suggest that in Europe and its colonies, the process of southernization laid the foundation for westernization."

Lynda Shaffer, historian, *Southernization*, 1994

181. a) Briefly explain ONE specific historical event or development from the period 600–1450 c.e. that could be used to support Shaffer's argument.

b) Briefly explain ONE specific historical event or development from the period 600–1450 C.E. that could be used to support Shaffer's claim that southernization laid the foundation for westernization.

c) Explain ONE way the process of southernization impacted the Mediterranean region by the year 1450 C.E.

Use the image below to answer all parts of the question that follows.

Sultanhani Caravanserai, Konya, Turkey, originally constructed in the thirteenth century

182. a) Identify ONE <u>change</u> that occurred in trade between 600 and 1450 C.E. that contributed to the need for the building shown in the image.

b) Explain ONE way the image reflects a <u>continuity</u> in economic patterns in the period 600–1450 C.E.

c) Explain ONE way interregional trade changed as a result of the rise of the Mongol Empire.

Long Essay Questions

183. In the period 600–1450 C.E., improved transportation technologies and commercial practices led to the intensification of trade.

Develop an argument that evaluates how improved technologies and commercial practices led to changes in one or more Eurasian trade networks.

184. In the period 600–1450 C.E., the expansion of empires facilitated Afro-Eurasian trade and communication.

Develop an argument that evaluates the effects of imperial expansion on the Afro-Eurasian trade networks.

Document-Based Question

185. Evaluate the extent to which the attitudes toward the spread of Christianity in the Roman Empire differed from the attitudes toward the spread of Islam in the West African kingdoms of Ghana and Mali in the period before 1450 C.E.

Document 1

Source: Tacitus, Roman historian, from the *Annals* written in 109 C.E. In 64 C.E., two-thirds of Rome was destroyed in a fire.

Yet no human effort, no princely largess nor offerings to the gods could make that infamous rumor disappear that Nero had somehow ordered the fire. Therefore, in order to abolish that rumor, Nero falsely accused and executed with the most exquisite punishments those people called Christians, who were infamous for their abominations. The originator of the name, Christ, was executed as a criminal by the procurator Pontius Pilate during the reign of Tiberius; and though repressed, this destructive superstition erupted again, not only through Judea, which was the origin of this evil, but also through the city of Rome, to which all that is horrible and shameful floods together and is celebrated. Therefore, first those were seized who admitted their faith, and then, using the information they provided, a vast multitude were convicted, not so much for the crime of burning the city, but for hatred of the human race. And perishing they were additionally made into sports: they were killed by dogs by having the hides of beasts attached to them, or they were nailed to crosses or set aflame, and, when the daylight passed away, they were used as nighttime lamps. Nero gave his own gardens for this spectacle and performed a Circus game, in the habit of a charioteer mixing with the plebs or driving about the race-course. Even though they were clearly guilty and merited being made the most recent example of the consequences of crime, people began to pity these sufferers, because they were consumed not for the public good but on account of the fierceness of one man.

Document 2

Source: Letter from Pliny the Younger, governor of the Roman province Bithynia, to the emperor Trajan in 112 c.e. concerning Christians who were brought to his court

Sir,
It is my constant method to apply myself to you for the resolution of all my doubts; for who can better govern my dilatory way of proceeding or instruct my ignorance? I have never been present at the examination of the Christians [by others], on which account I am unacquainted with what uses to be inquired into, and what, and how far they used to be punished; nor are my doubts small, whether there be not a distinction to be made between the ages [of the accused]? and whether tender youth ought to have the same punishment with strong men? Whether there be not room for pardon upon repentance?" or whether it may not be an advantage to one that had been a Christian, that he has forsaken Christianity? Whether the bare name, without any crimes besides, or the crimes adhering to that name, be to be punished? In the meantime, I have taken this course about those who have been brought before me as Christians. I asked them whether they were Christians or not? If they confessed that they were Christians, I asked them again, and a third time, intermixing threatenings with the questions. If they persevered in their confession, I ordered them to be executed; for I did not doubt but, let their confession be of any sort whatsoever, this posi-tiveness and inflexible obstinacy deserved to be punished....

Document 3

Source: Lactantius, Christian author, *Of the Manner in Which the Persecutors Died*, describing the edict issued by Emperor Diocletian in 303 c.e.

The next day an edict was published, depriving the Christians of all honours and dignities; ordaining also that, without any distinction of rank or degree, they should be subjected to tortures, and that every suit at law should be received against them; while, on the other hand, they were debarred from being plaintiffs in ques-tions of wrong, adultery, or theft; and, finally, that they should neither be capable of freedom, nor have right of suffrage. A certain person tore down this edict, and cut it in pieces, improperly indeed, but with high spirit, saying in scorn, "These are the triumphs of Goths and Sarmatians." Having been instantly seized and brought to judgment, he was not only tortured, but burnt alive, in the forms of law; and having displayed admirable patience under sufferings, he was consumed to ashes.

Document 4

Source: Eusebius of Caesarea, Greek historian and Bishop known as "The Father of Church History," *The Life of Constantine*, 337 c.e.

But at the time when he [Constantine] was struck with amazement at the extraordinary vision, and resolving to worship no other God than him who had appeared to him, he sent for those who were acquainted with the mysteries of his doctrines, and enquired who that God was, and what the vision meant. They affirmed that he was God, the only begotten Son of the one and only God: that the sign which had appeared was the symbol of immortality, and the trophy of that victory over death which he won in the past when visiting the earth. They told him about how he came to be born, and explained to him the true account of his incarnation. Constantine was in awe of the divine manifestation he had seen. Comparing the heavenly vision with the interpretation he was given, he found his judgment confirmed. Believing this knowledge had been given to him by God, he decided to devote himself from then on to the reading of the inspired writings. Moreover, he made the priests of God his advisers, and thought it his duty to honor the God who had appeared to him with all devotion. Then, being strengthened by this hope in God, he went quickly on to fight the fire of tyranny. . . .

Document 5

Source: Al-Bakri, a member of a prominent Spanish Arab family, description of the Kingdom of Ghana based on stories from merchants, 11th century c.e.

In the king's town, and not far from his court of justice, is a mosque where the Muslims who arrive at his court pray. Around the king's town are domed buildings and groves and thickets where the sorcerers of these people, men in charge of the religious cult, live. In them too are their idols and the tombs of their kings. . . .

The audience is announced by the beating of a drum which they call *duba* made from a long hollow log. When the people who profess the same religion as the king approach him, they fall on their knees and sprinkle dust on their head, for this is their way of greeting him. As for the Muslims, they greet him only by clapping their hands. . . . Their religion is paganism and the worship of idols.

Document 6

Source: Djingareyber Mosque built in Mali's capital, Timbuktu, in 1327. This is one of five mosques commissioned by Mansa Musa to be built in Timbuktu upon his return from his pilgrimage to Mecca.

Document 7

Source: Ibn Battuta, Muslim traveler, on meeting the King of Mali, Mansa Sulayman, in 1352

The sultan of Mali is Mansa Sulayman, "mansa" meaning [in Mandingo] sultan, and Sulayman being his proper name. He is a miserly king, not a man from whom one might hope for a rich present. It happened that I spent these two months without seeing him, on account of my illness. Later on he held a banquet in commemoration of our master [the late sultan of Morocco] Abu'l-Hasan, to which the commanders, doctors, *qadi* and preacher were invited, and I went along with them. Reading-desks were brought in, and the Koran was read through, then they prayed for our master Abu'l-Hasan and also for Mansa Sulayman.

When the ceremony was over I went forward and saluted Mansa Sulayman. The qadi, the preacher, and Ibn al-Faqih told him who I was, and he answered them in their tongue. They said to me, "The sultan says to you 'Give thanks to God,'" so I said, "Praise be to God and thanks under all circumstances."

(Answers on pages 327–332.)

Interactions Among New and Reconstituted States

Answers for Chapter 8 are on pages 332–336.

Key Concept 3.2—State formation and development demonstrated continuity, innovation, and diversity in various regions.

I. Empires collapsed in different regions of the world, and in some areas were replaced by new imperial states or political systems.

    A. Following the collapse of empires, imperial states were reconstituted in some regions, including the Byzantine Empire and the Chinese dynasties (Sui, Tang, and Song), combining traditional sources of power and legitimacy with innovations better suited to their specific local context.

    B. In some places, new political entities emerged, including those developed in various Islamic states; the Mongol khanates, new Hindu and Buddhist states in South, East, and Southeast Asia; city-states; and decentralized government (feudalism) in Europe and Japan.

    C. Some states synthesized local with foreign traditions.

    D. In the Americas, as in Afro-Eurasia, state systems expanded in scope and reach; networks of city-states flourished in the Maya region and, at the end of this period, imperial systems were created by the Mexica (Aztecs) and Inca.

II. Interregional contacts and conflicts between states and empires encouraged significant technological and cultural transfers.

    A. Technological and cultural transfers were taking place:

       • between Tang China and the Abbasids;

       • across the Mongol Empire;

       • between Muslims and Christians in the Mediterranean region during the Crusades; and

       • during Chinese maritime activity led by Ming Admiral Zheng He.

Following the decline and fall of early empires of the previous period, reconstituted states emerged that often drew upon previous state forms, such as the Byzantine Empire and Imperial China. Many historians refer to this period as the "Post-Classical" era for this reason. New government systems emerged in the Middle East, called the Islamic Caliphates. Hindu and Buddhist states formed in South, East, and Southeast Asia. In the Americas, imperial states were created for the first time. In other regions, such as Europe and Japan, decentralized governments remained and city-states developed in some areas. Due to the intensification of trade, these states shared knowledge and cultural elements.

Questions 186–189 refer to the passage below.

"Governing under the authority of God our empire, which was delivered to us by His Heavenly Majesty, we prosecute wars with success, we adorn peace, we bear up the frame of the State, and we so lift up our minds in contemplation of the aid of the omnipotent Deity that we do not put our trust in our arms, nor in our soldiers, nor in our leaders in war, nor in our own skill, but we rest all our hopes in the providence of the Supreme Trinity alone, from whence proceeded the elements of the whole universe, and their disposition throughout the orb of the world was derived.

1. Whereas then there is in all things nothing found so worthy of respect as the authority of enacted law, which disposes well things both divine and human, and expels all inequity, and yet we find the whole course of our statutes, such as they come down from the foundation of the city of Rome and from the days of Romulus, to be in a state of such confusion that they reach to an infinite length and surpass the bounds of all human capacity, it was therefore our first desire to make a beginning with the most sacred Emperors of old times, to amend their statutes, and to put them in a clear order, so that they might be collected together in one book, and, being divested of all superfluous repetition and most inequitable disagreement, might afford to all mankind the ready resource of their unalloyed character."

Introduction to *Corpus Juris Civilis*,
also known as Justinian's Code, 6th century C.E.

186. The reason for issuing this document as described in the <u>first paragraph</u> is best understood in the context of which of the following?

   (A) The rejection of Roman traditions by later governments
   (B) The role of the Catholic Church in creating legal codes
   (C) The desire to legitimize Justinian's rule of the Byzantine Empire
   (D) The decentralized nature of the Byzantine Empire

187. The passage reflects which of the following patterns of the period 600–1450 C.E.?

    (A) Imperial states synthesized local traditions with foreign traditions to strengthen their rule.
    (B) Imperial states combined traditional sources of power with innovations better suited to the local context.
    (C) Imperial states rejected previous forms of governance in order to avoid past mistakes.
    (D) Imperial states embraced all aspects of previous political entities, including legal codes.

188. Justinian's government as described in the passage <u>differs</u> most strongly from the political system of which of the following?

    (A) The feudal system of Western Europe
    (B) The rule of the Song dynasty in China
    (C) The West African kingdoms of Ghana and Mali
    (D) The Abbasid Caliphate in the Middle East

189. The reference to Roman statutes is a result of which of the following?

    (A) The Roman style of art and architecture influenced the Mediterranean region.
    (B) The Byzantine Empire traded with the Italian peninsula.
    (C) The Roman legal code required the statutes to be enforced for eternity.
    (D) The Byzantine Empire was formerly territory of the Eastern Roman Empire.

 Tip: You will most likely be nervous during the exam, but you should read carefully! If you misread one word of this question, you might choose an incorrect answer. Wrong answers are called distractors because they are designed to do just that.

Questions 190–192 refer to the map below.

INTERACTIONS IN EAST ASIA, CIRCA 600–1450 C.E.

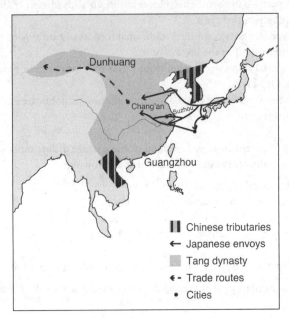

190. Which of the following developments on the map is a political innovation of the period 600–1450 C.E.?

(A) Centralized imperial rule of China
(B) Tributary relationships between China and Korea
(C) Trade relationships between China and Vietnam
(D) Chinese participation in Silk Road trade

191. Which of the following is the most direct effect of contact between China and Japan as shown on the map?

(A) Japan became a Chinese tributary state.
(B) China conquered the islands of Japan.
(C) Japan was influenced by Chinese traditions.
(D) China adopted Japanese religious traditions.

192. Which of the following was a result of China's participation in Eurasian land-based trade as shown on the map?

(A) Exchange of goods between the Tang and the Aztecs
(B) Transfer of religion between the Tang and the Byzantine Empire
(C) Exchange of goods between the Tang and Western Europe
(D) Transfer of knowledge between the Tang and the Abbasids

Questions 193–195 refer to the image below.

Mural in Malacca, Malaysia, of Admiral Zheng He and his fleet

193. A historian would most likely use the image as support for which of the following assertions?

(A) Zheng He's voyage to Malacca furthered trade relations between China and the Malay Peninsula.

(B) The Malaysian government benefited from contact with China via Zheng He's voyages.

(C) Malaysian artists often incorporated elements of Chinese history into their works.

(D) Zheng He's voyage was inconsequential in the history of Malacca.

194. Which of the following was an effect of the event shown in the image?

(A) The spread of Chinese ideas to West Africa

(B) The complete adoption of Chinese traditions by Malaysians

(C) The transfer of Malaysian religious beliefs to China

(D) The diffusion of Chinese knowledge to Southeast Asia

195. The end of the voyages depicted in the image led to which of the following in the period 1450–1750 C.E.?

(A) China's naval expeditions focused on maritime reconnaissance of the Pacific Ocean.

(B) European navies established trading posts in the Indian Ocean basin.

(C) China became completely isolated from Indian Ocean trade.

(D) Europeans adopted Chinese shipbuilding techniques.

Questions 196–198 refer to the passage below.

"When the ruler treats the elderly as the elderly should be treated, the people rise up with filiality. When the ruler treats those senior to him as those senior to him should be treated the people rise up with behavior fitting those who are younger. When the ruler treats the orphaned with compassion the people do not turn their backs. Hence the ruler fulfills the Dao of the carpenter's square. That which you detest in your superior, do not employ upon your subordinates. That which you detest in your subordinates, do not employ to serve your superior. That which you detest in those who are before you, do not employ to lead those behind you. That which you detest in those who are behind you, do not employ to follow those before you. That which you detest in him on your right, do not employ when engaged with him on your left. That which you detest in him on your left, do not employ when engaged with him on your right."

Zhu Xi, Chinese philosopher, 1190 C.E.

196. According to the passage, Zhu Xi was advocating an approach to government that most clearly illustrates the principles of

(A) Legalism
(B) Buddhism
(C) Neoconfucianism
(D) Hinduism

197. The passage reflects which of the following <u>continuities</u> in China's history?

(A) The belief that the ruler is above the law
(B) The influence of traditional religious beliefs on imperial rule
(C) The emphasis on the individual over family obligations
(D) The patriarchal nature of gender relations

198. Which of the following developments would disrupt the type of rule discussed in the passage?

(A) The conquest by the Mongols
(B) The rise of the Ming dynasty
(C) The fall of the Tang dynasty
(D) The conquest by Korea

Questions 199–200 refer to the image below.

**IMAGE FROM *THE BOOK OF GAMES* BY ALFONSO X,
SPANISH KING, CIRCA 1285**

The image shows a Christian and a Muslim playing chess.

199. The contact in the image is most likely the result of which of the following?

   (A) Byzantine expansion to the Middle East
   (B) Spanish conquest of North Africa
   (C) Trans-Saharan trade networks
   (D) The Crusades in the Mediterranean

200. Which of the following was a result of contact similar to the interaction shown in the image?

   (A) The creation of a new syncretic faith
   (B) The diffusion of ideas regarding forms of governance
   (C) The transfer of medical knowledge to Western Europe
   (D) The spread of Mongol technologies to the Middle East

Questions 201–203 refer to the following passage.

"As this kingdom was so vast, in each of the many provinces there were many storehouses filled with supplies and other needful things; thus, in times of war, wherever the armies went they drew upon the contents of these storehouses, without ever touching the supplies of their confederates or laying a finger on what they had in their settlements. . . . Then the storehouses were filled up once more with the tributes paid the Inca. If there came a lean year, the storehouses were opened and the provinces were lent what they needed in the way of supplies; then, in a year of abundance, they paid back all they had received. No one who was lazy or tried to live by the work of others was tolerated; everyone had to work. Thus on certain days each lord went to his lands and took the plow in hand and cultivated the earth, and did other things. Even the Incas themselves did this to set an example. And under their system there was none such in all the kingdom, for, if he had his health, he worked and lacked for nothing; and if he was ill, he received what he needed from the storehouses. And no rich man could deck himself out in more finery than the poor, or wear different clothing, except the rulers and the headmen, who, to maintain their dignity, were allowed great freedom and privilege."

Pedro de Cieza de Léon, Spanish conquistador,
Chronicles of the Incas, 1535

201. **The passage best supports which of the following conclusions?**

(A) The Inca were influenced by Marxist ideology.
(B) The Inca had a highly centralized government system.
(C) The Incan government promoted social inequality.
(D) The Inca Empire became too large to control efficiently.

202. **Which of the following best describes a limitation to the information presented in the passage?**

(A) The author was not a member of the society and may have misunderstood some of the workings of the government.
(B) The author did not have direct contact with the Inca, so the information presented may be incorrect.
(C) The author did not have access to information about the Inca due to the lack of a system of record keeping.
(D) The author was a conquistador, so he may have wanted to depict the Inca as primitive.

203. **Which of the following led to the end of the system described in the passage in the period 1450–1750 C.E.?**

(A) The fall of the Inca due to internal discontent and rebellions
(B) The decline of the Inca due to overexpansion
(C) The fall of the Incan Empire due to Spanish conquest
(D) The decline of the Incan Empire due to war with the Aztecs

Questions 204–206 refer to the diagrams below.

JAPANESE FEUDAL SYSTEM   **EUROPEAN FEUDAL SYSTEM**

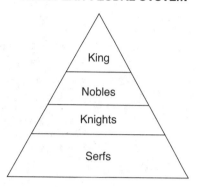

204. The diagrams best support which of the following comparative statements about Japan and Europe in the period 600–1450 C.E.?

(A) Elites in Japan were wealthier than elites in Europe.
(B) Warrior classes in both Europe and Japan were subjugated.
(C) European nobles were more influential than Japanese *daimyo*.
(D) Landowning classes in both Europe and Japan enjoyed a relatively high social status.

205. Which of the following factors led to the rise of the feudal system in Europe?

(A) The fall of the Roman Empire
(B) The prominence of the Roman Catholic Church
(C) The notion of divine right of kings
(D) The Crusades

206. Which of the following most directly led to changes in Japan's social structure in the <u>nineteenth century</u>?

(A) The arrival of foreigners following the Treaty of Kanagawa
(B) The rise of the Tokugawa Shogunate
(C) The restoration of the Meiji emperor
(D) The imperial rule by Western Europeans

Questions 207–209 refer to the map below.

MONGOL EMPIRE CIRCA 1300 C.E.

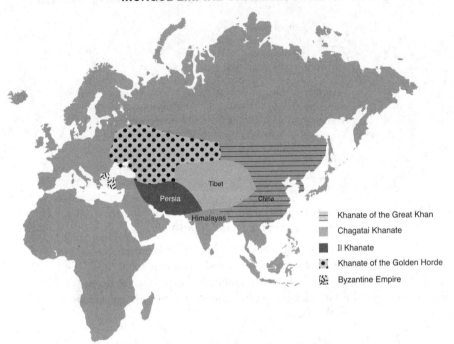

FUN FACT: The Mongols established the largest land empire
in history, controlling approximately 11 million square miles!

207. Which of the following best describes the political structure of the empire
shown on the map?

(A) Although each khanate was ruled separately, they reported to a central
Mongol ruler.

(B) The Mongol Empire was divided into khanates that were each ruled
individually.

(C) The division of the Mongol Empire into khanates was similar to the
division of power in a bureaucracy.

(D) Although each khanate was ruled separately, they all had similar
policies toward conquered groups.

208. Which of the following factors contributed to the Mongol expansion
shown on the map?

(A) A lack of centralized governments in the area

(B) Military strategies and access to gunpowder weapons

(C) Experience with administrative techniques and taxation systems

(D) Control of trade routes providing wealth to fund the military

209. Which of the following best describes an economic effect of the expansion of the Mongol Empire?

(A) Mongol rule facilitated the diffusion of goods and the transfer of information across the Silk Road.

(B) Mongol conquest of trading cities led to a decline in Silk Road trade networks.

(C) Mongol control of the Yuan dynasty led to decreased demand for Chinese goods.

(D) Mongol taxation policies increased the price of goods, lowering the volume of trade.

Questions 210–212 refer to the image below.

MAYAN VESSEL WITH SEATED LORD, CIRCA 7TH AND 8TH CENTURY C.E.

210. The object can best be used as evidence for which of the following that occurred in the period 600–1450 C.E.?

(A) States in some areas synthesized local with foreign traditions.

(B) Imperial systems emerged in the Americas that were similar to those in Afro-Eurasia.

(C) State systems in the Americas expanded in scope and reach from the previous period.

(D) Political systems in the Americas were dominated by the nobility due to the lack of monarchs.

211. The vessel can best be used as evidence for which of the following continuities in world history?

    (A) The use of art as propaganda by religious institutions
    (B) The diffusion of artistic traditions from Europe to the Americas
    (C) The sponsorship of art by merchants
    (D) The use of art to glorify elites

 **Tip: Continuity questions are usually pretty general. You
should always look at an image's caption for clues.**

212. Based on your knowledge of world history, which of the following best
describes the political organization of the Maya?

    (A) A network of city-states
    (B) A highly centralized empire
    (C) A tributary system
    (D) A feudal system

Questions 213–215 refer to the image below.

ANGKOR WAT TEMPLE, CAMBODIA, CONSTRUCTED
CIRCA 12TH CENTURY C.E.

213. The temple shown in the image best illustrates which of the following
developments of the period 600–1450 c.e.?

    (A) The emergence of reconstituted imperial states following the collapse
        of empires
    (B) The rise of new Hindu and Buddhist states in Southeast Asia
    (C) The transfer of European architectural knowledge to Southeast Asia
    (D) The extension of Chinese political rule beyond East Asia

214. The temple depicted in the image was initially devoted to the Hindu god Vishnu but later became a Buddhist temple. Which of the following best explains this?

    (A) Religious beliefs in Southeast Asia changed frequently due to control by foreigners.

    (B) Indian traditions spread to Southeast Asia via the Silk Road.

    (C) Areas of Southeast Asia developed tributary relationships with China.

    (D) Southeast Asia was influenced by the Indian Ocean trade network.

215. The presence of the temple shown in the image best exemplifies which of the following historical processes?

    (A) The spread of religious traditions beyond their place of origin

    (B) The conflict between religion and secular governments

    (C) The intolerance of religious beliefs by rulers

    (D) The financial support of foreign merchants by governments

Short-Answer Questions

Use the map below to answer all parts of the question that follows.

ZHENG HE'S VOYAGES, 1405–1433

216. a) Describe ONE change that resulted from the voyages depicted on the map.

    b) Describe ONE continuity in the Indian Ocean basin from 600 to 1450.

    c) Describe ONE way the decision to end the voyages impacted China in the period 1450–1900 C.E.

Answer all parts of the question that follows.

217. a) Identify ONE similarity in the administrative techniques used by imperial states in the period 600–1450 C.E.

b) Explain ONE reason for the use of similar administrative techniques of imperial states in the period 600–1450 C.E.

c) Identify ONE difference in the political systems of imperial states and decentralized regions in the period 600–1450 C.E.

Long Essay Questions

218. In the period 600–1450 C.E., new states and empires demonstrated continuity, innovation, and diversity as they developed in various regions such as the Mediterranean, the Middle East, and East Asia.

Develop an argument that evaluates how one or more new states or empires consolidated power and administered their territory in this time period.

219. In the period 600–1450 C.E., the decline and reconstitution of empires in regions such as the Mediterranean, the Middle East, and East Asia affected the expansion or decline of cities across Afro-Eurasia.

Develop an argument that evaluates how the growth of empires led to the change in urban growth in Afro-Eurasia in the period circa 600–1450 C.E.

Document-Based Question

220. Evaluate the extent to which political systems impacted commerce in the period circa 300–1500 C.E.

Document 1

Source: *The New History of the Tang Dynasty*, published in 1060 C.E., discussing the taxation system before a Twice-a-Year Tax was proposed

Very little of the tax revenue that should have gone to the emperor was actually presented. Altogether there were several hundred kinds of taxation: those that had been formally abolished were never dropped, and those that duplicated others were never eliminated. Old and new taxes piled up, and there seemed to be no limit to them. The people drained the last drop of their blood and marrow; they sold their loved ones. ... Rich people with many able-bodied adults in their families sought to obtain exemption from labor services by having them become officials, students, Buddhist monks, and Daoist priests. The poor had nothing they could get into [to obtain such an exemption] and continued to be registered as able-bodied adults liable to labor service. The upper class had their taxes forgiven, while the lower class had their taxes increased. Thereupon the empire was ruined and in distress, and the people wandered around like vagrants. Fewer than four or five out of a hundred lived in their own villages and stayed on their own land.

Document 2

Source: *The Chronicle of Zuo*, Chinese history book, circa 350 B.C.E. during the second Warring States period

An ambassador from another [Chinese] state desired a jade ring that belonged to a merchant who resided in the Chinese state of Lu. So the ambassador begged Zi Chan, a Lu official, to have the ring confiscated from the merchant and given to him. Zi Chan, however, refused, saying, "One of our ancient rulers made a pact with the merchants in our state, to last through all generations. The pact said, 'If you do not revolt against me, I will not violently interfere with your commerce. I will not beg or take anything from you, and you may have your profitable markets, precious things, and substance, without my taking any knowledge of them.'"

Document 3

Source: Excerpts from *Corpus Iurus Civilis*, Byzantine legal code, circa 535 C.E.

41. But things sold and delivered are not acquired by the buyer until he has paid the seller the price, or satisfied him in some way or other, as by procuring some one to be security, or by giving a pledge. And, although this is provided by a law of the Twelve Tables, yet it may be rightly said to spring from the law of nations, that is, the law of nature. But if the seller has accepted the credit of the buyer, the thing then becomes immediately the property of the buyer ...

44. Sometimes, too, the mere wish of the owner, without tradition, is sufficient to transfer the property in a thing, as when a person has lent, or let to you anything, or deposited anything with you, and then afterwards sells or gives it to you. For, although he has not delivered it to you for the purpose of the sale or gift, yet by the mere fact of his consenting to it becoming yours, you instantly acquire the property in it, as fully as if it had actually been delivered to you for the express purpose of passing the property.

45. So, too, anyone who has sold goods deposited in a warehouse, as soon as he has handed over the keys of the warehouse to the buyer, transfers to the buyer the property in the goods ...

Document 4

Source: Qu'ran, Islamic holy text, Surah Al Nisa' (4), Aayah 29, 7th century C.E.

"O ye who believe! Eat not up your property among yourselves in vanities; but let there be among you traffic and trade by mutual good-will."

Document 5

Source: Fra Angelico, *St. Nicholas with the Emperor's Envoy and the Miraculous Rescue of a Sailing Vessel*, between 1437 and 1449

Document 6

Source: Ganapatideva, ruler of South Indian Kakatiya state, circa 1245 c.e.

By the glorious king Ganapatideva the following edict assuring safety had been granted to sea traders starting for and arriving from all continents, islands, foreign countries, and cities:

Formerly kings used to take away by force the whole cargo—elephants, horses, gems, etc.—carried by ships and vessels which, after they had started from one country to another, were attacked by storms and wrecked ashore.

But we, out of mercy, for the sake of glory and merit, hereby pledge to leave everything except the fixed duty to those who have incurred the great risk of a sea voyage with the thought that wealth is more valuable than even life.

The rate of this duty is one thirtieth on all exports and imports.

Document 7

Source: Ibn Battuta, Muslim traveler, 14th century, describing East African city-states

We stayed one night in this island [Mombasa], and then pursued our journey to Kulwa, which is a large town on the coast. The majority of its inhabitants are Zanj, jet-black in colour, and with tattoo marks on their faces. I was told by a merchant that the town of Sufala lies a fortnight's journey [south] from Kulwa and that gold dust is brought to Sufala from Yufi in the country of the Limis, which is a month's journey distant from it. Kulwa is a very fine and substantially built town, and all its buildings are of wood. Its inhabitants are constantly engaged in military expeditions, for their country is contiguous to the heathen Zanj.

The sultan at the time of my visit was Abu'l-Muzaffar Hasan, who was noted for his gifts and generosity. He used to devote the fifth part of the booty made on his expeditions to pious and charitable purposes, as is prescribed in the Koran, and I have seen him give the clothes off his back to a mendicant who asked him for them. When this liberal and virtuous sultan died, he was succeeded by his brother Dawud, who was at the opposite pole from him in this respect. Whenever a petitioner came to him, he would say, "He who gave is dead, and left nothing behind him to be given." Visitors would stay at his court for months on end, and finally he would make them some small gift, so that at last people gave up going to his gate.

(Answers on pages 332–336.)

Increased Economic Productivity and Its Consequences

CHAPTER 9

Answers to Chapter 9 are on pages 336–339.

 Key Concept 3.3—Changes in trade networks resulted from and stimulated increasing productive capacity, with important implications for social and gender structures and environmental processes.

I. Innovations stimulated agricultural and industrial production in many regions.

    A. Agricultural production increased significantly due to technological innovations.

    B. Demand for foreign luxury goods increased in Afro-Eurasia. Chinese, Persian, and Indian artisans and merchants expanded their production of textiles and porcelains for export; industrial production of iron and steel expanded in China.

II. The fate of cities varied greatly, with periods of significant decline and periods of increased urbanization buoyed by rising productivity and expanding trade networks.

    A. Multiple factors contributed to the decline of urban areas in this period, including invasions, disease, and the decline of agricultural productivity.

    B. Multiple factors contributed to urban revival, including the end of invasions, the availability of safe and reliable transport, the rise of commerce and warmer temperatures between 800 and 1300 C.E., increased agricultural productivity and subsequent rising population, and greater availability of labor.

III. Despite significant continuities in social structures and in methods of production, there were also some important changes in labor management and in the effect of religious conversion on gender relations and family life.

    A. The diversification of labor organization that began with settled agriculture continued in this period. Forms of labor organization included free peasant agriculture, nomadic pastoralism, craft production and guild organization, various forms of coerced and unfree labor, government-imposed labor taxes, and military obligations.

B. As in the previous period, social structures were shaped largely by class and caste hierarchies. Patriarchy continued; however, in some areas, women exercised more power and influence, most notably among the Mongols and in West Africa, Japan, and Southeast Asia.

C. New forms of coerced labor appeared, including serfdom in Europe and Japan and the elaboration of the *mit'a* in the Inca Empire. Peasants resisted attempts to raise dues and taxes by staging revolts. The demand for slaves for both military and domestic purposes increased, particularly in central Eurasia, parts of Africa, and the eastern Mediterranean.

D. Buddhism, Christianity, Islam, and Neoconfucianism were adopted in new regions and often caused significant changes in gender relations and family structure.

Agricultural and manufacturing productivity increased in this period due to the intensification of trade, leading to population growth and urbanization. This led to new forms of forced labor, such as serfdom, and the continuation of previous forms of labor, such as peasant agriculture and slavery. Societies remained stratified and patriarchal. However, in some regions, women took on new roles that gave them more power.

Questions 221–224 refer to the image below.

MAP OF MEXICO UNDER MEXICA RULE, CIRCA 1519

Madman © 2001

FUN FACT: You may have learned about the Aztec Empire rather than the Mexica. The term Aztec was not commonly used until the 18th century, when a Jesuit monk wrote a history of the indigenous people of the Americas. The name derived from the Azteca people who left the city of Atzlan and moved to the valley of Mexico in the 14th century and founded the cities that became the basis of the empire.

221. The location of cities depicted on the map best reflects which of the following characteristics of the Mexica?

   (A) Their location enabled them to defend urban areas from outside invaders.
   (B) Their use of draft animals enabled them to construct large cities with monumental architecture.
   (C) They used technologies to adapt to their environment and improve agricultural production.
   (D) They needed to import food crops from North America due to a lack of areas for cultivation.

222. Which of the following factors contributed to urban revival in the period 600–1450 C.E.?

   (A) The need for protection from invasions plaguing the countryside
   (B) The rise of commerce and increased agricultural productivity
   (C) The concentration of industrial labor in cities
   (D) The decline in trade and lower levels of production

223. Which of the following best describes the Mexica civilization?

   (A) The empire had a tributary relationship with conquered groups.
   (B) The decentralized government was divided into individual city-states.
   (C) The empire was highly centralized with bureaucratic institutions.
   (D) The government had little control beyond Tenochtitlan.

224. The map best illustrates which of the following patterns of world history?

   (A) Cities are often self-sufficient and have little contact with surrounding areas.
   (B) Cities are often economic centers rather than residential areas.
   (C) Cities are often built in locations that provide access to lakes, swamps, and islands.
   (D) Cities often serve as centers of commerce, religious rituals, and political institutions.

Questions 225–227 refer to the passage below.

"To that magnificent lord _____, I, _____. Since it is known familiarly to all how little I have whence to feed and clothe myself, I have therefore petitioned your piety, and your good-will has decreed to me that I should hand myself over or commend myself to your guardianship, which I have thereupon done; that is to say in this way, that you should aid and succor [secure] me as well with food as with clothing, according as I shall be able to serve you and deserve it.

And so long as I shall live I ought to provide service and honor to you, suitably to my free condition; and I shall not during the time of my life have the ability to withdraw from your power or guardianship; but must remain during the days of my life under your power or defence. Wherefore it is proper that if either of us shall wish to withdraw himself from these agreements, he shall pay _____ shillings to the other party (*pari suo*), and this agreement shall remain unbroken."

Frankish formula of commendation, Western Europe, 7th century C.E.

225. **The passage best represents which of the following?**

(A) Military conscription
(B) Indentured servitude
(C) Slavery
(D) Serfdom

226. **Which of the following occurred as a direct reaction against the system described in the passage?**

(A) Revolts were staged by those opposed to higher dues.
(B) Monarchies were overthrown by serfs who sought natural rights.
(C) Rebellions were organized by nobles unwilling to clothe and feed laborers.
(D) Mutinies were staged by armies seeking better fighting conditions.

227. **Which of the following factors contributed to agreements similar to the one in the passage?**

(A) The end of social welfare systems led to mass poverty and famine.
(B) The spread of epidemic diseases led to decentralized governments.
(C) Invasions caused the decline of urban areas and the desire for protection.
(D) Labor-saving devices lowered the demand for unskilled workers.

Questions 228–230 refer to the sources below.

Source 1

SCROLL DEPICTING SERICULTURE, CHINA, EARLY 13TH CENTURY C.E.

Sericulture is the process of producing silk cloth.

Source 2

"It is a fact that all over the country of Cathay [China] there is a kind of black stones existing in beds in the mountains, which they dig out and burn like firewood. If you supply the fire with them at night, and see that they are well kindled, you will find them still alight in the morning; and they make such capital fuel that no other is used throughout the country. It is true that they have plenty of wood also, but they do not burn it, because those stones burn better and cost less.

[Moreover with that vast number of people, and the number of hot baths that they maintain—for every one has such a bath at least three times a week, and in winter if possible every day, whilst every nobleman and man of wealth has a private bath for his own use—the wood would not suffice for the purpose.]"

Marco Polo, Italian traveler, *The Book of Ser Marco Polo: The Venetian Concerning Kingdoms and Marvels of the East*, 13th century c.e.

228. The image in Source 1 supports which of the following assertions about the time period 600–1450 c.e.?

(A) Silk production relied on slave labor to produce large quantities.
(B) Production of silk expanded to meet the increased demand for luxury goods.
(C) Silk production was mainly carried out in large state-run factories.
(D) Production of silk depended on environmental and political factors.

229. <u>Source 2</u> supports which of the following assertions about China in the period 600–1450 C.E.?

(A) Coal was used due to a lack of alternative sources of energy.
(B) Landowning elites were less susceptible to diseases.
(C) Water shortages existed due to high demand.
(D) Industrial production of coal and iron expanded.

230. Which of the following factors most likely contributed to Marco Polo's ability to travel to China?

(A) The Yuan dynasty's expansion westward decreased the distance between Europe and China.
(B) Italian city-states grew more influential as a result of the Crusades.
(C) Mongol control of the Silk Road trade networks facilitated travel across Eurasia.
(D) European exploration in the Indian Ocean basin led to the establishment of sea routes to China.

Questions 231–234 refer to the passage below.

"The Arabs were responsible for moving sugarcane cultivation and sugar manufacturing westward from southern Iraq into other relatively arid lands. Growers had to adapt the plant to new conditions, and they had to develop more efficient irrigation technologies. By 1000 or so sugarcane had become an important crop in the Yemen; in Arabian oases; in irrigated areas of Syria, Lebanon, Palestine, Egypt, and the Mahgrib; in Spain; and on Mediterranean islands controlled by Muslims. By the tenth century cotton also had become a major crop in the lands of the caliphate, from Iran and Central Asia to Spain and the Mediterranean islands. Cotton industries sprang up wherever the plant was cultivated, producing for both local and distant markets.

The introduction of Indian crops, such as sugar and cotton, led to a much more intensive agriculture in the Middle East and some parts of the Mediterranean. Before the arrival of these crops, farmers had planted in the fall to take advantage of autumn rains and harvested in the spring. In the heat of the summer their fields usually lay fallow. But the new southern crops preferred the heat of the summer, and thus farmers began to use their fields throughout the year. They also began to use a system of multiple cropping, a practice that seems to have come from India. This led to an increased interest in soil fertility, and to manuals that advised farmers about adding such things as animal dung and vegetable and mineral materials to the soil to maintain its productivity."

Lynda Shaffer, historian, *Southernization*, 1994

231. Which of the following factors most likely contributed to the shift in sugarcane cultivation as discussed in the passage?

    (A) The diffusion of crops along Eurasian trade routes, such as the Indian Ocean networks

    (B) The contact between Christians and Muslims as a result of the Crusades

    (C) The tributary relationship established between the Abbasids and Tang China

    (D) The intensification of trans-Saharan trade and increased contacts with West African kingdoms

232. The passage best reflects which of the following characteristics of the period 600–1450 C.E.?

    (A) Commercial growth was facilitated by state practices and trading organizations.

    (B) Increased cross-cultural interactions resulted in the diffusion of literary and artistic traditions.

    (C) Crop production increased significantly due to technological innovations.

    (D) Demand for luxury goods led to increased production of Chinese porcelains and textiles.

 Tip: Each of these four answer choices comes directly from the key concepts for this period, so you must decide which one best relates to the passage.

233. Which of the following best describes an effect of the agricultural practices described in the passage?

    (A) Demand for slaves in the Middle East decreased due to improved soil fertility.

    (B) Increased production led to a variety of forms of labor organization.

    (C) Surplus food crops led to population growth in the Middle East.

    (D) The Middle East became more self-sufficient due to the expansion of production.

234. Increased demand for crops referred to in the passage led to which of the following in the period 1450–1750 C.E.?

    (A) The creation of guilds to organize artisans

    (B) The rise of indentured servitude in Europe

    (C) The first use of slave labor for cultivation of cash crops

    (D) The establishment of plantations in the Caribbean

Questions 235–237 refer to the passage below.

"Because a great part of the people and especially of the, workmen and servants has now died in that pestilence, some, seeing the straights of the masters and the scarcity of servants, are not willing to serve unless they receive excessive wages, and others, rather than through labour to gain their living, prefer to beg in idleness: We, considering the grave inconveniences which might come from the lack especially of ploughmen and such labourers, have held deliberation and treaty concerning this with the prelates and nobles and other learned men sitting by us; by whose consentient counsel we have seen fit to ordain: that every man and woman of our kingdom of England, of whatever condition, whether bond or free, who is able bodied and below the age of sixty years, not living from trade nor carrying on a fixed craft, nor having of his own the means of living, or land of his own with regard to the cultivation of which he might occupy himself, and not serving another, if he, considering his station, be sought after to serve in a suitable service, he shall be bound to serve him who has seen fit so to seek after him; and he shall take only the wages liveries, meed or salary which, in the places where he sought to serve, were accustomed to be paid in the twentieth year of our reign of England, or the five or six common years next preceding."

The Statute of Laborers, issued by King Edward III, 1351

235. The restrictions described in the passage are best understood in the context of which of the following?

   (A) Migrations to urban areas by peasants in search of industrial labor
   (B) Labor shortages following the spread of the bubonic plague
   (C) Famine as a result of the Little Ice Age contributing to lower populations
   (D) Rebellions following the implementation of serfdom

236. Which of the following best describes the likely intent of the statute?

   (A) To secure an affordable labor force for the nobility
   (B) To ensure a reliable staff of servants at the king's palace
   (C) To improve wages for workers to stop rebellions
   (D) To stabilize the government following civil war

237. Which of the following is most likely an effect of the pestilence mentioned in the passage?

   (A) The desire to seek maritime routes to Asia
   (B) The rise of commerce due to warmer temperatures
   (C) The invention of labor-saving devices
   (D) The complete isolation of England

Questions 238–240 refer to the graph below.

CHINA'S POPULATION, 600–1200 C.E.

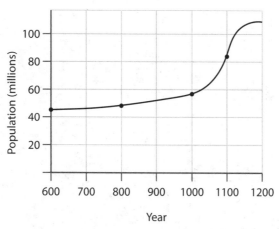

238. Which of the following factors most likely contributed to the changes on the graph between 1000 and 1200 C.E.?

(A) The government provided incentives for families to bear children.

(B) The lack of effective forms of birth control led to large families.

(C) The construction of the Great Wall resulted in an absence of outside threats and war.

(D) Increased agricultural production resulted in the availability of more food crops.

239. Which of the following was an effect of the trend shown on the graph?

(A) Rebellions occurred as food supply could not meet the demand of the growing population.

(B) Slavery increased due to greater demand for workers on plantations.

(C) Urban areas grew due to rising productivity and expanding trade networks.

(D) Conquest of Vietnam and Japan occurred to meet the need for more arable land.

240. Which of the following continuities occurred in China throughout this period despite the changes on the graph?

(A) A single family controlled the central government.

(B) Patriarchy and a rigid social hierarchy remained.

(C) The government used violence to enforce its rule.

(D) Social mobility was common due to the education system.

Questions 241–242 refer to the image below.

STATUE OF MURASAKI SHIKIBU, KYOTO, JAPAN

Murasaki wrote the world's first novel, Tale of Genji, *in the 11th century c.e.*

241. The statue represents which of the following characteristics of the period 600–1450 C.E.?

    (A) Women in Japan exercised influence on society, despite the persistence of patriarchy elsewhere.
    (B) Women in Japan of all classes had equal opportunities like men.
    (C) Japanese society was highly patriarchal, much like Chinese society.
    (D) Chinese views of women influenced Japanese gender roles.

242. The role of women in Japanese society as shown in the image is <u>most different from</u> the role of women in which of the following in the period 600–1450 C.E.?

    (A) Southeast Asia
    (B) West Africa
    (C) The Mongol Empire
    (D) Tang China

Questions 243–246 refer to the graph below.

EUROPEAN POPULATION, 800–1300 C.E.

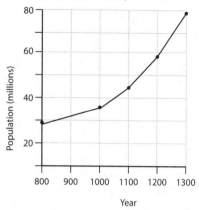

243. Which of the following best explains the overall population trend shown on the graph?

    (A) Less warfare and lack of invasions led to fewer casualties.
    (B) Agricultural output increased as a result of innovations.
    (C) Increased immigration to Europe occurred as a result of the Crusades.
    (D) Family size increased due to the introduction of Christianity.

244. All of the following are consequences of the trend shown on the graph EXCEPT

    (A) greater availability of labor
    (B) urban revival
    (C) widespread famine
    (D) increased commerce

245. The historical trend shown on the graph is <u>most similar to</u> which of the following?

    (A) The impact of the Green Revolution on India
    (B) The impact of the Columbian Exchange on the Americas
    (C) The impact of Mongol rule on China
    (D) The impact of European immigration to North America

246. Which of the following changed the trend shown on the graph in the 14th century C.E.?

    (A) The continuous invasions of Germanic tribes
    (B) The outbreak of wars among European kingdoms
    (C) The immigration to the Americas by Europeans
    (D) The spread of pathogens as a result of trade contacts

Questions 247–250 refer to the passage below.

"Cities on China's southern coasts became centers of overseas commerce. Silk remained an important export, and by the Tang dynasty it had been joined by a true porcelain, which was developed in China sometime before 400 C.E. China and its East Asian neighbors had a monopoly on the manufacture of true porcelain until the early eighteenth century. Many attempts were made to imitate it, and some of the resulting imitations were economically and stylistically important. China's southern ports were also exporting to Southeast Asia large quantities of ordinary consumer goods, including iron hardware, such as needles, scissors, and cooking pots. Although iron manufacturing was concentrated in the north, the large quantity of goods produced was a direct result of the size of the market in southern China and overseas. Until the British Industrial Revolution of the eighteenth century, no other place ever equaled the iron production of Song China."

Lynda Shaffer, historian, *Southernization*, 1994

247. Which of the following factors contributed to the development of Chinese commerce as described in the passage?

(A) The lack of iron deposits throughout much of Eurasia

(B) The decline of the production of goods in Southeast Asia

(C) The expansion of empires across Eurasia

(D) The sponsorship of businesses by the government

248. Which of the following best reflects a consequence of increased production as described in the passage?

(A) Migrations to the mining regions of Northern China

(B) Urbanization due to increased commerce

(C) Fewer farmers due to the demand for mine workers

(D) Monopolies formed in the porcelain industry

249. Contact between China and Southeast Asia as described in the passage is most similar to contact between which of the following?

(A) Britain and India in the nineteenth century

(B) Spain and Portugal in the fifteenth century

(C) West Africa and India in the twelfth century

(D) Japan and the United States in the nineteenth century

250. Contact between Chinese and Southeast Asian merchants would most likely result in which of the following?

   (A) Cultural conservatism and the rejection of foreign ideas
   (B) Increased tension due to competition for control of trade
   (C) The diffusion of Hinduism from Southeast Asia to China
   (D) The spread of Neoconfucian values to Southeast Asia

Short-Answer Questions

Answer all parts of the question that follows.

251. a) Identify ONE factor that led to the development of serfdom as a form of labor between 600 and 1450 C.E.

   b) Explain ONE similarity in the role of serfs and slaves in labor systems in the period 600–1450 C.E.

   c) Explain ONE difference between the role of serfs and slaves in labor systems in the period 600–1450 C.E.

Answer all parts of the question that follows.

252. a) Identify ONE change that occurred in agricultural production in the period 600–1450 C.E.

   b) Identify ONE factor that contributed to changes in agricultural production in the period 600–1450 C.E.

   c) Identify ONE continuity that occurred in agricultural production in the period 600–1450 C.E.

Long Essay Questions

253. In the period 600–1450 C.E., changes in trade networks resulted from and stimulated increasing productive capacity, with important implications for social and gender structures.

   Develop an argument that evaluates the changes in social and gender structures in the period 600–1450 C.E.

254. In the period 600–1450 C.E., despite significant continuities in social structures and in methods of production, there were also some important changes in labor management.

   Develop an argument that evaluates the changes in labor systems in the period 600–1450 C.E.

(Answers on pages 336–339.)

PERIOD 4
(c. 1450–1750 C.E.)
Global
Interactions

Globalizing Networks of Communication and Exchange

Answers to Chapter 10 are on pages 339–344.

Key Concept 4.1—The interconnection of the Eastern and Western Hemispheres, made possible by transoceanic voyaging, transformed trade and religion and had a significant economic, cultural, social, and demographic impact on the world.

I.   Existing regional patterns of trade intensified in the context of the new global circulation of goods.

    A.   The intensification of trade brought prosperity and economic disruption to the merchants and governments in the trading regions of the Indian Ocean, the Mediterranean, the Sahara, and overland Eurasia.

II. European technological developments in cartography and navigation built on previous knowledge developed in the Classical, Islamic, and Asian worlds.

    A.   The developments included the production of new tools, innovations in ship designs, and an improved understanding of global wind and current patterns—all of which made transoceanic travel and trade possible.

III. Remarkable new transoceanic maritime reconnaissance occurred in this period.

    A.   Portuguese development of maritime technology and navigational skills led to increased travel to and trade with West Africa and resulted in the construction of a global trading-post empire.

    B.   Spanish sponsorship of the first Columbian and subsequent voyages across the Atlantic and Pacific dramatically increased European interest in transoceanic travel and trade.

    C.   Northern Atlantic crossings for fishing and for the purpose of settlement continued and spurred European searches for multiple routes to Asia.

IV. The new global circulation of goods was facilitated by chartered European monopoly companies and the flow of silver from Spanish colonies in the

Americas to purchase Asian goods for the Atlantic markets. Regional markets continued to flourish in Afro-Eurasia by using established commercial practices and new transoceanic shipping services developed by European merchants.

    A. European merchants' role in Asian trade was characterized mostly by transporting goods from one Asian country to another market in Asia or the Indian Ocean region.

    B. Commercialization and the creation of a global economy were intimately connected to new global circulation of silver from the Americas.

    C. Mercantilist policies and practices were used by European rulers to expand and control their economies and claim overseas territories, and joint-stock companies, influenced by these mercantilist policies, were used by rulers and merchants to finance exploration and compete against one another in global trade.

    D. The Atlantic system involved the movement of goods, wealth, and free and unfree laborers and the mixing of African, American, and European cultures and peoples.

V. The new connections between the Eastern and Western Hemispheres resulted in the Columbian Exchange.

    A. European colonization of the Americas led to the spread of diseases that were endemic in the Eastern Hemisphere—including smallpox, measles, and influenza—to Amerindian populations and the unintentional transfer of disease vectors, including mosquitoes and rats.

    B. American foods became staple crops in various parts of Europe, Asia, and Africa. Cash crops were grown primarily on plantations with coerced labor and were exported mostly to Europe and the Middle East in this period.

    C. Afro-Eurasian fruit trees, grains, sugar, and domesticated animals were brought by Europeans to the Americas, while other foods were brought by African slaves.

    D. Populations in Afro-Eurasia benefited nutritionally from the increased diversity of American food crops.

    E. European colonization and the introduction of European agriculture and settlement practices in the Americas often affected the physical environment through deforestation and soil depletion.

VI. The increase in interactions between newly connected hemispheres and intensification of connections within hemispheres expanded the spread and reform of existing religions and contributed to both religious conflicts and the creation of syncretic belief systems and practices.

VII. As merchants' profits increased and governments collected more taxes, funding for the visual and performing arts, even for popular audiences, increased along with an expansion of literacy and increased focus on innovation and scientific inquiry.

Technological innovations enabled European explorers to insert themselves into existing Afro-Eurasian trade networks. At the same time, Columbus's arrival in the Caribbean set the stage for the integration of the Eastern and Western Hemispheres. New contact between these previously unconnected worlds led to the Columbian Exchange, or the transfer of pathogens, plants, animals, ideas, culture, and people. The indigenous peoples of the Americas were devastated by diseases, while the clearing of land for plantations led to environmental degradation. Throughout Afro-Eurasia, the introduction of new food crops from the Americas led to more varied diets and larger populations. Existing trade networks expanded with the influx of goods from the Americas, especially cash crops. European merchants served as the carriers of goods among regional markets, aided greatly by silver from the Americas. As trade intensified, existing religions spread, and new syncretic belief systems formed. Governments taxed trade and used the revenue to fund the arts.

Questions 255–258 refer to the passage below.

"Europe's Dutch and English East India Companies are often viewed as prototypes of modern multinational corporations. The scholarly literature recognizes that huge quantities of silver flowed to Asia, but this phenomenon is considered a reflection of Europe's balance-of-trade deficit with east Asia; Europeans developed a far greater taste for Asian finery than the other way around, according to conventional wisdom, so treasure had to flow from west to east to pay for Europe's trade deficit. In short, all the key issues are normally framed in terms of European perspectives. Acceptance of a global perspective instead of the predominant Eurocentric view outlined above yields a startlingly different view. It becomes clear that Europeans did indeed play an important role in the birth of world trade, but their role was as middlemen in the vast silver trade; they were prime movers on neither the supply side (except Spain in America) nor the demand side of the worldwide silver market. Europeans were intermediaries in the trade between the New World and China. Massive amounts of silver traversed the Atlantic. After it had reached European soil, the Portuguese in the sixteenth century and Dutch in the seventeenth century became dominant distributors of silver by a multitude of routes into Asia."

> Dennis O. Flynn and Arturo Giráldez, historians,
> *Born with a "Silver Spoon": The Origin of World Trade in 1571*, 1995

255. **Which of the following most directly led to the increased presence of Europeans in Asian trade?**

   (A) European maritime reconnaissance in the Indian Ocean basin
   (B) British conquest of India
   (C) European colonization of North America
   (D) The establishment of trading posts in coastal West Africa

256. **Which of the following would best support the author's assertion that Europeans were middlemen in the global silver trade?**

   (A) Silver mined in South America was transported to Spain.
   (B) Europeans had a great demand for Asian luxury items.
   (C) Chinese goods were purchased by Europeans with silver mined in South America.
   (D) European monarchies required silver to finance large building projects.

257. **Which was an important effect of the process described in the passage?**

   (A) Imperial rule in China weakened as European interference in China's economy strengthened.
   (B) Europeans conquered and colonized indigenous peoples of Latin America.
   (C) Demand for European manufactured goods in Asia increased.
   (D) Europeans established trading post empires in Africa and Asia.

258. **The contact between Europeans and Asians described in the passage contributed most directly to which of the following?**

   (A) The complete adoption of Western culture by Asian peoples
   (B) The diffusion of existing religions, such as Christianity
   (C) Chinese sponsorship of the voyages of Zheng He
   (D) European conquest of Africa in order to acquire slaves

Questions 259–261 are based on the image below.

SLAVERY: WEST INDIES, 1596

The image above, by European artist Theodor de Bry, shows African slaves processing sugarcane on the Caribbean island of Hispaniola, 1596.

 Tip: When working with artwork, read the captions carefully. Most of the information you need to answer the questions tends to be in the captions.

259. The presence of a sugar plantation in Hispaniola is most likely due to which of the following?

(A) Widespread migration of indentured servants
(B) The Atlantic trade system
(C) Indian Ocean basin networks
(D) Trans-Saharan caravans

260. Which of the following changes occurred as a result of the cultivation depicted in the image?

(A) The decline of Amerindian populations as a result of African diseases
(B) Population growth throughout Eurasia
(C) Environmental degradation, such as soil depletion
(D) European colonization in Africa

261. The conditions on plantations as shown in the image contributed most directly to which of the following in the period 1750–1850?

(A) Slave resistance challenged the existing authorities in the Americas.
(B) African cultural elements were completely eliminated from Caribbean culture.
(C) Slavery and relative conformity to the institution was accepted by Africans.
(D) Epidemic diseases, such as smallpox, spread.

Questions 262–263 are based on the image below.

DISCOVERY OF NORTH AMERICA BY JOHN CABOT

This image depicts the landing of John Cabot in Canada and his claiming it for England in 1497.

262. Which of the following made the event shown in the image possible?

   (A) Improvements in European cartography and navigation
   (B) The availability of steamships due to the Industrial Revolution
   (C) Access to knowledge from the Chinese acquired through Zheng He's voyages
   (D) Profits from the slave trade enabling Europeans to invest in voyages

263. Which most likely explains the motivation of the English monarchy to fund Cabot's voyage?

   (A) The desire to establish cotton plantations due to industrialization
   (B) The establishment of Portuguese trading posts throughout the Indian Ocean basin
   (C) The need to acquire land for settlement due to rapid population growth
   (D) Spanish sponsorship of the voyages of Columbus and other explorers

Questions 264–266 are based on the following two images.

Image 1

CARAVEL SHIP, C. 1500

Image 2

COMPASS USED BY EUROPEAN EXPLORERS
IN THE 15TH AND 16TH CENTURIES

264. The object in <u>Image 1</u> contributed to which of the following developments in the period 1450–1750 c.e.?

(A) The creation of the first trade link between Europe and Asia

(B) The disappearance of previously established trade networks

(C) The creation of a global economy and the rise of mercantilism

(D) The diffusion of Chinese technology to Europeans as a result of the Crusades

265. The object in Image 2 best illustrates which of the following developments in the period 1450–1750 C.E.?

   (A) The diffusion of knowledge from Islamic and Asian Empires to European navigators
   (B) The development of new syncretic cultural traditions
   (C) The intensification of existing trade networks
   (D) The influence of the Columbian Exchange on technological knowledge

266. When taken together, the two images best support which of the following conclusions?

   (A) Europeans developed entirely new technologies to begin maritime expeditions.
   (B) Improved technology enabled Europeans to undertake transoceanic voyages.
   (C) European technology in this era was completely adopted from other regions.
   (D) Improved technology was the result of new contact between Europeans and the Americas.

Questions 267–270 are based on the map below.

GLOBAL TRADE, C. 1500–1800

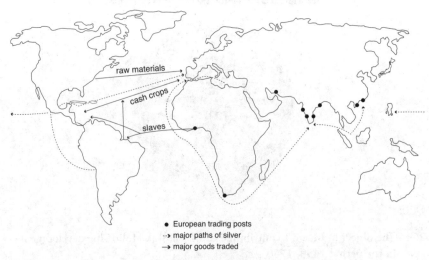

- European trading posts
- major paths of silver
- major goods traded

 Tip: Be sure to take note of the map's title and to examine the key carefully. They could include important dates to help you in answering the questions!

267. Which of the following factors contributed to the increased circulation of goods shown on the map in the period 1500–1750 C.E.?

   (A) The development of industrial technologies, such as steamships
   (B) The control of trade routes by gunpowder civilizations, such as the Ottomans
   (C) The rise of royal-chartered European trading companies, such as the British East India Company
   (D) The expansion of land-based caravan trade, such as trans-Saharan routes

268. Based on your knowledge of world history, how were European societies affected by an increased presence in global trade?

   (A) European governments used increased tax revenues to fund the arts.
   (B) European governments declined as European trading companies grew more powerful.
   (C) European empires contracted as managing global maritime empires became more difficult.
   (D) European empires expanded rapidly due to new industrial technologies.

269. Due to the contacts illustrated on the map, which of the following cultural processes occurred in the period 1450–1750 C.E.?

   (A) The adoption of Western cultural elements throughout Asia
   (B) The spread of existing belief systems
   (C) The diffusion of Islamic cultural elements in West Africa
   (D) The adoption of Chinese technologies by Japan

270. Which of the following best describes an effect of the increased European presence in global trade?

   (A) The decline in Indian Ocean trade networks as Atlantic routes became more widespread
   (B) The increased global demand for goods native to Europe
   (C) The decline in European exports to regional Asian markets
   (D) The creation of a truly global economy due to the integration of the Americas

Questions 271–274 are based on the following passage.

"One of the principal effects of those discoveries [the Americas and a route to Asia] has been to raise the mercantile system to a degree of splendour and glory which it could never otherwise have attained to. It is the object of that system to enrich a great nation rather by trade and manufactures than by the improvement and cultivation of land, rather by the industry of the towns than by that of the country. But, in consequence of those discoveries, the commercial towns of

Europe, instead of being the manufacturers and carriers for but a very small part of the world (that part of Europe which is washed by the Atlantic Ocean, and the countries which lie round the Baltic and Mediterranean seas), have now become the manufacturers for the numerous and thriving cultivators of America, and the carriers, and in some respects the manufacturers too, for almost all the different nations of Asia, Africa, and America. Two new worlds have been opened to their industry, each of them much greater and more extensive than the old one, and the market of one of them growing still greater and greater every day. . . ."

Adam Smith, British economist, *Wealth of Nations*, 1776

271. The growth in European manufacturing as described in the passage was most likely due to which of the following?

(A) The mechanization of European industry
(B) Imperial policies established in African colonies
(C) Mercantilist policies of European mother countries
(D) The establishment of spheres of influence in China

272. Which of the following commercial practices led to the economic changes as described in the passage?

(A) The development of joint-stock companies
(B) The rise of guilds in Europe
(C) The growth of feudal society
(D) The creation of a universal currency

273. Based on your knowledge of world history, which of the following factors contributed to the expansion of European global trade in the period circa 1450–1750 C.E.?

(A) The development of the factory system
(B) Access to silver from the Americas
(C) The process of urbanization in Europe
(D) The development of European land-based empires

274. Which of the following most directly contributed to the disruption of European trade in the Western Hemisphere in the nineteenth century?

(A) The increase in European immigrants in the Americas
(B) The development of new transportation technologies
(C) The spread of Enlightenment ideas in the Americas
(D) The increased demand for American silver in China

Questions 275–277 are based on the graph below.

AFRO-EURASIAN POPULATION, 1500–1800

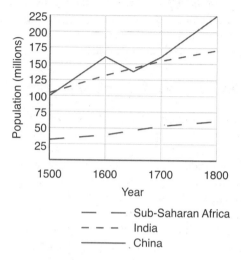

Sub-Saharan Africa
India
China

275. Which of the following explains the overall population trend on the graph?

  (A) The increased consumption of cash crops improved diets in
      Afro-Eurasia
  (B) The use of African slaves on plantations throughout Afro-Eurasia
  (C) The rise of indentured servitude throughout Afro-Eurasia
  (D) Populations in Afro-Eurasia benefiting nutritionally from American
      food crops

276. Which of the following may explain the changes in population in sub-
     Saharan Africa relative to China and India?

  (A) Although all three regions were exposed to new food crops, African
      populations were decimated by the spread of diseases such as smallpox,
      measles, and influenza.
  (B) China and India were exposed to new food crops due to contacts
      with European merchants, while most of sub-Saharan Africa remained
      isolated from contact with Europeans.
  (C) Although all three regions were exposed to new food crops, Africa was
      the only one facing a forced diaspora.
  (D) Centralized governments in China and India promoted the adoption
      of crops from the Americas, while African governments actively resisted
      Western encroachment.

277. Which of the following most likely explains the changes in China's population between 1600 and 1700?

(A) The spread of the Black Death along the Silk Road
(B) Widespread famine and war at the end of the Ming dynasty
(C) China's defeat in the Opium Wars
(D) The environmental effects of the Little Ice Age

Questions 278–281 are based on the passage below.

"As I saw that they [native peoples of the Caribbean] were very friendly to us, and perceived that they could be much more easily converted to our holy faith by gentle means than by force, I presented them with some red caps, and strings of beads to wear upon the neck, and many other trifles of small value, wherewith they were much delighted, and became wonderfully attached to us. . . . Weapons they have none, nor are acquainted with them, for I showed them swords which they grasped by the blades, and cut themselves through ignorance. They have no iron, their javelins being without it, and nothing more than sticks, though some have fish-bones or other things at the ends. They are all of a good size and stature, and handsomely formed. . . . I thought then, and still believe, that these were from the continent. It appears to me, that the people are ingenious, and would be good servants and I am of opinion that they would very readily become Christians, as they appear to have no religion. They very quickly learn such words as are spoken to them. If it please our Lord, I intend at my return to carry home six of them to your Highnesses, that they may learn our language. I saw no beasts in the island, nor any sort of animals except parrots."

Christopher Columbus, European explorer, 1492

278. The contact described in the passage led most directly to which of the following?

(A) The decline of Amerindian populations due to exposure to European diseases
(B) The growth of the African slave trade and the rise of capitalism
(C) The establishment of European trading posts in the Indian Ocean basin
(D) The rise in the global silver trade and the establishment of European maritime empires

279. **The author's description of the natives he encountered most directly reflects the influence of which of the following?**

    (A) His desire to find a direct route to Asia by sailing across the Atlantic
    (B) His understanding of the culture of Native Americans
    (C) His Christian beliefs about proper dress
    (D) His desire to please the monarchs who sponsored his voyages

280. **Which of the following best explains the author's description of the technology of the indigenous peoples?**

    (A) His desire to study the cultural heritage of the people of the Caribbean
    (B) His desire to teach natives how to use European-style weapons
    (C) His desire to profit from the expedition he led by subjugating natives
    (D) His desire to teach natives the Spanish language

281. **Which of the following was the most direct effect of the contact described in the passage?**

    (A) The growth of European cities
    (B) The mixing of African, American, and European cultures and peoples
    (C) The establishment of colonies in Africa
    (D) The rise of European joint-stock companies

Questions 282–285 are based on the passage below.

"The common ways mainly employed by the Spaniards who call themselves Christian and who have gone there to extirpate those pitiful nations and wipe them off the earth is by unjustly waging cruel and bloody wars.

Their reason for killing and destroying such an infinite number of souls is that the Christians have an ultimate aim, which is to acquire gold, and to swell themselves with riches in a very brief time and thus rise to a high estate disproportionate to their merits. It should be kept in mind that their insatiable greed and ambition, the greatest ever seen in the world, is the cause of their villainies. And also, those lands are so rich and felicitous, the native peoples so meek and patient, so easy to subject, that our Spaniards have no more consideration for them than beasts. And I say this from my own knowledge of the acts I witnessed. . . . And never have the Indians in all the Indies committed any act against the Spanish Christians, until those Christians have first and many times committed countless cruel aggressions against them or against neighboring nations. For in the beginning the Indians regarded the Spaniards as angels from Heaven. Only after the Spaniards had used violence against them, killing, robbing, torturing, did the Indians ever rise up against them. . . ."

Bartolomé de Las Casas, Spanish missionary,
Brief Account of the Devastation of the Indies, 1542

 Tip: As you read a passage, note the tone of the document and underline any words that indicate that tone. For example, Las Casas refers to the natives as "pitiful," "meek," and "patient." For the Spaniards, he uses words like "tyranny," "unjustly," and "enslave."

282. Which of the following most likely influenced Las Casas's view of the actions of the Spaniards as described in the passage?

(A) His Spanish heritage
(B) His desire to profit personally
(C) His role as a Christian missionary
(D) His anger toward the natives

283. Spanish treatment of Native Americans as described in the passage contributed most directly to which of the following?

(A) The independence of Latin America
(B) Widespread slave rebellions throughout the Americas
(C) The rise of the trans-Atlantic slave trade
(D) The spread of Enlightenment ideas

284. Which of the following factors contributed most directly to the situation described in the passage?

(A) The Spanish view of the natives as an inferior group
(B) The desire of the Spanish to spread Christianity
(C) Competition among European conquerors for control of the natives
(D) Retaliation for large-scale rebellions by natives

285. Which of the following most directly led to the end of the labor system described in the passage in the period 1750–1900 C.E.?

(A) The spread of Enlightenment ideas
(B) The overthrow of colonial governments by slaves
(C) The colonization of Africa
(D) The Atlantic Revolutions

Short-Answer Questions

Use the passage below to answer all parts of the question that follows.

> "Europe's Dutch and English East India Companies are often viewed
> as prototypes of modern multinational corporations. The scholarly
> literature recognizes that huge quantities of silver flowed to Asia, but
> this phenomenon is considered a reflection of Europe's balance-of-
> trade deficit with east Asia; Europeans developed a far greater taste for
> Asian finery than the other way around, according to conventional
> wisdom, so treasure had to flow from west to east to pay for Europe's
> trade deficit. In short, all the key issues are normally framed in terms
> of European perspectives. Acceptance of a global perspective instead
> of the predominant Eurocentric view outlined above yields a star-
> tlingly different view. It becomes clear that Europeans did indeed play
> an important role in the birth of world trade, but their role was as
> middlemen in the vast silver trade; they were prime movers on neither
> the supply side (except Spain in America) nor the demand side of the
> worldwide silver market. Europeans were intermediaries in the trade
> between the New World and China. Massive amounts of silver tra-
> versed the Atlantic. After it had reached European soil, the Portuguese
> in the sixteenth century and Dutch in the seventeenth century became
> dominant distributors of silver by a multitude of routes into Asia."
>
> Dennis O. Flynn and Arturo Giráldez, historians, *Born with a*
> *"Silver Spoon": The Origin of World Trade in 1571*, 1994

286. a) Explain ONE historically specific example of Europeans' role in global trade in the period 1500–1750 C.E. that supports the authors' assertion in the passage above.

b) Explain ANOTHER historically specific example of Europeans' role in global trade in the period 1500–1750 C.E. that supports the authors' assertion in the passage above.

c) Explain ONE piece of evidence about global trade in the period 1500–1750 C.E. that <u>undermines</u> the authors' assertion in the passage above.

Answer all parts of the question that follows.

287. a) Explain ONE demographic change that occurred as a result of the Columbian Exchange.

b) Explain ONE environmental change that occurred as a result of the Columbian Exchange.

c) Explain ONE economic change that occurred as a result of the Columbian Exchange.

Long Essay Questions

288. In the period 1450–1750 c.e., new connections between the Eastern and Western Hemispheres resulted in the Columbian Exchange.

Develop an argument that evaluates how the Columbian Exchange changed one or more regions in this time period.

289. In the period 1450–1750 c.e., existing regional patterns of trade intensified in the context of the new global circulation of goods.

Develop an argument that evaluates how one or more trade networks changed as a result of the new global circulation of goods in this time period.

Document-Based Question

290. Evaluate the extent to which European conquest and colonization changed societies in Latin America from 1492 to circa 1750.

Document 1

Source: Juan Gines de Sepulveda, *Concerning the Just Cause of the War Against the Indians*, 1547

The Spanish have a perfect right to rule these barbarians of the New World and the adjacent islands, who in prudence, skill, virtues, and humanity are as inferior to the Spanish as children to adults, or women to men; for there exists between the two as great a difference as between savage and cruel races and the most merciful, between the most and the moderate and temperate, and, I might even say, between apes and men....

Furthermore these Indians were otherwise so cowardly and timid that they could barely endure the presence of our soldiers, and many times thousands upon thousands of them scattered in flight like women before Spaniards so few that they did not even number one hundred....

Document 2

Source: An excerpt from the journal of Christopher Columbus, European explorer, describing the natives he encountered in the Caribbean, 1492

Weapons they have none, nor are acquainted with them, for I showed them swords which they grasped by the blades, and cut themselves through ignorance. They have no iron, their javelins being without it, and nothing more than sticks, though some have fish-bones or other things at the ends. They are all of a good size and stature, and handsomely formed.... It appears to me, that the people are ingenious, and would be good servants and I am of opinion that they would very readily become Christians, as they appear to have no religion. They very quickly learn such words as are spoken to them. If it please our Lord, I intend at my return to carry home six of them to your Highnesses, that they may learn our language. I saw no beasts in the island, nor any sort of animals except parrots.

Document 3

Source: Guaman Poma de Ayala, descendant of royal Inca, illustrated letter to the Spanish king, 1615

"The Execution of Atahualpa Inka in Cajamarca"

Document 4

Source: Bartolomé de Las Casas, a Spanish priest, account addressed to the King of Spain hoping for new laws to prevent the brutal exploitation of Native Americans, 1542

Now this infinite multitude of Men are by the Creation of God innocently simple, altogether void of and averse to all manner of Craft, Subtlety and Malice, and most Obedient and Loyal Subjects to their Native Sovereigns; and behave themselves very patiently, submissively and quietly towards the Spaniards, to whom they are subservient and subject; so that finally they live without the least thirst after revenge, laying aside all litigiousness, Commotion and hatred ...

The natives are capable of Morality or Goodness and very apt to receive the principles of Catholic Religion; nor are they averse to Civility and good Manners ..., I myself have heard the Spaniards themselves (who dare not assume the Confidence to deny the good Nature in them) declare, that there was nothing wanting in them for the acquisition of eternal grace, but the sole Knowledge and Understanding of the Deity. ...

Document 5

Source: Aztec accounts of the conquest by the Spanish, 1519

During this time, the people asked Motecuhzoma how they should celebrate their god's fiesta. He said: "Dress him in all his finery, in all his sacred ornaments."

During this same time, The Sun commanded that Motecuhzoma and Itzcohuatzin, the military chief of Tlatelolco, be made prisoners. The Spaniards hanged a chief from Acolhuacan named Nezahualquentzin. They also murdered the king of Nauhtla, Cohualpopocatzin, by wounding him with arrows and then burning him alive.

When this had been done, the celebrants began to sing their songs. That is how they celebrated the first day of the fiesta. On the second day they began to sing again, but without warning they were all put to death. The dancers and singers were completely unarmed.

The Spaniards attacked the musicians first, slashing at their hands and faces until they had killed all of them. The singers—and even the spectators—were also killed. This slaughter in the Sacred Patio went on for three hours. Then the Spaniards burst into the rooms of the temple to kill the others: those who were carrying water, or bringing fodder for the horses, or grinding meal, or sweeping, or standing watch over this work.

The king Motecuhzoma, who was accompanied by Itzcohuatzin and by those who had brought food for the Spaniards, protested: "Our lords, that is enough! What are you doing? These people are not carrying shields or macanas. Our lords, they are completely unarmed!"

The Sun had treacherously murdered our people on the twentieth day after the captain left for the coast. We allowed the Captain to return to the city in peace. But on the following day we attacked him with all our might, and that was the beginning of the war.

Document 6

Source: Hernan Cortés, Spanish conquistador, letter to the Spanish king Charles V, describing Mexico City, 1520

Three halls are in this grand temple, which contain the principal idols; these are of wonderful extent and height, and admirable workmanship, adorned with figures sculptured in stone and wood; leading from the halls are chapels with very small doors, to which the light is not admitted, nor are any persons except the priests, and not all of them. In these chapels are the images of idols, although, as I have before said, many of them are also found on the outside; the principal ones, in which the people have greatest faith and confidence, I precipitated from their pedestals, and cast them down the steps of the temple, purifying the chapels in which they had stood, as they were all polluted with human blood, shed ill the sacrifices. In the place of these I put images of Our Lady and the Saints, which excited not a little feeling in Moctezuma and the inhabitants, who at first remonstrated, declaring that if my proceedings were known throughout the country, the people would rise against me; for they believed that their idols bestowed on them all temporal good, and if they permitted them to be ill-treated, they would be angry and without their gifts, and by this means the people would be deprived of the fruits of the earth and perish with famine. I answered, through the interpreters, that they were deceived in expecting any favors from idols, the work of their own hands, formed of unclean things; and that they must learn there was but one God, the universal Lord of all, who had created the heavens and earth, and all things else, and had made them and us; that He was without beginning and immortal, and they were bound to adore and believe Him, and no other creature or thing.

Document 7

Source: Antonio Vazquez de Espinosa, Spanish monk, *Compendium and Description of the West Indies*, circa 1620

The ore was very rich black flint, and the excavation so extensive that it held more than 3,000 Indians working away hard with picks and hammers, breaking up that flint ore; and when they have filled their little sacks, the poor fellows, loaded down with ore, climb up those ladders or rigging, some like masts and others like cables, and so trying and distressing that a man empty-handed can hardly get up them. That is the way they work in this mine, with many lights and the loud noise of the pounding and great confusion. Nor is that the greatest evil and difficulty; that is due to the thievish and undisciplined superintendents. . . .

These Indians are sent out every year under a captain whom they choose in each village or tribe, for him to take them and oversee them for the year each has to serve; every year they have a new election, for as some go out, others come in. This works out very badly, with great losses and gaps in the quotas of Indians, the villages being depopulated; and this gives rise to great extortions and abuses on the part of the inspectors toward the poor Indians, ruining them and thus depriving the chief Indians of their property and carrying them off in chains because they do not fill out the mita assignment, which they cannot do, for the reason given and for others which I do not bring forward.

(Answers are on pages 339–344.)

New Forms of Social Organization and Modes of Production

Answers for Chapter 11 are on pages 344–348.

Key Concept 4.2—Although the world's productive systems continued to be heavily centered on agriculture, major changes occurred in agricultural labor, the systems and locations of manufacturing, gender and social structures, and environmental processes.

I. Beginning in the fourteenth century, there was a decrease in mean temperatures, often referred to as the Little Ice Age, around the world that lasted until the nineteenth century, contributing to changes in agricultural practices and the contraction of settlement in parts of the Northern Hemisphere.

II. Traditional peasant agriculture increased and changed, plantations expanded, and demand for labor increased. These changes both fed and responded to growing global demand for raw materials and finished products.

    A. Peasant and artisan labor intensified in many regions.

    B. Slavery in Africa continued both the traditional incorporation of mainly female slaves into households and the export of slaves to the Mediterranean and the Indian Ocean.

    C. The growth of the plantation economy increased the demand for slaves in the Americas.

    D. Colonial economies in the Americas depended on a range of coerced labor.

III. As new social and political elites changed, they also restructured new ethnic, racial, and gender hierarchies.

    A. Both imperial conquests and widening global economic opportunities contributed to the formation of new political and economic elites.

    B. The power of existing political and economic elites fluctuated as they confronted new challenges to their ability to affect the policies of the increasingly powerful monarchs and leaders.

    C. Some notable gender and family restructuring occurred, including the demographic changes in Africa that resulted from the slave trades.

Questions 291–294 refer to the map below.

AFRICAN SLAVE TRADE, CIRCA 1500–1800

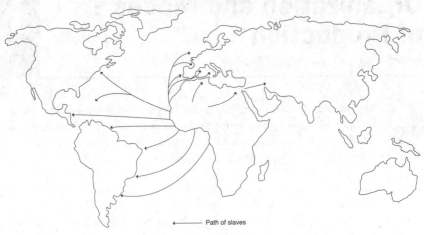

←——— Path of slaves

291. **Which of the following developments contributed most directly to the pattern shown on the map?**

   (A) The demand for domestic servants in Europe increased due to the bubonic plague.
   (B) The establishment of silver mines in the Americas led to a greater demand for slaves.
   (C) The growth of the plantation economy increased the demand for slaves in the Americas.
   (D) The industrialization of Europe increased the demand for a cheap labor force.

292. **The pattern shown on the map had which of the following effects in the period 1450–1750 C.E.?**

   (A) Gender imbalance in West Africa
   (B) Social restructuring in Western Europe
   (C) The formation of new economic elites in Spanish America
   (D) The increasing power of monarchs in Ghana and Mali

293. **Which of the following best describes a change that occurred as a result of the interactions depicted on the map?**

   (A) The diffusion of Bantu languages throughout Western Europe
   (B) The growth of the merchant class throughout sub-Saharan Africa
   (C) The decline of coerced labor in the Americas and West Africa
   (D) The spread of existing religions and the creation of syncretic belief systems

294. **Which of the following represents a major continuity in labor systems shown on the map in the period <u>600–1750</u> C.E.?**

(A) Slaves worked on large plantations in the Caribbean and Brazil.

(B) Slaves were exchanged in the Mediterranean and Indian Ocean basin trade networks.

(C) Slaves were used as the main form of labor on farms in Western Europe.

(D) Slaves mainly served in domestic roles in European households.

Questions 295–297 refer to the passage below.

"We have fire-arms, bows and arrows, broad two-edged swords and javelins: we have shields also which cover a man from head to foot. All are taught the use of these weapons; even our women are warriors, and march boldly out to fight along with the men. Our whole district is a kind of militia: on a certain signal given, such as the firing of a gun at night, they all rise in arms and rush upon their enemy. . . . I was once a witness to a battle in our common. We had been all at work in it one day as usual, when our people were suddenly attacked. I climbed a tree at some distance, from which I beheld the fight. There were many women as well as men on both sides; among others my mother was there, and armed with a broad sword. After fighting for a considerable time with great fury, and after many had been killed our people obtained the victory, and took their enemy's Chief prisoner. He was carried off in great triumph, and, though he offered a large ransom for his life, he was put to death. . . . Those prisoners which were not sold or redeemed we kept as slaves: but how different was their condition from that of the slaves in the West Indies! With us they do no more work than other members of the community, even their masters; their food, clothing and lodging were nearly the same as theirs, (except that they were not permitted to eat with those who were free-born); and there was scarce any other difference between them, than a superior degree of importance which the head of a family possesses in our state, and that authority which, as such, he exercises over every part of his household. Some of these slaves have even slaves under them as their own property, and for their own use."

Olaudah Equiano, *The Interesting Narrative of the Life of Olaudah Equiano,* or Gustavus Vassa, describing life in Africa, 1789

295. The passage is best used as evidence for which of the following?

    (A) Warfare and social stratification on African plantations
    (B) Weapons and family relationships in the West Indies
    (C) Gender roles among European slaveholders
    (D) Military strategies and labor systems of West Africa

296. The passage best illustrates which of the following <u>continuities</u> in the period 600–1750 C.E.?

    (A) The use of gunpowder weapons by West African tribes
    (B) The exchange of African slaves within sub-Saharan Africa and the Indian Ocean basin
    (C) The trans-Atlantic slave trade and commerce with European merchants
    (D) The egalitarian nature of sub-Saharan African tribal groups

297. The passage by Equiano is best understood in the context of which of the following?

    (A) Increased demand for slaves by Europeans led to slave raids in West Africa
    (B) The initial development of slavery in Africa due to the establishment of European trading posts
    (C) The establishment of social stratification in Africa due to the wealth from the slave trade
    (D) The increase in slave raids as a result of the spread of European diseases in West Africa

Questions 298–300 refer to the graph below.

ESTIMATED POPULATION BY REGION, 1500–1800

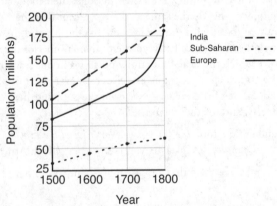

Source: Jerry H. Bentley, *Traditions & Encounters: A Global Perspective on the Past*, 4th ed., Vol. I, McGraw-Hill, 2008, pp. 649, 705, 765

Tip: Population growth throughout history has almost always been due to the introduction of new crops or agricultural innovations. More food means more people!

298. Which of the following best explains the overall trend shown on the graph?

    (A) Populations in Eurasia benefited from the increased availability of American food crops.

    (B) Death rates decreased as warfare and invasions throughout Eurasia ceased.

    (C) Population growth was moderated by the desire for smaller families.

    (D) Birth rates increased due to government-sponsored programs promoting large families.

299. Which of the following best explains the difference in the population trends of sub-Saharan Africa and Europe?

    (A) Population growth in Europe was higher due to the widespread importation of slaves.

    (B) Sub-Saharan Africa's population was limited by the spread of epidemic diseases.

    (C) Population growth in sub-Saharan Africa was lower due to the exportation of slaves overseas.

    (D) Europe's population grew due to climate change as a result of the Little Ice Age.

300. The trend shown on the graph most likely had which of the following effects on India?

    (A) Slavery increased as the number of wealthy families grew.

    (B) Peasant and artisan labor intensified as the population grew.

    (C) Warfare increased due to competition for resources.

    (D) Famines occurred as a result of the limited availability of land.

Questions 301–304 refer to the following passage.

"The ore was very rich black flint, and the excavation so extensive that it held more than 3,000 Indians working away hard with picks and hammers, breaking up that flint ore; and when they have filled their little sacks, the poor fellows, loaded down with ore, climb up those ladders or rigging, some like masts and others like cables, and so trying and distressing that a man empty-handed can hardly get up them. That is the way they work in this mine, with many lights and the loud noise of the pounding and great confusion. . . .

These Indians are sent out every year under a captain whom they choose in each village or tribe, for him to take them and oversee them for the year each has to serve; every year they have a new election, for as some go out, others come in. This works out very badly, with great losses and gaps in the quotas of Indians, the villages being depopulated; and this gives rise to great extortions and abuses on the part of the inspectors toward the poor Indians, ruining them and thus depriving the chief Indians of their property and carrying them off in chains because they do not fill out the *mita* assignment, which they cannot do, for the reason given and for others which I do not bring forward."

Antonio Vazquez de Espinosa, Spanish monk,
Compendium and Description of the West Indies, circa 1620

 Tip: As you read, note any language that seems to be biased. In this case, Espinosa referred to the Indians as "poor fellows." He implied that the system the Spanish forced the Native Americans to live under was evil and that the overseers were thieves. This shows that Espinosa was against the system and felt sympathetic toward the Native Americans.

301. The author's point of view regarding the Native Americans was likely influenced by which of the following?

(A) The role he played as a missionary representing the Roman Catholic Church

(B) The Spanish view that Native Americans were inferior and could withstand harsh treatment

(C) The desire of the Spanish government for a cheap labor force to mine silver

(D) The *encomienda* system ensuring that indigenous laborers were protected by plantation owners

302. Which of the following economic conditions was most important in creating the increased demand for silver that resulted in the labor system described in the passage?

(A) The sponsorship of expeditions by the Spanish crown

(B) The demand for laborers for plantation agriculture

(C) Europeans' desire to participate in trade with East Asia

(D) Spanish merchants' investment in industrial production

303. Which of the following can best be inferred about the author's primary purpose in writing this account of mining conditions?

(A) To show the reasons for the population decline in Latin America

(B) To bring attention to the poor treatment of indigenous peoples in the *mita* system

(C) To depict indigenous peoples as inferior and weak as compared to the Spanish

(D) To show the primitive technology used by workers in silver mines

304. The passage can best be used as evidence for which of the following world historical trends that took place during the period 1450–1750 c.e.?

(A) Peasant labor intensified in many regions, including the Americas.

(B) The growth of the plantation economy increased the demand for slaves in the Americas.

(C) The power of existing political and economic elites fluctuated as they confronted challenges.

(D) Colonial economies in the Americas depended on a range of coerced labor.

Questions 305–306 refer to the table below.

POPULATION OF ICELAND, 1095–1790

Year	Population
1095	77,500
1311	72,000
1703	50,000
1790	38,000

Source: H. H. Lamb, *Climate, History, and the Modern World*, 1995, p. 189

305. Which of the following best explains the overall population trend shown in the table?

(A) The spread of epidemic diseases, such as bubonic plague, showed lack of immunity.

(B) The Little Ice Age contributed to the contraction of settlements in the Northern Hemisphere.

(C) The colonization of the Americas led to widespread migration out of Iceland.

(D) The raids by Vikings led to the relocation of many in the Northern Hemisphere.

306. Which of the following was an effect of the trend shown in the table?

(A) Agricultural practices changed.
(B) New trade routes were established.
(C) The family size in Iceland increased.
(D) A lack of resources led to civil war.

Questions 307–309 refer to the passage below.

"This indenture witnesseth, that John Reid, of Freehold, in the
County of Mounmouth, hath put himself, and by these presents
doth voluntarily and of his own free Will and Accord put himself
an Apprentice to Robert Livingston of New York, with him to live,
and (after the Manner of an Apprentice) to serve from the first day
of November, 1742 till the full term of five years be complete and
ended. During all which term the said apprentice his said master
faithfully shall serve, his secrets keep, his lawful Commands gladly
everywhere obey: he shall do no damage to his said master he shall
not waste his said master's goods, nor lend them unlawfully to any,
he shall not contract matrimony within the said term. At cards, dice,
or any other unlawful game he shall not play, whereby his said master
may have damage with his own goods, nor the goods of others within
the said term, without license from his said master he shall neither
buy nor sell, he shall not absent himself day or night from his said
master's service without his leave, nor haunt ale houses, taverns or
play houses, but in all things as a faithful apprentice he should behave
himself to his said master and all his during the said term."

Indenture agreement, British North America, 1742

307. The terms set forth by the indenture agreement most directly reflect which
of the following?

(A) Indentured servants were treated in a manner similar to peasant
laborers.
(B) Various forms of coerced labor were used in colonial economies
throughout the Americas.
(C) Coerced laborers in the Americas were protected by legal documents.
(D) Indentured servitude was practiced solely in North American colonies.

308. Which of the following factors contributed to the demand for labor
illustrated by the agreement?

(A) The abolition of the slave trade and slavery
(B) The increased demand for workers in silver mines
(C) The global demand for cash crops and finished products
(D) The decline in Europe's working-class population

309. Which of the following best describes a <u>difference</u> between indentured servitude as described in the passage and slavery on plantations in the period 1450–1750 C.E.?

(A) Indentured servitude was for a prescribed amount of time.
(B) The leisure time of plantation slaves was less controlled.
(C) Indentured servants often worked as domestic servants.
(D) Slaves on plantations often resented the terms of the labor contract.

Questions 310–314 refer to the excerpts below.

"8.
Marriage must not be contracted in private [without approval from the shogun]. . . . To form a factional alliance through marriage is the root of treason. . . .

10.
The regulations with regard to dress materials must not be breached. Lords and vassals, superiors and inferiors, must observe what is proper within their positions in life. Without authorization, no retainer may indiscriminately wear fine white damask, white wadded silk garments, purple silk kimono, purple silk linings, and kimono sleeves which bear no family crest. . . .

12.
The *samurai* of all domains must practice frugality. When the rich proudly display their wealth, the poor are ashamed of not being on par with them. There is nothing which will corrupt public morality more than this, and therefore it must be severely restricted.

13.
The lords of the domains must select as their officials men of administrative ability. The way of governing a country is to get the right men. If the lord clearly discerns between the merits and faults of his retainers, he can administer due rewards and punishments. If the domain has good men, it flourishes more than ever. If it has no good men, it is doomed to perish. This is an admonition which the wise men of old bequeathed to us."

The Edicts of the Tokugawa Shogunate:
Excerpts from Laws of Military Households, 1615

310. The edicts issued by the Tokugawa Shogunate are best seen as evidence for which of the following?

   (A) Landowning classes caused significant challenges to state consolidation and expansion.
   (B) Peasant labor intensified in many regions as a result of growing demand for raw materials.
   (C) Widening global economic opportunities contributed to the formation of new economic elites.
   (D) The power of existing elites fluctuated in response to increasingly powerful leaders.

311. Which of the following can best be inferred about the purpose in issuing the edicts for the military households?

   (A) The *shogun* wanted to justify the creation of an imperial examination system.
   (B) The *samurai* strained resources in a time of economic depression.
   (C) The *shogun* wanted to consolidate power and lessen attempts at rebellion.
   (D) The *daimyo* refused to pledge loyalty to the Tokugawa Shogun.

312. The edicts by the Tokugawa Shogunate are best understood in the context of which of the following?

   (A) The period of civil war among *daimyo* prior to the rise of the shogunate
   (B) The arrival of European merchants in Japanese ports
   (C) The trading agreements forcibly imposed by Western powers
   (D) The spread of Neoconfucian values as a result of a tributary relationship with China

313. Which of the following was the most immediate effect of the edicts issued by the Tokugawa Shogun?

   (A) The power of the *shogun* was threatened by the supporters of the emperor.
   (B) Japan became dominated by European merchants wishing to control the silver trade.
   (C) The government of Japan was overthrown by resentful *daimyo*.
   (D) Japan experienced a period of relative peace and political stability.

314. The rule of the Tokugawa Shogunate in Japan was disrupted by which of the following during the nineteenth century?

   (A) The conquest of the Tokugawa Shogunate by Western imperial powers
   (B) The emergence of Meiji Japan as a result of U.S. and European influence
   (C) The defeat of Japan in a series of wars with Chinese naval forces
   (D) The collapse of Japan's economy as a result of regulations on construction and commerce

Questions 315–317 refer to the passage below.

"Long before Europeans arrived, maritime Southeast Asia (including present-day Malaysia, Indonesia and the Philippines) carried on a substantial long-distance trade. Many of the merchants were women—in some cases because commerce was thought too base an occupation for upper-class men, but too lucrative for elite families to abstain from completely. . . .

. . . the Portuguese, the first Europeans to establish themselves in this world, had found intermarrying with such women to be an indispensable part of creating profitable and defensible colonies. When the VOC* gave up on importing Dutch women. . . . It turned to the daughters of these earlier Portuguese-Asian unions: they at least spoke a Western language and were at least nominally Christian. Many had also learned from their mothers how useful a European husband could be for protecting their business interests in an increasingly multinational and often violent trading world. . . .

The VOC's principal goal, of course, was profit, and profit was best secured by monopolizing the export of all sorts of Asian goods—from pepper to porcelain—back to Europe. In theory, the company also claimed—at least intermittently—the right to license and tax (or sink) all the ships participating in the much larger intra-Asian trade, including those of Southeast Asia's women traders. But the realities of huge oceans and numerous rivals made enforcing such a system impossible, and the VOC also faced powerful enemies within. Most company servants soon discovered that while smuggling goods back to Holland was risky and difficult, they could earn sums by trading illegally (or semi-legally) within Asia that dwarfed their official salaries. Here their wives were a perfect vehicle for making a fortune: they were well connected in and knowledgeable about local markets, often possessed considerable capital and able to manage the family business continuously without being susceptible to sudden transfer by the company."

Kenneth Pomeranz and Steven Topik, historians,
The World That Trade Created: Society, Culture, and the World Economy, 1400 to the Present, 2006

*The VOC, also known as the Dutch East India Company, was a joint-stock company.

315. **Based on Pomeranz and Topik's argument, Dutch merchants in Southeast Asia were most clearly motivated by which of the following?**

    (A) The opportunity to bring profit to their employer
    (B) The desire to improve diplomatic relations with local governments by marrying native women
    (C) The promise of economic gain by circumventing regulations established by their employer
    (D) The lack of availability of Dutch women and the desire to establish families

316. **Which of the following enabled the Dutch to establish and enforce a monopoly on the Southeast Asian spice trade in the seventeenth century?**

    (A) The establishment of powerful joint-stock companies
    (B) The development of exclusive inventions for navigation
    (C) Increased scientific knowledge leading to medicines to treat malaria
    (D) Population growth as a result of the Columbian Exchange

317. **The role of women described in the passage is best seen as a continuation of which of the following patterns that developed in the period 600–1450 C.E.?**

    (A) Patriarchy persisted due to defined gender roles in societies that were primarily agricultural.
    (B) Women in Southeast Asia exercised more power and influence than women in other regions.
    (C) Female merchants were the primary traders in the Indian Ocean basin due to social norms.
    (D) Women became merchants due to Neoconfucian values that viewed trade as harmful.

Questions 318–320 refer to the image below.

PORTRAIT OF A SENIOR MERCHANT OF THE DUTCH EAST INDIA COMPANY AND HIS WIFE, LATE 17TH CENTURY

The portrait depicts the merchant, his wife, and a servant in the port of Batavia, Dutch East Indies

318. The painting would be most useful to a historian studying which of the following?

(A) The factors that contributed to the rise of the Dutch East India Company

(B) The clothing styles of European commoners in the early modern period

(C) The innovations in sailing as a result of the Dutch Scientific Revolution

(D) The formation of new economic elites due to widening global economic opportunities

319. Which of the following best describes the primary role of the merchant depicted in the image?

(A) The trade of goods from one Asian country to another market in the Indian Ocean region

(B) The capture of slaves in West Africa for sale in the Americas

(C) Overseeing the sale of European manufactured goods in China

(D) Transporting silver from mines in the Americas to markets in Europe

320. Which of the following best represents a motivation for the creation of royal chartered companies like the Dutch East India Company?

(A) European merchants could operate without government interference.

(B) Joint-stock companies were used to establish colonial rule in Latin America.

(C) Individual merchants could avoid taxation and ensure larger profits for themselves.

(D) European rulers could collect more taxes to fund their governments.

Short-Answer Questions

Use the passage below to answer all parts of the question that follows.

"In the fourteenth century, Europe was a rural continent with only the most rudimentary infrastructure of roads, harbors, and local mills. Kings and queens reigned over kingdoms and crowded cities haunted by the constant threat of insufficient food. Nine of every ten workers were engaged in growing food, and still the entire continent lived only from year to year. But the exigencies of the Little Ice Age helped bring about an agricultural revolution, which began during the fifteenth and sixteenth centuries in the Low Countries, then spread to England a hundred years later. Many English landowners embraced the new agriculture as larger, enclosed farms changed the landscape. Innovative crops like turnips and clover provided insurance for herds and people against winter hunger. Britain, Flanders, and the Netherlands were self-sufficient in grain and livestock by the onset of the Industrial Revolution in the late eighteenth century."

Brian Fagan, historian, *The Long Summer: How Climate Changed Civilization*, 2004

321. a) Identify ONE historically specific example of an innovation in agriculture in the period 1450–1800 C.E. that supports the author's argument.

b) Explain ONE cause of limited food suppy referred to in the passage.

c) Explain ONE specific effect of the agricultural revolution described in the passage in the period from 1750–1900 C.E.

Answer all parts of the question that follows.

322. a) Identify ONE form of coerced labor that was used in colonial economies in the period 1450–1750 C.E.

b) Explain ONE change in agricultural labor in the period 1450–1750 C.E.

c) Explain ONE continuity in agricultural labor in the period 1450–1750 C.E.

Long Essay Questions

323. In the period 1450–1750, traditional peasant agriculture increased and changed, plantations expanded, and demand for labor increased.

   Develop an argument that evaluates how one or more labor systems changed as a result of increased demand for labor in this period.

324. In the period 1450–1750, as social and political elites changed, they also restructured ethnic, racial, and gender hierarchies.

   Develop an argument that evaluates how one or more social hierarchies changed as a result of the formation of new elites in this period.

(Answers on pages 344–348.)

State Consolidation and Imperial Expansion

Answers for Chapter 12 are on pages 348–353.

Key Concept 4.3—Empires expanded around the world, presenting new challenges in the incorporation of diverse populations and in the effective administration of new coerced labor systems.

I.   Rulers used a variety of methods to legitimize and consolidate their power.

   A.   Rulers continued to use religious ideas, art, and monumental architecture to legitimize their rule.

   B.   Many states adopted practices to accommodate the different ethnic and religious diversity of their subjects or to utilize the economic, political, and military contributions of different ethnic or religious groups.

   C.   Recruitment and use of bureaucratic elites, as well as the development of military professionals, became more common among rulers who wanted to maintain centralized control over their populations and resources.

   D.   Rulers used tribute collection and tax farming to generate revenue for territorial expansion.

II. Imperial expansion relied on the increased use of gunpowder, cannons, and armed trade to establish large empires in both hemispheres.

   A.   Europeans established new trading-post empires in Africa and Asia, which proved profitable for the rulers and merchants involved in new global trade networks, but the impact of these empires was limited by the authority of local states including the Ashanti and Mughal Empires.

   B.   Land empires—including the Manchu, Mughal, Ottoman, and Russian—expanded dramatically in size.

   C.   European states established new maritime empires in the Americas, including the Portuguese, Spanish, Dutch, French, and British.

III. Competition over trade routes, state rivalries, and local resistance all provided significant challenges to state consolidation and expansion.

In this era, both land and maritime empires expanded. They became increasingly centralized by rulers who used a variety of methods to legitimize their power and extend bureaucratic institutions. Due to their increased size, empires became more ethnically and religiously diverse. This led to new practices to accommodate these subjects. European maritime empires were characterized by trading posts in Africa and the Indian Ocean basin and by colonies in the Americas. Challenges occurred as some subjects resisted policies of the state, competition in international trade made expansion difficult, and empires had rivalries with one another.

Questions 325–326 refer to the images below.

Image 1

PALACE OF VERSAILLES, CONSTRUCTED IN THE 17TH CENTURY OUTSIDE OF PARIS, FRANCE

Image 2

THE TAJ MAHAL, CONSTRUCTED IN THE 17TH CENTURY IN AGRA, INDIA

325. **Image 1 best illustrates which of the following political developments in the period 1450–1750 C.E.?**

     (A) The development of military professionals to increase centralized control over populations
     (B) The contraction of empires as a result of challenges to imperial authority
     (C) The increase in tax revenues as a result of the establishment of Eurasian empires
     (D) The rise of Asian land empires due to access to gunpowder weapons

326. **The images best illustrate which of the following continuities in world history?**

     (A) The construction of fortifications for defensive purposes
     (B) The use of monumental architecture by rulers
     (C) The universal adoption of Greco-Roman architectural features
     (D) The use of religious ideas to legitimize the rule of monarchs

Questions 327–329 refer to the passage below.

"The state of monarchy is the supremest thing upon earth; for kings are not only God's lieutenants upon earth, and sit upon God's throne, but even by God himself are called gods. . . .

Kings are justly called gods, for that they exercise a manner or resemblance of divine power upon earth: for if you will consider the attributes to God, you shall see how they agree in the person of a king. God hath power to create or destroy, make or unmake at his pleasure, to give life or send death, to judge all and to be judged nor accountable to none; to raise low things and to make high things low at his pleasure, and to God are both souls and body due. And the like power have kings: they make and unmake their subjects, they have power of raising and casting down, of life and of death, judges over all their subjects and in all causes and yet accountable to none but God only. . . ."

King James I, English monarch, address to Parliament, 1609

327. **The passage by King James I reflects which of the following characteristics common to empires in the period 1450–1750 C.E.?**

     (A) The implementation of legal codes based on Enlightenment ideas
     (B) The recruitment of bureaucratic elites to centralize power
     (C) The worship of political rulers as deities
     (D) The use of religious ideas to justify imperial rule

328. The power of the king as described in the passage is <u>most similar</u> to which of the following?

    (A) The Mandate of Heaven in imperial China
    (B) The Pope's position in the Roman Catholic Church
    (C) The role of nobles in the European feudal system
    (D) The power of Egyptian pharaohs in the Nile Valley

329. Which of the following developments of the <u>nineteenth century</u> directly challenged ideas presented in the passage?

    (A) The rise of nationalist ideas to unite diverse populations
    (B) The abolitionist movement in the Americas
    (C) The Enlightenment notion of consent of the governed
    (D) The women's suffrage movement

Questions 330–332 refer to the following sources.

Source 1

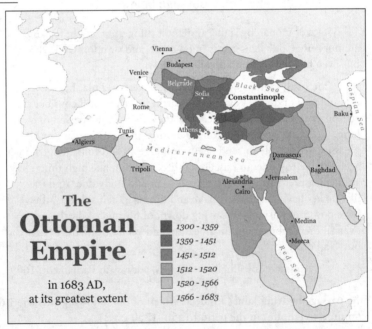

Source 2

"No distinction is attached to birth among the Turks; the deference [respect] to be paid to a man is measured by the position he holds in the public service. There is no fighting for precedence; a man's place is marked out by the duties he discharges. In making his appointments the *Sultan* pays no regard to any pretensions on the score of wealth or rank, nor does he take into consideration recommendations or popularity; he considers each case on its own merits, and examines carefully into the character, ability, and disposition of the man whose promotion is in question. It is by merit that men rise in the service, a system which ensures that posts should only be assigned to the competent. Each man in Turkey carries in his own hand his ancestry and his position in life, which he may make or mar as he will."

> Ogier Ghiselin de Busbecq, Austrian diplomat to the
> Ottoman Empire, letters to a friend, 1555–1562 C.E.

330. **Which of the following factors most directly contributed to the changes shown on the map in Source 1?**

   (A) The power vacuum that resulted from the collapse of the Mongol Empire
   (B) The Ottoman Empire's use of gunpowder technologies and superior naval forces
   (C) The alliance between the Ottomans and Russians against western European powers
   (D) The decline of European maritime empires as a result of competition and state rivalries

331. **The system described in Source 2 had which of the following purposes?**

   (A) To prevent the political influence of individuals who were not related to the *sultan*
   (B) To reinforce the existing social hierarchy to ensure stability
   (C) To ensure that landowning elites maintained political influence
   (D) To recruit bureaucratic elites in order to maintain centralized control

332. **The political structure described in Source 2 is most similar to which of the following?**

   (A) The Chinese imperial examination system
   (B) The bureaucracy of the Spanish Empire in the Americas
   (C) The use of *boyars* in imperial Russia
   (D) The tribute system of the Mongol Empire

Questions 333–335 refer to the map below.

EMPIRES IN THE AMERICAS, CIRCA 1750 C.E.

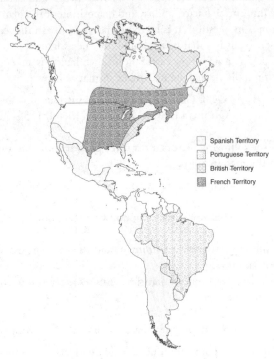

333. **Which of the following contributed to the establishment of empires shown on the map?**

    (A) Colonization as a result of the complete destruction of native populations
    (B) Cooperation between indigenous peoples of the Americas and European settlers
    (C) Improvements in transoceanic travel and the use of gunpowder weapons and cannons
    (D) The power vacuum resulting from the collapse of the Aztec and Incan Empires

334. **Which of the following best describes a result of the rise of empires shown on the map?**

    (A) Joint-stock companies developed in order to monopolize all trade in the region.
    (B) Colonists exported manufactured goods to Europe.
    (C) Mercantilist policies were used to expand European economies.
    (D) Trans-Atlantic trade increased as trade networks in the Indian Ocean basin declined.

335. **The establishment of empires shown on the map led to the development of which of the following?**

(A) The adoption of a racial classification system by the Spanish due to the diversity of the empire

(B) The collection of tribute from colonists and indigenous peoples in British North America

(C) The decline in European imperial rule due to difficulty in administering vast empires

(D) The lessening of tensions among European maritime powers

Questions 336–339 refers to the edicts below.

Edict 1

> "*Decree on the Invitation of Foreigners*, 1702
> Since our accession to the throne all our efforts and intentions have tended to govern this realm in such a way that all of our subjects should, through our care for the general good, become more and more prosperous. For this end we have always tried to maintain internal order, to defend the state against invasion, and in every possible way to improve and to extend trade. With this purpose we have been compelled to make some necessary and salutary changes in the administration, in order that our subjects might more easily gain a knowledge of matters of which they were before ignorant, and become more skillful in their commercial relations. We have therefore given orders, made dispositions, and founded institutions indispensable for increasing our trade with foreigners, and shall do the same in the future. . . ."
>
> Edict of Russian Emperor Peter I (Peter the Great)
> of Russia (reigned 1682–1725)

Edict 2

> "*Decree on Promotion to Officer's Rank*, 1714
> Since there are many who promote to officer rank their relatives and friends—young men who do not know the fundamentals of soldiering, not having served in the lower ranks—and since even those who serve [in the ranks] do so for a few weeks or months only, as a formality; therefore . . . let a decree be promulgated that henceforth there shall be no promotion [to officer rank] of men of noble extraction or of any others who have not first served as privates in the Guards. This decree does not apply to soldiers of lowly origin who, after long service in the ranks, have received their commissions through honest service or to those who are promoted on the basis of merit, now or in the future. . . ."
>
> Edict of Russian Emperor Peter I (Peter the Great)
> of Russia (reigned 1682–1725)

336. Based on <u>Edict 1</u>, Peter the Great's policy on trade had which of the following purposes?

    (A) To establish trade links after a period of isolation
    (B) To encourage exploration to establish a sea route to Asia
    (C) To obtain colonies in the Americas for plantation agriculture
    (D) To promote trade in order to increase tax revenues

337. Based on <u>Edict 2</u>, the Russian Empire exhibited which of the following characteristics common to empires in the period 1450–1750 c.e.?

    (A) The supremacy of landholding elites in political and military affairs continued despite the increasing power of hereditary leaders.
    (B) The power of existing political elites fluctuated as they confronted challenges to their ability to affect the policies of increasingly powerful monarchs.
    (C) The weakening of militaries occurred due to the use of gunpowder weaponry, and a period of relative peace resulted from fewer rivalries.
    (D) Practices were adopted to incorporate diverse ethnic and religious groups into the expanding empire.

338. <u>Edict 1</u> is best understood in the context of which of the following?

    (A) The intensification of trade due to the creation of global economy
    (B) The isolation of Russia as a result of continued Mongol control
    (C) The competition between Russia and the Ottoman Empire for control of Mediterranean trade
    (D) The collapse of the Silk Road network ending overland Eurasian trade

 Tip: Remember to be wary of answers containing extremes—in this case "collapse" and "ending."

339. The economic and military policies described in the edicts resulted in which of the following?

    (A) Increased influence of the Russian nobility
    (B) Less control over trade and a lack of centralized rule
    (C) Consolidation of power by Russian rulers
    (D) The decline of serfdom and economic liberalization

Questions 340–342 refer to the map below.

QING DYNASTY, 1644–1760

340. **Which of the following best explains the changes on the map between 1660 and 1760?**

   (A) The decline of surrounding land empires led to a power vacuum in East Asia.
   (B) The Manchu used gunpowder technology and effective military strategies.
   (C) Control of Eurasian land trade generated profits that financed the Qing military.
   (D) The Manchu and Mughal Empires were allied together against Tibet.

341. **Which of the following challenges occurred as a result of the changes shown on the map?**

   (A) The Manchu had to legitimize their rule and accommodate diverse ethnic groups.
   (B) Increased population led to a strain on resources and a civil war.
   (C) The Manchu had to secure their borders from attacks by neighboring land empires.
   (D) Ethnic and religious diversity led to the fall of the dynasty in the late eighteenth century.

342. **How did the Qing Empire shown on the map differ from European empires in the period 1450–1750 c.e.?**

   (A) The Qing Empire was less centralized than European empires due to the Qing's large land area.
   (B) European maritime empires were in a period of decline as they lost overseas territories.
   (C) The Qing Empire was less tolerant of the religious beliefs and customs of conquered groups.
   (D) European empires controlled overseas colonies and trading posts.

Questions 343–345 refer to the passage below.

"The Ottoman Empire's long history, large size, and pivotal location offer multiple angles of approach to historians. Western historians have commonly seen the Ottomans as an alien threat, part of the Turkic third wave of Islamic aggression against Christendom. From the perspective of Islamic history, it was part of the second political and cultural flowering of the Islamic world. From a geographic perspective, it appears as a reassertion of the imperial pattern of the Eastern Roman (Byzantine) Empire. . . . Arab historians, like the Europeans, regard the Ottomans as intruding aliens. Each of these views of the Ottomans has an element of truth. The Ottomans carried the traditions and conflicts of the post-Abbasid Turko-Irano-Islamic political matrix into the fertile ground—literally and figuratively—of western Anatolia and the Balkans. Its geographic setting, the specific circumstances of its development, the quality of its leadership, its institutional development, and its military organization permitted the Ottoman polity to overcome the chronic weaknesses of post-Abbasid political formations and establish an enduring and extensive empire. The Ottomans integrated themselves into the political and economic environments of Europe and the Mediterranean."

Douglas E. Streusand, historian, *Islamic Gunpowder Empires: Ottomans, Safavids, Mughals*, 2011

343. The author's argument regarding the strengths of the Ottoman Empire is likely based on which of the following?

(A) The separation of religious affairs from political affairs and the intolerance of minorities

(B) The conquest of areas in Western Europe previously under Arab control

(C) The implementation of a legal code and use of gunpowder technology for expansion

(D) The incorporation of Byzantine and Abbasid policies regarding non-Muslims

344. The point of view of Western historians regarding the Ottomans, as described by the author, is most likely the result of which of the following?

(A) Competition between the Ottomans and Mughals over control of Mesopotamia

(B) Ottoman conquest of former Abbasid territories in North Africa

(C) Competition between Ottomans and Russians over the Black Sea

(D) Ottoman expansion into Eastern Europe as a result of Ottoman naval supremacy

345. Which of the following developments of the <u>nineteenth century</u> challenges the author's argument that the Ottoman Empire was able to overcome weaknesses of its predecessors?

   (A) Ethnic nationalism and contraction of the empire
   (B) Western imperialism and the incorporation of Enlightenment ideas
   (C) The increasing power of *sultans* and weakening of the bureaucracy
   (D) The loss of territory and the overthrow of the monarchy

Questions 346–348 refer to the excerpts below.

"1. Japanese ships are strictly forbidden to leave for foreign countries.

2. No Japanese is permitted to go abroad. If there is anyone who attempts to do so secretly, he must be executed. The ship so involved must be impounded and its owner arrested, and the matter must be reported to the higher authority.

3. If any Japanese returns from overseas after residing there, he must be put to death....

8. All incoming ships must be carefully searched for the followers of *padres* [priests].

9. No single trading city shall be permitted to purchase all the merchandise brought by foreign ships.

10. *Samurai* are not permitted to purchase any goods originating from foreign ships directly from Chinese merchants in Nagasaki....

You are hereby required to act in accordance with the provisions set above. It is so ordered."

Tokugawa Ieyasu, Japanese shogun, Excerpts from
the *Sakoku Policy* (Closed Country Edict), 1635

346. The *shogun's* policies regarding foreign trade as described in the excerpts had which of the following purposes?

   (A) To limit foreign ideas and prevent threats to the *shogun's* power
   (B) To become dominant in East Asian trading networks
   (C) To stop Japanese merchants from evading taxation on trade goods
   (D) To prevent individual ports from monopolizing trade

347. This edict is best seen as evidence for which of the following developments of the period 1450–1750 C.E.?

(A) The intensification of connections within hemispheres created syncretic belief systems.

(B) Traditional peasant agriculture and the plantation economy continued to grow.

(C) Rulers used religious ideas to legitimize their rule.

(D) State consolidation and centralization of power increased.

348. Which of the following was an effect of the Japanese seclusion policies described in the excerpts?

(A) The Tokugawa Shogunate faced rebellions as a result of economic decline.

(B) Japan had limited knowledge of foreign technology and culture.

(C) The Tokugawa Shogunate was overthrown by Japanese merchants.

(D) Japan was completely isolated from regional trade networks.

Questions 349–351 refer to the following images.

Image 1

A MUGHAL PAINTING DEPICTING THE EMPEROR AURANGZEB AND HIS ROYAL HUNTING PARTY

Aurangzeb is the central figure being carried on a palanquin.

Image 2

A QING DYNASTY PORTRAIT OF THE YONGZHENG EMPEROR IN COURT DRESS, 18TH CENTURY

349. Image 1 would be most useful to a historian studying which of the following?

(A) The means of acquiring food and the typical diet of Mughal India

(B) The policies implemented regarding conquered groups

(C) The methods used by Mughal rulers to display their power

(D) The technologies used for maritime transportation

350. A historian would most likely use Image 2 as support for which of the following assertions?

(A) Manchu rulers adopted Chinese cultural aspects in order to legitimize their rule.

(B) Manchu art was mainly abstract and symbolic in nature, as opposed to realistic.

(C) Manchu rulers rejected traditional Chinese beliefs and practices.

(D) Manchu subjects resented the emperors' unwillingness to adapt to Chinese traditions.

351. When taken together, the two images best support which of the following conclusions?

(A) Asian rulers maintained more direct control over their subjects than did European monarchs.

(B) Rulers used art to legitimize their political authority.

(C) Mughal and Manchu rulers recruited bureaucratic elites to control their populations.

(D) Art is often used by rulers to display their divine status.

Questions 352–354 refer to the passage below.

"By this personal *ukaz* [proclamation] We bestow on all those who formerly were peasants and in subjugation to the landowners, along with our monarchic and paternal compassion, to be dutiful slaves subject directly to our crown. We grant them the ancient cross and prayer, haircut and beard, freedom and liberty, and they are to be Cossacks forever, not liable to recruitment into the army or to the soul tax or other money taxes, and We grant them tenure of the land and the forests and the hay meadows and the fisheries and the salt lakes, without purchase and without *obrok* [tax], and we liberate all the aforementioned from the villainous nobles and from the bribe takers in the city—the officials who imposed taxes and other burdens on the peasants and the whole people. . . . We accordingly do ordain by this personal *ukaz*: those who formerly were nobles living on estates are enemies to our power and disrupters of the empire and oppressors of the peasantry, and they should be caught, executed and hanged, they should be treated just as they, who have no Christianity, dealt with you peasants. When these enemies and villains have been eliminated, all may enjoy peace and a quiet life that will last for all time."

Yemelyan Pugachev, leader of a rebellion
against Catherine the Great, Russia, 1774

352. The proclamation by Pugachev is most likely a response to which of the following?

(A) Imperial policies promoting the adoption of Western cultural elements
(B) The mutually beneficial relationship between nobles and peasants
(C) Resentment of the regulations regarding traditional religious practices
(D) Anger against landholding elites and imperial taxation policies

353. The passage by Pugachev best illustrates which of the following?

(A) States adopted practices to accommodate various religious groups.
(B) Military professionals were used to maintain centralized control.
(C) Local resistance provided significant challenges to state consolidation.
(D) Landholding elites resisted imperial taxation policies.

354. Rebellions similar to the one organized by Pugachev led to which of the following in the Russian empire during the <u>nineteenth century</u>?

(A) The abolition of serfdom
(B) The overthrow of the imperial government
(C) The rise of a communist government
(D) The improvement of living conditions for peasants

FUN FACT: Pugachev claimed to be the dead husband of Catherine the Great, Emperor Peter III, in order to give legitimacy to his movement. Peasants who were upset at increased tax burdens did not question this man who promised to abolish serfdom.

Short-Answer Questions

Answer all parts of the question that follows.

355. a) Identify ONE way rulers in the period 1450–1750 consolidated power and legitimized their rule.

b) Explain ONE way the establishment of European maritime empires in the period 1450–1750 changed the previous patterns of empire building.

c) Explain ONE way the establishment of European maritime empires in the period 1450–1750 continued previous patterns of empire building.

Answer all parts of the question that follows.

356. a) Identify ONE factor that facilitated the growth of empires in the period 1450–1750.

b) Explain ONE way in which empire building among European maritime empires was similar to empire building among Asian land empires in the period 1450–1750.

c) Explain ONE way empire building among European maritime empires was different from empire building among Asian land empires in the period 1450–1750.

Long Essay Questions

357. In the period 1450–1750 c.e., rulers used a variety of methods to legitimize and consolidate their power.

Develop an argument that evaluates how one or more rulers consolidated and legitimized their power in this period.

358. In the period 1450–1750, imperial expansion relied on the increased use of gunpowder, cannons, and armed trade to establish large empires in both hemispheres.

Develop an argument that evaluates the extent to which empire building among European powers was different from empire building by the Ottoman Empire in this period.

Document-Based Question

359. Evaluate the factors that enabled Eurasian rulers to consolidate power in the period 1450–1750 C.E.

Document 1

Source: Tokugawa Ieyasu, *shogun*, Laws Governing the Military Households, 1615

6. The castles in various domains may be repaired, provided the matter is reported without fail. New construction of any kind is strictly forbidden. . . . "Big castles are a danger to the state." Walls and moats are the cause of great disorders. . . .

8. Marriage must not be contracted in private [without approval from the *bakufu*]. . . . Marriage follows the principle of harmony between *yin* and *yang*, and must not be entered into lightly. . . . The Peach Blossom Ode in *The Book of Poetry* also says that "When men and women are proper in their relationships and marriage is arranged at the correct time; then throughout the land there will be no loose women." To form a factional alliance through marriage is the root of treason.

9. Visits of the *daimyo* to the capital are to be in accordance with regulations. . . . *Daimyo* should not be accompanied by a large number of soldiers.

10. The regulations with regard to dress materials must not be breached. Lords and vassals, superiors and inferiors, must observe what is proper within their positions in life. Without authorization, no retainer may indiscriminately wear fine white damask, white wadded silk garments, purple silk kimono, purple silk linings, and kimono sleeves which bear no family crest. . . .

12. The samurai of all domains must practice frugality. When the rich proudly display their wealth, the poor are ashamed of not being on par with them. There is nothing which will corrupt public morality more than this, and therefore it must be severely restricted.

Document 2

Source: Edicts of Russian Emperor Peter I (the Great) of Russia
(reigned 1682–1725)

Decree on the Invitation of Foreigners, 1702
Since our accession to the throne all our efforts and intentions have tended to
govern this realm in such a way that all of our subjects should, through our care for
the general good, become more and more prosperous. For this end we have always
tried to maintain internal order, to defend the state against invasion, and in every
possible way to improve and to extend trade. With this purpose we have been compelled to make some necessary and salutary changes in the administration, in order
that our subjects might more easily gain a knowledge of matters of which they were
before ignorant, and become more skillful in their commercial relations. We have
therefore given orders, made dispositions, and founded institutions indispensable
for increasing our trade with foreigners, and shall do the same in the future.

Decree on Promotion to Officer's Rank, 1714
Since there are many who promote to officer rank their relatives and friends—
young men who do not know the fundamentals of soldiering, not having served
in the lower ranks—and since even those who serve [in the ranks] do so for a few
weeks or months only, as a formality; therefore ... let a decree be promulgated
that henceforth there shall be no promotion [to officer rank] of men of noble
extraction or of any others who have not first served as privates in the Guards....

Document 3

Source: Hongwu, first emperor of the Ming Dynasty, imperial edict

To all civil and military officials:
I have told you to refrain from evil. Doing so would enable you to bring glory to your
ancestors, your wives, your children and yourselves. With your virtue, you then could
assist me in my endeavors to bring good fortune and prosperity to the people. You
would establish names for yourselves in Heaven and on earth, and for thousands
and thousands of years, you would be praised as worthy men.

However, after assuming your posts, how many of you really followed my instruc-
tions? Those of you in charge of money and grain have stolen them yourselves;
those of you in charge of criminal laws and punishments have neglected the regulations. In this way grievances are not redressed and false charges are ignored.
Those with genuine grievances have nowhere to turn; even when they merely wish
to state their complaints, their words never reach the higher officials. Occasionally
these unjust matters come to my attention. After I discover the truth, I capture and
imprison the corrupt, villainous, and oppressive officials involved. I punish them
with the death penalty or forced labor or have them flogged with bamboo sticks in
order to make manifest the consequences of good or evil actions....

Document 4

Source: Jacques Bossuet, French Bishop, court preacher to Louis XIV of France, seventeenth century

The person of the king is sacred, and to attack him in any way is an attack on God itself. Kings represent the Divine Majesty and have been appointed by Him to carry out His purposes. Serving God and respecting kings are bound together.

Document 5

Source: Ogier Ghiselin de Busbecq, Austrian diplomat to the Ottoman Empire, letters to a friend, 1555–1562

No distinction is attached to birth among the Turks; the deference [respect] to be paid to a man is measured by the position he holds in the public service. There is no fighting for precedence; a man's place is marked out by the duties he discharges. In making his appointments the Sultan pays no regard to any pretensions on the score of wealth or rank, nor does he take into consideration recommendations or popularity; he considers each case on its own merits, and examines carefully into the character, ability, and disposition of the man whose promotion is in question. It is by merit that men rise in the service, a system which ensures that posts should only be assigned to the competent. Each man in Turkey carries in his own hand his ancestry and his position in life, which he may make or mar as he will.

Document 6

Source: Russian satirical cartoon of Peter the Great as a barber cutting off a boyar's beard, c. 1705

Document 7

Source: King James I, English monarch, address to Parliament, 1609

The state of monarchy is the supremest thing upon earth; for kings are not only God's lieutenants upon earth, and sit upon God's throne, but even by God himself are called gods....

Kings are justly called gods, for that they exercise a manner or resemblance of divine power upon earth: for if you will consider the attributes to God, you shall see how they agree in the person of a king. God hath power to create or destroy, make or unmake at his pleasure, to give life or send death, to judge all and to be judged nor accountable to none; to raise low things and to make high things low at his pleasure, and to God are both souls and body due. And the like power have kings: they make and unmake their subjects, they have power of raising and casting down, of life and of death, judges over all their subjects and in all causes and yet accountable to none but God only....

(Answers on pages 348–353.)

PERIOD 5
(c. 1750–1900 C.E.)
Industrialization and Global Integration

Industrialization and Global Capitalism

CHAPTER 13

Answers for Chapter 13 are on pages 353–357.

 Key Concept 5.1—The process of industrialization changed the way in which goods were produced and consumed, with far-reaching effects on the global economy, social relations, and culture.

I. Industrialization fundamentally changed how goods were produced.

    A. A variety of factors that led to the rise of industrial production and eventually resulted in the Industrial Revolution included:

- Europe's location on the Atlantic Ocean
- The geographical distribution of coal, iron, and timber
- European demographic changes
- Urbanization
- Improved agricultural productivity
- Legal protection of private property
- An abundance of rivers and canals
- Access to foreign resources
- The accumulation of capital

    B. The development of machines, including steam engines and the internal combustion engine, made it possible to take advantage of vast new resources of energy stored in fossil fuels, specifically coal and oil. The fossil fuels revolution greatly increased the energy available to human societies.

    C. The development of the factory system concentrated labor in a single location and led to an increasing degree of specialization of labor.

    D. As the new methods of industrial production became more common in parts of Northwestern Europe, they spread to other parts of Europe and the United States, Russia, and Japan.

    E. The "Second Industrial Revolution" led to new methods in the production of steel, chemicals, electricity, and precision machinery during the second half of the nineteenthth century.

II. New patterns of global trade and production developed and further integrated the global economy as industrialists sought raw materials and new markets for the increasing amount and array of goods produced in their factories.

   A. The need for raw materials for the factories and increased food supplies for the growing population in urban centers led to the growth of export economies around the world that specialized in commercial extraction of natural resources and the production of food and industrial crops. The profits from these raw materials were used to purchase finished goods.

   B. The rapid development of steam-powered industrial production in European countries and the U.S. contributed to the increase in these regions' share of global manufacturing during the First Industrial Revolution. While Middle Eastern and Asian countries continued to produce manufactured goods, these regions' share in global manufacturing declined.

   C. The global economy of the nineteenth century expanded dramatically from the previous period due to increased exchanges of raw materials and finished goods in most parts of the world. Trade in some commodities was organized in a way that gave merchants and companies based in Europe and the United States a distinct economic advantage.

III. To facilitate investments at all levels of industrial production, financiers developed and expanded various financial institutions.

   A. The ideological inspiration for economic changes lies in the development of capitalism and classical liberalism associated with Adam Smith and John Stuart Mill.

   B. The global nature of trade and production contributed to the proliferation of large-scale transnational businesses that relied on various financial instruments.

IV. There were major developments in transportation and communication, including railroads, steamships, telegraphs, and canals.

V. The development and spread of global capitalism led to a variety of responses.

   A. In industrialized states, many workers organized themselves, often in labor unions, to improve working conditions, limit hours, and gain higher wages. Workers' movements and political parties emerged in different areas, promoting alternative visions of society, including Marxism.

B. In response to the expansion of industrializing states, some governments in Asia and Africa, such as the Ottoman Empire and Qing China, sought to reform and modernize their economies and militaries. Reform efforts were often resisted by some members of government or established elite groups.

C. In a small number of states, governments promoted their own state-sponsored visions of industrialization.

D. In response to the social and economic changes brought about by industrial capitalism, some governments promoted various types of political, social, educational, and urban reforms.

VI. The ways in which people organized themselves into societies also underwent significant transformations in industrialized states due to the fundamental restructuring of the global economy.

A. New social classes, including the middle class and the industrial working class, developed.

B. Family dynamics, gender roles, and demographics changed in response to industrialization.

C. Rapid urbanization that accompanied global capitalism often led to a variety of challenges.

The process of industrialization transformed the way goods were produced and revolutionized travel. However, it also greatly affected economies around the world, global trade, societies, philosophy, and the role of government. In industrialized states, new social classes emerged, and lifestyles changed drastically. This led to poor conditions in cities and major changes in family relationships. In industrialized areas, governments and workers responded to the harsh working and living conditions with unions and legislation. Some questioned capitalism and promoted alternatives, such as Marxism. Although industrialization began in Europe, the effects were felt around the world, furthered the process of globalization, and led to imperialism in Africa and Asia to meet the demand for raw materials and markets. By the end of this time period, the United States, Western Europe, Russia, and Japan were industrialized.

Questions 360–364 refer to the images below.

Image 1

**SOME OF THE DOFFERS AND THE SUPERINTENDENT
OF CATAWBA COTTON MILL, UNITED STATES, 1908**

Image 2

**PATENT FOR THE COTTON GIN FILED
BY ELI WHITNEY, UNITED STATES, 1794**

360. Image 1 best illustrates which of the following economic transformations
that began circa 1750?

(A) The transition from industrial manufacturing to the putting-out system
of manufacturing

(B) The transition from production in multiple locations to the concentration
of labor in factories

(C) The transition from an industrial economy to the military-industrial
complex

(D) The transition from the use of child labor to the use of machines

361. Which of the following was an effect of the invention of machines similar to the one shown in Image 2?

    (A) The growth of export economies around the world due to the demand for raw materials

    (B) The increased production of manufactured goods in the Middle East and India

    (C) The decreased demand for unskilled workers due to the implementation of machines

    (D) The sponsorship of industrialization in overseas colonies by European imperial powers

362. In the second half of the 19th century, the conditions depicted in Image 1 served as inspiration for those arguing that

    (A) state-sponsored industrialization was necessary to end abuses by private business owners

    (B) the capitalist system was beneficial to both business owners and factory workers

    (C) the use of fossil fuels was damaging the environment by contributing to pollution

    (D) governments should implement reforms in order to address the negative effects of capitalism

363. Which of the following was the most immediate effect of the economic transformation illustrated in the images?

    (A) The emergence of revolutions based on Marxist ideology

    (B) The development of anti-imperial movements in Asian colonies

    (C) The rise of a new working class and changing family dynamics

    (D) The implementation of new political systems and legal codes

364. The development of production as shown in the images had which of the following impacts on the global economy?

    (A) Prices of cash crops were significantly lower.

    (B) India's share in global manufacturing declined.

    (C) Prices of textiles increased significantly.

    (D) European merchants no longer dominated trade routes.

Questions 365–367 refer to the passage below.

"Steam-engines furnish the means not only of their support but of
their multiplication. They create a vast demand for fuel; and, while
they lend their powerful arms to drain the pits and to raise the
coals, they call into employment multitudes of miners, engineers,
shipbuilders, and sailors, and cause the construction of canals and
railways. Thus therefore, in enabling these rich fields of industry
to be cultivated to the utmost, they leave thousands of fine arable
fields free for the production of food to man, which must have been
otherwise allotted to the food of horses. Steam-engines moreover, by
the cheapness and steadiness of their action, fabricate cheap goods,
and procure in their exchange a liberal supply of the necessaries and
comforts of life produced in foreign lands."

Andrew Ure, Scottish doctor, *The Philosophy of Manufactures*,
published in London, 1835

365. The passage is best seen as evidence for which of the following?

(A) The implementation of the factory system led to increased demand for
skilled laborers.

(B) The limited supply of fossil fuels led to innovations in transportation.

(C) The rise of industrial technology improved living conditions for all
members of society.

(D) The development of machines led to increased agricultural yields and
population growth.

366. Which of the following groups in industrial societies of the nineteenth
century would be most likely to <u>disagree</u> with the author's view of
machines?

(A) Industrial capitalists

(B) Government officials

(C) Landholding elites

(D) Industrial workers

367. Which of the following factors contributed to the rise of industrial
production described in the passage?

(A) The accumulation of capital for investment and legal protection of
private property

(B) The conquest of overseas colonies in Africa and access to slaves

(C) The reduction of Europe's population and the need for labor-saving
devices

(D) The decline in agricultural productivity and a lack of skilled workers

Questions 368–370 refer to the map below.

SPREAD OF INDUSTRIAL TECHNOLOGY
IN EUROPE, 1750–1900 C.E.

368. Which of the following factors contributed to the spread of industrial production shown on the map?

(A) The use of railroads to transport machines to new regions

(B) Access to colonies in North America and East Asia

(C) The geographical distribution of coal, iron, and timber

(D) The abundance of cotton, oil, and rubber in those regions

369. Which of the following was a result of the rapid urbanization shown on the map?

(A) Unsanitary living conditions and environmental pollution

(B) Lack of available land for agricultural production

(C) Political revolutions and more democratic governments

(D) The rise of financial instruments and transnational businesses

370. **Which of the following best describes the effect of increased industrial production on workers in areas shown on the map?**
    (A) Distinctions between the workers and factory owners became less pronounced.
    (B) Access to railroads and steamships enabled factory workers to take vacations.
    (C) Living conditions improved due to access to cheap goods and fossil fuels.
    (D) Unions formed to improve working conditions, limit hours, and gain higher wages.

Questions 371–374 refer to the passage below.

"You are horrified at our intending to do away with private property. But in your existing society, private property is already done away with for nine-tenths of the population; its existence for the few is solely due to its non-existence in the hands of those nine-tenths. You reproach us, therefore, with intending to do away with a form of property, the necessary condition for whose existence is the non-existence of any property for the immense majority of society.

In one word, you reproach us with intending to do away with your property. Precisely so; that is just what we intend.

From the moment when labor can no longer be converted into capital, money, or rent, into a social power capable of being monopolized, i.e., from the moment when individual property can no longer be transformed into bourgeois property, into capital, from that moment, you say individuality vanishes.

You must, therefore, confess that by 'individual' you mean no other person than the bourgeois, than the middle-class owner of property. This person must, indeed, be swept out of the way, and made impossible.

Communism deprives no man of the power to appropriate the products of society; all that it does is to deprive him of the power to subjugate the labor of others by means of such appropriation."

Friedrich Engels and Karl Marx, German political theorists,
The Communist Manifesto, 1848

371. The views expressed in the passage best illustrate which of the following processes?

    (A) The development of alternative visions of society in response to the spread of global capitalism
    (B) The spread of ideologies similar to those of John Stuart Mill and Adam Smith
    (C) The rise of the middle class as a result of the spread of industrial technology
    (D) The organization of workers into labor unions to improve working conditions

372. Which of the following occurred in the late nineteenth and early twentieth centuries in Western Europe that diminished the appeal of ideas such as those expressed in the passage?

    (A) Marxist revolutions led to government control of the means of production.
    (B) Labor unions and government reforms improved living and working conditions.
    (C) Migration to overseas colonies alleviated crowded conditions and created job opportunities.
    (D) State-sponsored industrialization improved working conditions in factories and mines.

373. The authors' point of view regarding private property was likely influenced by which of the following developments at the time they were writing?

    (A) The rise of government-owned factories as a result of state-sponsored industrialization
    (B) Government reforms to improve living conditions and make elementary education compulsory
    (C) The increase in the United States' share of global manufacturing
    (D) The unequal distribution of wealth as a result of *laissez-faire* capitalism

374. Ideas similar to those expressed in the passage led to which of the following in the early twentieth century?

    (A) The overthrow of the Russian monarchy
    (B) The abolition of private property in Germany
    (C) World War I beginning in order to combat Marxist ideas
    (D) Revolutions led by those prohibited from owning property

Questions 375–377 refer to the following images.

Image 1

CHILOK STATION, TRANS-SIBERIAN RAILROAD, 1903

Image 2

GINZA STREET, TOKYO, 1921

The image shows electrical poles, a car, and a rickshaw.

375. Which of the following best describes the primary purpose of the construction of the railroad featured in Image 1?

    (A) To increase trade with nations of Southern Asia

    (B) To transport migrants from western cities to eastern areas for settlement

    (C) To connect coal- and iron-producing regions with industrial centers

    (D) To export manufactured goods to the United States and Western Europe

376. The technologies shown in Image 2 are the result of which of the following?

    (A) The spread of industrial technologies as a result of World War I

    (B) The invention of steam-powered machines by Japanese engineers

    (C) The conquest of Japan by the United States and European powers

    (D) The Meiji Restoration and the spread of industrial technology

377. The objects in the images are the result of which of the following processes?
  (A) State-sponsored industrialization in Japan and Russia
  (B) Private ownership of transportation technologies
  (C) Military reforms in response to Western imperialism
  (D) Urbanization as a result of private investment in industrial production

Questions 378–380 refer to the passage below.

"One industrial initiative in India developed around Calcutta, where British colonial rule had centered since the East India Company founded the city in 1690. A Hindu Brahman family, the Tagores, established close ties with many British administrators. . . . Tagore's dominant idea was a British-Indian economic and cultural collaboration that would revitalize his country. He enjoyed a high reputation in Europe and for a short time made a success of his economic initiatives. Tagore died on a trip abroad, and his financial empire declined soon after.

This first taste of Indian industrialization was significant, but it brought few immediate results. The big news in India, even as Tagore launched his companies, was the rapid decline of traditional textiles under the bombardment of British factory competition; millions of Indian villages were thrown out of work. Furthermore, relations between Britain and the Indian elite worsened after the mid-1830s as British officials sought a more active economic role and became more intolerant of Indian culture. One British official, admitting no knowledge of Indian scholarship, wrote that 'all the historical information' and science available in Sanskrit was 'less valuable than what may be found in the most paltry abridgements used at preparatory schools in England.' With these attitudes, the kind of collaboration that might have aided Indian appropriation of British industry became impossible."

Peter N. Stearns, historian,
The Industrial Revolution in World History, 1993

378. The British view of Indian culture discussed in the passage is best understood in the context of which of the following?
  (A) Changes in Indian government as a result of the Enlightenment
  (B) Emerging racial ideologies that were used to justify imperialism
  (C) The rise of Marxist ideas regarding the working class
  (D) The migration of Indian laborers overseas for plantation labor

379. Which of the following was an effect of the decline in Indian industries discussed in the passage?

    (A) India's economy became dependent on Britain for natural resources and commodities.
    (B) India's participation in global trade declined significantly.
    (C) India's economy shifted from producing manufactured goods to exporting commodities.
    (D) India's economy relied on the import of British food supplies and raw materials.

380. The economic changes described in the passage led to which of the following in the twentieth century?

    (A) Indian nationalism and desire for economic self-sufficiency
    (B) British migrations to India for long-term settlement
    (C) Civil war between British officials and Indian merchants
    (D) Indian independence and economic isolation from the West

Questions 381–383 refer to the passage below.

"'Heaven helps those who help themselves' is a welltried maxim, embodying in a small compass the results of vast human experience. The spirit of selfhelp is the root of all genuine growth in the individual; and, exhibited in the lives of many, it constitutes the true source of national vigour and strength. Help from without is often enfeebling in its effects, but help from within invariably invigorates. Whatever is done *for* men or classes, to a certain extent takes away the stimulus and necessity of doing for themselves; and where men are subjected to over-guidance and over-government, the inevitable tendency is to render them comparatively helpless.

Even the best institutions can give a man no active aid. Perhaps the utmost they can do is, to leave him *free* to develop himself and improve his individual condition. But in all times men have been prone to believe that their happiness and well being were to be secured by means of institutions rather than by their own conduct. Hence the value of legislation as an agent in human advancement has always been greatly overestimated."

Samuel Smiles, Scottish author, *Self-Help*, 1859

381. Smiles's argument is best understood in the context of which of the following?

    (A) Discontent among the owners of transnational businesses over trade regulations

    (B) Disputes among factory owners over wages and working hours

    (C) Conflicting visions of Marxists and union members in addressing working conditions

    (D) Debates over the role of government in implementing social and urban reforms

382. Smiles's view regarding legislation would most likely be supported by which of the following?

    (A) Factory workers

    (B) Marxist socialists

    (C) *Laissez-faire* capitalists

    (D) Parliament members

383. Smiles's view toward legislation would most likely be <u>opposed</u> by which of the following?

    (A) Factory owners

    (B) Landholding elites

    (C) Factory workers

    (D) Rural peasants

Questions 384–386 refer to the graph below.

RELATIVE SHARE OF WORLD MANUFACTURING OUTPUT, 1750–1900

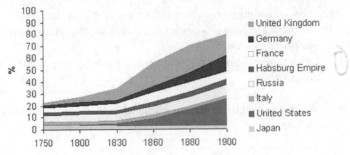

Source: *Two One Two at English Wikipedia*

Tip: Before looking at the questions, be sure that you understand what the graph is showing. The big shift that is occurring is that Europe's share of manufacturing was approximately 25 percent in 1750 but was close to 80 percent by 1900.

384. Which of the following explains the change in Europe's share of global manufacturing between 1750 and 1900?

    (A) The availability in Europe of raw materials such as oil and cotton
    (B) The concentration of labor in factories and the fossil fuels revolution
    (C) The organization of workers into labor unions and the rise of Marxists
    (D) The rise of new social classes and changing family dynamics

385. Which of the following was the most immediate effect of the trend shown on the graph?

    (A) The proliferation of large-scale transnational businesses
    (B) The spread of industrial technology to South and East Asia
    (C) The conquest of colonies in the Americas and the Caribbean
    (D) The contraction of the global economy

386. How did the expansion of Japanese and Russian manufacturing differ from manufacturing by Western European powers?

    (A) Japanese and Russian manufacturing was hindered by strict regulations to discourage production.
    (B) Japanese and Russian manufacturing was mainly focused on the production of food instead of consumer goods.
    (C) Japanese and Russian industrialization was funded by private investors rather than with support from the state.
    (D) Japanese and Russian industrialization was sponsored by the government rather than private investors.

Questions 387–389 refer to the tables below.

Table 1

INVENTIONS OF THE FIRST INDUSTRIAL REVOLUTION

Innovation	Year
Steam engine	1775
Cotton gin	1793
Puddling process for iron production	1784
Locomotive	1804

Table 2

INVENTIONS OF THE SECOND INDUSTRIAL REVOLUTION

Innovation	Year
Bessemer process for steel production	1856
Electrical current (DC)	1882
Diesel engine	1892
Automobile	1885

387. Which of the following contributed to the rise of the innovations of the First Industrial Revolution as shown in Table 1?

   (A) The abandonment of rural areas and resulting urbanization
   (B) The backing of monarchs and new navigation technologies
   (C) The decline in population and access to iron and coal from the Americas
   (D) The accumulation of capital for investment and the rise of the factory system

388. Which of the following was an effect of the development of the innovations of the Second Industrial Revolution shown in Table 2?

   (A) Overseas migration declined due to greater access to domestic jobs.
   (B) The global population grew due to the role of these technologies in food production.
   (C) The global economy was further integrated due to the innovations in transportation.
   (D) European colonies became increasingly motivated by nationalist ideologies.

389. Which of the following occurred in response to the expansion of industrializing states as a result of the innovations shown in both tables?

(A) The governments of the Ottoman Empire and Qing China sought to modernize their economies.

(B) Factory workers and peasants in Western Europe overthrew existing governments.

(C) Nationalist leaders in areas that were colonized by Europeans utilized the colonists in their movements.

(D) Reform movements in industrialized states failed to gain the support of government.

Short-Answer Questions

Answer all parts of the question that follows.

390. a) Identify ONE way the development and spread of industrial technology changed patterns of global trade in the period 1750–1900 C.E.

b) Explain ONE change in the social structure of industrialized states of Western Europe in the period 1750–1900 C.E.

c) Describe ONE significant continuity that occurred in the social structure of industrialized states of Western Europe in the period 1750–1900 C.E.

Answer all parts of the question that follows.

391. a) Identify ONE economic effect of the spread of industrial technology in Europe in the period 1750–1900 C.E.

b) Explain ONE similarity in the responses of governments and the responses of workers to the development and spread of global capitalism in the period 1750–1900 C.E.

c) Explain ONE difference in the responses of governments and the responses of workers to the development and spread of global capitalism in the period 1750–1900 C.E.

Long Essay Questions

392. In the period 1750–1900, the process of industrialization changed the way in which goods were produced and consumed, with far-reaching effects on the global economy.

    Develop an argument that evaluates how the process of industrialization transformed the global economy in this period.

393. In the period 1750–1900, the process of industrialization changed the way in which goods were produced and consumed, with far-reaching effects on the global economy, social relations, and culture.

    Develop an argument that evaluates the factors that contributed to the rise of industrialization in Europe in this period.

Document-Based Question

394. Evaluate the differences in responses to the negative effects of industrialization on European workers in the period 1750–1900 c.e.

Tip: In a DBQ you should:
- Use 6 documents to support your argument
- Explain the significance of the source (historical situation, audience, point of view, purpose) for 3 documents
- Include 1 specific piece of outside historical evidence that relates to your argument and the prompt

Document 1

Source: Thomas Malthus, English economist, *An Essay on the Principle of Population*, second edition, 1803

The principal and most permanent cause of poverty has little or no relation to forms of government, or the unequal division of property; and as the rich do not in reality possess the power of finding employment and maintenance for [all] the poor, the poor cannot, in the nature of things, possess the right to demand them; [these] are important truths flowing from the principle of population....And it is evident that every man in the lower classes of society, who became acquainted with these truths, would be disposed to bear the distresses in which he might be involved with more patience.

Document 2

Source: Karl Marx and Friedrich Engels, *The Communist Manifesto*, 1848

...The Communists everywhere support every revolutionary movement against the existing social and political order of things.

In all these movements, they bring to the front, as the leading question in each, the property question, no matter what its degree of development at the time....

The Communists disdain to conceal their views and aims. They openly declare that their ends can be attained only by the forcible overthrow of all existing social conditions. Let the ruling classes tremble at a Communistic revolution. The proletarians have nothing to lose but their chains. They have a world to win.

Working Men of All Countries, Unite!

Document 3

Source: David Ricardo, English economist, *Principles of Political Economy and Taxation*, 1817

Like all other contracts, wages should be left to the fair and free competition of the market, and should never be controlled by the interference of the legislature. The clear and direct tendency of the Poor Laws* is in direct opposition to these obvious principles: ...instead of making the poor rich, they are calculated to make the rich poor....The comforts and well-being of the poor cannot be permanently secured without some regard on their part, or some effort on the part of the legislature, to regulate the increase of their numbers.

*British laws that provided a government subsidy to workers who received less than a certain amount of wages

Document 4

Source: Leeds Woolen Workers Petition to the merchants and clothiers, 1786

... the Scribbling-Machines have thrown thousands of your petitioners out of employ, whereby they are brought into great distress, and are not able to procure a maintenance for their families, and deprived them of the opportunity of bringing up their children to labour: We have therefore to request, that prejudice and self-interest may be laid aside, and that you may pay that attention to the following facts, which the nature of the case requires.

How are those men, thus thrown out of employ to provide for their families;—and what are they to put their children apprentice to, that the rising generation may have something to keep them at work, in order that they may not be like vagabonds strolling about in idleness? Some say, Begin and learn some other business.—Suppose we do; who will maintain our families, whilst we undertake the arduous task; and when we have learned it, how do we know we shall be any better for all our pains; for by the time we have served our second apprenticeship, another machine may arise, which may take away that business also; so that our families, being half pined whilst we are learning how to provide them with bread, will be wholly so during the period of our third apprenticeship.

These things impartially considered will we hope, be strong advocates in our favour; and we conceive that men of sense, religion and humanity, will be satisfied of the reasonableness, as well as necessity of this address, and that their own feelings will urge them to espouse the cause of us and our families. ...

Document 5

Source: Factory Act of 1833, Britain

...no person under eighteen years of age shall [work] between half-past eight in the evening and half-past five in the morning, in any cotton, woollen, worsted, hemp, flax, tow, linen or silk mill. ...

...no person under the age of eighteen shall be employed in any such mill ... more than twelve hours in ... one day, nor more than sixty-nine hours in ... one week. ...

It shall be lawful for His Majesty to appoint four Inspectors of factories where ... children and young persons under eighteen years of age [are] employed, empowered to enter any ... mill, and any school ... belonging thereto, at all times ... by day or by night, when such ... factories are at work.

The Inspectors shall have power to make such rules as may be necessary for the execution of this act, binding on all persons subject to the provisions of this act; and are authorised to enforce the attendance at school of children employed in factories according to the provisions of this act.

Every child restricted to the performance of forty-eight hours of labour in any one week shall attend some school.

Document 6

Source: Label from The American Federation of Labor (AFL), circa 1900

The AFL was a group of unions that formed in 1886. *Labor omnia vincit* is a Latin phrase meaning "work conquers all," and was used as a slogan for the labor movement.

Document 7

Source: Robert Owen, utopian socialist, *Observations on the Effect of the Manufacturing System: With Hints for the Improvement of Those Parts of It Which Are Most Injurious to Health and Morals*, 1817

It is thence evident that human nature can be improved and formed into the character which it is for the interest and happiness of all it should possess, solely by directing the attention of mankind to the adoption of legislative measures judiciously calculated to give the best habits, and most just and useful sentiments to the rising generation;—and in an especial manner to those who are placed in situations, which, without such measures, render them liable to be taught the worst habits, and the most useless and injurious sentiments.

(Answers on pages 353–357.)

Imperialism and Nation-State Formation

CHAPTER 14

Answers for Chapter 14 are on pages 357–362.

Key Concept 5.2—As states industrialized, they also expanded existing overseas empires and established new colonies and transoceanic relationships.

I. Industrializing powers established transoceanic empires.

    A. States with existing colonies strengthened their control over those colonies.

    B. European states, as well as the United States and Japan, established empires throughout Asia and the Pacific, while Spanish and Portuguese influence declined.

    C. Many European states used both warfare and diplomacy to establish empires in Africa.

    D. In some parts of their empires, Europeans established settler colonies.

    E. Industrialized states practiced neocolonialism in Latin America and economic imperialism in some parts of the world.

II. Imperialism influenced state formation and contraction around the world.

    A. The expansion of U.S. and European influence over Tokugawa Japan led to the emergence of Meiji Japan.

    B. The United States, Russia, and Japan expanded their land borders by conquering and settling neighboring territories.

    C. Anti-imperial resistance took various forms, including direct resistance within empires and the creation of new states on the peripheries.

III. In some imperial societies, emerging cultural, religious, and racial ideologies, including Social Darwinism, were used to justify imperialism.

Industrialization led to the establishment of large overseas empires by industrial powers. The process of industrialization fueled greater demand for markets and raw materials. Transportation technologies enabled industrial powers faster access to their overseas colonies. Mass-produced weapons facilitated conquest. Colonies were obtained for a variety of reasons. They were sources of raw materials, minerals, and cash crops. They were areas for resettlement for growing

European populations. They also served as markets for mass-produced goods. Imperial powers often justified control due to ideologies such as scientific racism and Social Darwinism.

Questions 395–398 refer to the maps below.

Map 1

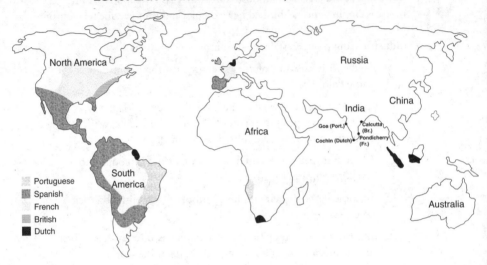

MARITIME EMPIRES, CIRCA 1900 C.E.

Map 2

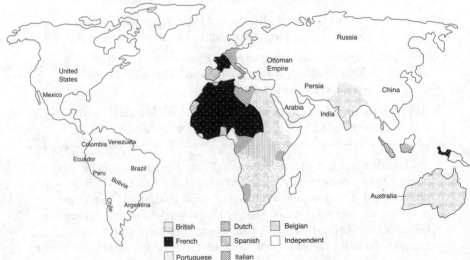

395. The maritime empires shown on Map 1 are mainly the result of which of the following?

    (A) The use of gunpowder weapons to subjugate indigenous populations of the Americas
    (B) The lack of centralized governments throughout the Americas and Southeast Asia
    (C) The use of steamships and mass-produced weapons to conquer Indonesia and the Philippines
    (D) The lack of resistance and cooperation of native populations in conquered regions

396. Which of the following motivated Europeans to conquer the areas shown on Map 2?

    (A) The desire to secure coal, iron ore, and timber for industrial production
    (B) Access to finished goods, such as textiles, weapons, and carpets
    (C) The availability of coerced laborers to work in European factories
    (D) Access to raw materials for industrial production, such as rubber, cotton, and metals

397. Which of the following contributed to the different patterns of imperial rule shown on the maps?

    (A) Access to gunpowder weapons by indigenous peoples of the Americas led to rebellion.
    (B) Nationalist movements developed among conquered groups in Afro-Eurasia.
    (C) Enlightenment ideas contributed to revolutions in the Atlantic world.
    (D) The consolidation of power by European monarchs facilitated conquest of new regions.

398. Which of the following was the primary response of indigenous peoples to encroachment by imperial powers between 1500 and 1900 C.E.?

    (A) Complete adoption of many aspects of European culture
    (B) Violent and nonviolent forms of resistance against Europeans
    (C) Movements that used civil disobedience and passive forms of resistance
    (D) Cooperation with conquerors and complete acceptance of foreign rule

Questions 399–401 refer to the passage below.

"The essential point in dealing with Africans is to establish a respect
for the European. Upon this—the prestige of the white man—
depends his influence, often his very existence, in Africa. If he shows
by his surroundings, by his assumption of superiority, that he is far
above the native, he will be respected, and his influence will be pro-
portionate to the superiority he assumes and bears out by his higher
accomplishments and mode of life. In my opinion—at any rate with
reference to Africa—it is the greatest possible mistake to suppose that
a European can acquire a greater influence by adopting the mode
of life of the natives. In effect, it is to lower himself to their plane,
instead of elevating them to his."

F. D. Lugard, British colonial administrator,
The Rise of Our East African Empire, 1893

399. The interactions described in the passage best illustrate which of the
following processes?

(A) The mass conversion of Africans to Christianity
(B) The expansion of the trans-Atlantic slave trade
(C) The establishment of transoceanic empires by industrializing
powers
(D) The transformation of Africa's economy due to industrial
technology

400. The author's point of view regarding natives was likely influenced by which
of the following?

(A) Marxist philosophy
(B) Racial ideologies
(C) Enlightenment ideas
(D) Capitalist economic theories

401. Which of the following resulted from interactions among Africans and
Europeans as described in the passage?

(A) The outbreak of violent resistance movements among Africans
(B) The creation of a syncretic religion by Africans
(C) The elevation of impoverished Africans to higher status
(D) The abandonment of African cultural and religious traditions

Questions 402–404 refer to the images below.

Image 1

PORTRAIT OF THE EMPEROR MEIJI, 1888

Image 2

NEGOTIATIONS AMONG THE JAPANESE, CHINESE, AND KOREANS, YOSAI (WATANABE) NOBUKAZU, 1894

Japanese print showing negotiations between the Japanese (on the left), Chinese (on the right), and Koreans (behind the table) to end the Sino-Japanese War, 1894

 Tip: The title and caption of Image 2 provide helpful information. Always read them first before examining the image so you can look at it with a more critical eye.

402. <u>Image 1</u> best reflects which of the following processes?

   (A) The use of the Japanese emperor as a figurehead by European imperial powers
   (B) The blending of traditional Japanese and Western clothing styles and furnishings
   (C) The implementation of centralized rule for the first time in Japanese history
   (D) The adoption of Western cultural elements as a result of increased interactions

403. <u>Image 2</u> best illustrates which of the following developments?

   (A) The rapid industrialization and imperialism of Japan
   (B) The interference of European powers in East Asian affairs
   (C) The creation of an alliance between Japan and China
   (D) The conquest of China by a modernized Japanese military

404. The developments illustrated by the images led to which of the following in the first half of the <u>twentieth century?</u>

   (A) The rejection of foreign cultural traditions as a result of Japan's isolation
   (B) The increased cooperation of industrializing powers in an effort to reduce trade barriers
   (C) The expansion of the Japanese Empire due to the demand for natural resources
   (D) The rise of a Japanese nationalist movement sparked by the desire for independence

Questions 405–407 refer to the passage below.

"The reason the West became so affluent and dominant in the modern era is that it invented three institutions: science, democracy and capitalism. All these institutions are based on universal impulses and aspirations, but those aspirations were given a unique expression in Western civilization. . . .

Science provides the knowledge that leads to invention, and capitalism supplies the mechanism by which the invention is transmitted to the larger society, as well as the economic incentive for inventors to continue to make new things. . . .

The wealth and power of European nations made them arrogant and stimulated their appetite for global conquest. Colonial possessions added to the prestige, and to a much lesser degree to the wealth, of Europe. But the primary cause of Western affluence and power is internal—the institutions of science, democracy, and capitalism acting in concert.

Consequently it is simply wrong to maintain that the rest of the world is poor because the West is rich or that the West grew rich off 'stolen goods' from Asia, Africa and Latin America, because the West created its own wealth, and still does."

Dinesh D'Souza, political commentator,
"Two Cheers for Colonialism," 2002

405. The author's argument regarding Western imperialism is likely based on which of the following?

(A) The diffusion of socialism and ownership of the means of production
(B) The spread of Enlightenment ideas and private enterprise
(C) The diffusion of Christian values and industrial technology
(D) The spread of Greco-Roman technology and economic attributes

406. Which of the following would most directly <u>challenge</u> the author's argument that the West created its own wealth?

(A) The export of raw materials from overseas colonies fueled European industrialization.
(B) The major centers of industrial production were located in Europe.
(C) The rise of capitalism facilitated investment in factories by entrepreneurs.
(D) The use of the scientific method contributed to industrial technology.

407. Based on the title of the article, which group would most likely <u>disagree</u> with the author's argument?

(A) Christian fundamentalists
(B) Advocates for neocolonialism
(C) European nationalist philosophers
(D) Anti-imperialist intellectuals

Questions 408–410 refer to the following images.

Image 1

**FROM "AN ABC FOR BABY PATRIOTS,"
PUBLISHED IN ENGLAND IN 1898**

B b   ℬ b

B stands for Battles
    By which England's name
Has for ever been covered
    With glory and fame.

C c   ℰ c

C is for Colonies.
    Rightly we boast,
That of all the great nations
    Great Britain has most.

Image 2

**FROM "AN ABC FOR BABY PATRIOTS,"
PUBLISHED IN ENGLAND IN 1898**

408. The images would be most useful to a historian studying which of the following?

(A) Clothing style of Europeans
(B) Educational strategies used by the British
(C) Nationalist attitudes among imperialist power
(D) British military technologies and literature

Tip: Images always require interpretation, so do not just accept what is shown as the entire truth. Consider the point of view of the artist and the historical situation at the time.

409. Which of the following was the likely purpose of the images?

(A) To promote Enlightenment ideas
(B) To develop loyal British citizens
(C) To glorify British parliamentary government
(D) To justify military conquest

410. Which of the following contributed to British imperialism in the nineteenth century?

(A) The process of industrialization and increased nationalism
(B) The desire to sponsor industrialization efforts overseas
(C) The emergence of Asian and African land empires
(D) The transition from manufacturing to the putting-out system

Questions 411–413 refer to the passage below.

"1. The establishment of a university at Peking.

2. The sending of imperial clansmen to foreign countries to study the forms and conditions of European and American government.

3. The encouragement of the arts, sciences and modern agriculture. . . .

7. Urged that the Lu-Han railway should be prosecuted with more vigour and expedition.

8. Advised the adoption of Western arms and drill for all the Tartar troops.

9. Ordered the establishment of agricultural schools in all the provinces to teach the farmers improved methods of agriculture. . . .

12. Special rewards were offered to inventors and authors.

13. The officials were ordered to encourage trade and assist merchants. . . .

15. Bureaus of Mines and Railroads were established.

16. Journalists were encouraged to write on all political subjects.

17. Naval academies and training-ships were ordered. . . .

20. Commercial bureaus were ordered in Shanghai for the encouragement of trade."

> Reforms proposed by Guangxu, Chinese emperor in the late
> 19th century, as summarized by Issac Taylor Headland,
> a professor studying in China, 1909

411. **The proposed reforms shown in the passage were most likely issued in reaction to which of the following?**

    (A) Colonization by Western powers and the desire for independence
    (B) Enlightenment ideas and the willingness of the emperor to abdicate
    (C) The collapse of the Qing dynasty and the resulting period of disorder
    (D) Encroachment by industrializing states and subsequent economic imperialism

412. **The reforms outlined in the passage were most similar to which of the following?**

    (A) The Russian Revolution
    (B) The Meiji Restoration
    (C) The Mexican Revolution
    (D) The Second Industrial Revolution

413. The conditions in the early twentieth century in China that these reforms attempted to address led to which of the following later developments?

    (A) Industrialization and the establishment of a stable democracy
    (B) The fall of the existing monarchy and rise of a new dynasty
    (C) A civil war and communist revolution
    (D) The rise of a foreign-ruled totalitarian state

Questions 414–415 refer to the image below.

POLITICAL CARTOON, TITLED "THE WORLD'S CONSTABLE," PUBLISHED IN THE UNITED STATES IN 1905

The image shows United States President Theodore Roosevelt as a constable standing between Europe and Latin America, with a club labeled "The New Diplomacy."

414. The image best illustrates which of the following developments in the period circa 1900?

    (A) Imperialism practiced by the United States and decline of Spanish and Portuguese influence
    (B) Using diplomacy to expand Western transoceanic empires as violent conflicts declined
    (C) The use of warfare and diplomacy to expand American colonies in Africa
    (D) The establishment of settler colonies in Africa and Asia by industrializing powers

415. The economic influence of the United States in Latin America best reflects which of the following?

    (A) Liberalism
    (B) Communism
    (C) Neocolonialism
    (D) Nationalism

Questions 416–418 refer to the passage below.

"In spite of the fact that we have no such fleet as we should have, we have conquered for ourselves a place in the sun. It will now be my task to see to it that this place in the sun shall remain our undisputed possession, in order that the sun's rays may fall fruitfully upon our activity and trade in foreign parts, that our industry and agriculture may develop within the state and our sailing sports upon the water, for our future lies upon the water. The more Germans go out upon the waters, whether it be in races or regattas, whether it be in journeys across the ocean, or in the service of the battle flag, so much the better it will be for us. . . .

As head of the Empire I therefore rejoice over every citizen, whether from Hamburg, Bremen, or Lübeck, who goes forth with this large outlook and seeks new points where we can drive in the nail on which to hang our armor. . . ."

Kaiser Wilhelm II, German emperor, Speech to the
North German Regatta Association, 1901

416. The speech by Wilhelm II best illustrates which of the following patterns of the period 1750–1900 C.E.?

(A) The growing demand for settler colonies to alleviate population pressures
(B) The establishment of transoceanic empires by industrializing powers
(C) The rise of resistance movements opposing imperialism
(D) The use of religious ideologies to justify the imperial expansion

417. The speech by Wilhelm II is promoting which of the following?

(A) Social Darwinism and racism
(B) Marxism and socialism
(C) Aggression and appeasement
(D) Imperialism and nationalism

418. The passage by Wilhelm II is best understood in the context of which of the following?

(A) Weakening industrial states attempting to reassert their dominance
(B) Growing militarism in response to border changes within Europe
(C) Increasing competition among industrializing powers over access to natural resources
(D) Economic decline within Asian states as a result of industrialization in Europe

Questions 419–421 refer to the image below.

**POLITICAL CARTOON PUBLISHED IN *PUCK* MAGAZINE
IN THE AFTERMATH OF THE BOXER REBELLION IN
CHINA, UNITED STATES, 1900**

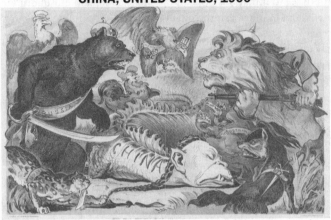

The cartoon, which is captioned, "The real trouble will come with the 'wake,'" shows international powers (Britain, Russia, Austria, Italy, Germany, and France) as animals that are subjugating the Chinese dragon as the United States, represented by the eagle, looks on.

419. The illustration would be most useful to a historian studying which of the following?

 (A) Responses to uprisings by European states
 (B) Chinese views of economic imperialism
 (C) Tactics used by imperial powers to conquer territories
 (D) Advances in military technology as a result of industrialization

420. Which of the following was the most immediate effect of the process illustrated in the image?

 (A) China adopted communism with a capitalist economy.
 (B) Reform movements led to rapid Chinese industrialization.
 (C) European powers took control of China's government.
 (D) China's monarchy was overthrown in a revolution.

421. Which of the following occurred in the early twentieth century that was predicted by the artist?

 (A) Cooperation among European states and China in response to the Great Depression
 (B) Competition by European powers over access to China during World War I
 (C) New forms of economic imperialism practiced by European powers in China
 (D) Expansion of China's borders at the expense of European powers

Questions 422–424 refer to the poem below.

"Take up the White Man's burden—
Send forth the best ye breed—
Go send your sons to exile
To serve your captives' need
To wait in heavy harness
On fluttered folk and wild—
Your new-caught, sullen peoples,
Half devil and half child

Take up the White Man's burden
In patience to abide
To veil the threat of terror
And check the show of pride;
By open speech and simple
An hundred times made plain
To seek another's profit
And work another's gain"

Rudyard Kipling, British novelist and poet,
"White Man's Burden," 1899

422. The description of the captives referred to in the poem is best understood in the context of which of the following?

(A) Emerging racial ideologies
(B) Growing nationalism
(C) The increase in slavery
(D) The spread of Enlightenment ideas

423. Imperial powers would most likely use ideas similar to those in the poem for which of the following purposes?

(A) To criticize the actions of other imperial powers
(B) To support the use of diplomacy in international affairs
(C) To justify their actions with regard to indigenous populations
(D) To explain capitalist economic policies

424. The attitude toward colonists reflected in the poem would result in which of the following reactions by conquered peoples?

(A) Anti-imperial resistance movements
(B) Cooperation with imperializing powers
(C) A decline in nationalist feelings
(D) Abolitionist movements

Short-Answer Questions

Use the passage below to answer all parts of the question that follows.

> "The British Empire helped not only to create many of the nation-states of the contemporary world, it was also instrumental in forging many of the transnational economic and cultural links that bound them together in complex and often unstable ways, and therefore the study of the British empire can enable historians to transcend the boundaries of the nation-state which have proven to be such a constraint on the historical imagination. . . . This is not to say that imperial history is necessarily any less Eurocentric than other forms of history: in fact, in its earliest iterations imperial history was excessively preoccupied with Europe at the expense of non-European forces and factors. Imperial territories in such instances were often little more than an exotic field upon which European superiority could be displayed in sharp relief."

> Douglas M. Peers, "Is Humpty Dumpty Back Together Again?: The Revival of Imperial History and the 'Oxford History of the British Empire,'"
> *Journal of World History*, 2002

425. a) Explain how ONE piece of evidence <u>supports</u> Peers's argument regarding the influence of the British Empire on transnational cultural or economic links.

 b) Explain how ONE piece of evidence <u>undermines</u> Peers's argument regarding the influence of the British Empire on transnational cultural or economic links.

 c) Identify ONE reason why the early imperial history described in the passage was typically Eurocentric.

The second short-answer question contains a primary source or graphic. It assesses either the skill of change and continuity over time or the skill of comparison.

Use the image below to answer all parts of the question that follows.

This cartoon by Thomas Nast, titled "The World's Plunderers," appeared in Harper's Weekly, *an American magazine, in 1885.*

426. a) Identify ONE change that occurred in Africa between 1750 and 1900 C.E. as a result of European actions shown in the image.

b) Explain ONE way the political cartoon reflects a continuity in European political and military actions between 1500 and 1900 C.E.

c) Explain ONE reaction of Africans in response to the European actions shown in the image.

Long Essay Questions

427. In the period 1750–1900 C.E., industrializing powers established transoceanic empires.

Develop an argument explaining the factors that contributed to the rise of transoceanic empires by industrializing powers in the period 1750–1900 C.E.

428. In the period 1750–1900 C.E., as states industrialized, they also expanded existing overseas empires and established new colonies and transoceanic relationships.

Develop an argument that evaluates how the establishment of overseas empires by industrializing states changed one or more regions in this period.

Document-Based Question

429. Evaluate the responses of native peoples to the expansion of overseas empires by industrializing states.

Document 1

> Source: Rammohun Roy, Indian reformer, *Letter to Lord Amherst*, 1823
>
> To His Excellency the Right Honorable Lord Amherst, Governor-General in Council
>
> My Lord,
> The present rulers of India, coming from a distance of many thousand miles to govern a people whose language, literature, manners, customs, and ideas, are almost entirely new and strange to them, cannot easily become so intimately acquainted with their real circumstances as the natives of the country are themselves. We should therefore be guilty of a gross dereliction of duty to ourselves and afford our rulers just grounds of complaint at our apathy did we omit, on occasions of importance like the present, to supply them with such accurate information as might enable them to devise and adopt measures calculated to be beneficial to the country, and thus second by our local knowledge and experience their declared benevolent intentions for its improvement. . . .
>
> We find that the government is establishing a Sanskrit school under Hindu pandits [wise men] to impart such knowledge as is already current in India. . . . The pupils will there acquire what was known two thousand years ago with the addition of vain and empty subtleties since then produced by speculative men such as is already commonly taught in all parts of India. . . .
>
> . . . But as the improvement of the native population is the object of the government, it will consequently promote a more liberal and enlightened system of instruction, embracing mathematics, natural philosophy, chemistry, anatomy, with other useful sciences, which may be accomplished with the sums proposed by employing a few gentlemen of talent and learning educated in Europe and providing a college furnished with necessary books, instruments, and other apparatus.

Document 2

> Source: Ndansi Kumalo, survivor of the Ndebele rebellion against British rule in southern Africa, 1896
>
> We surrendered to the white people and were told to go back to our homes and live our usual lives and attend to our crops. But the white men sent native police who did abominable things; they were cruel and assaulted a lot of our people and helped themselves to our cattle and goats. . . . They interfered with our wives and molested them. . . . We thought it best to fight and die rather than bear it. . . .
>
> We knew that we had very little chance because their weapons were so much superior to ours. But we meant to fight to the last, feeling that even if we could not beat them we might at least kill a few of them and so have some sort of revenge. . . .
>
> I remember a fight in the Matoppos when we charged the white men. There were some hundreds of us; the white men also were many. We charged them at close quarters: we thought we had a good chance to kill them but the Maxims [a type of gun] were too much for us. . . . Many of our people were killed in this fight. . . .

Document 3

Source: Baba, a Hausa woman of Nigeria, personal account, recorded in 1948

When I was a maiden the Europeans first arrived. Ever since we were quite small the malams [Muslim scholars] had been saying that the Europeans would come with a thing called a train, they would come with a thing called a motor-car...they would stop wars, they would repair the world, they would stop oppression and lawlessness, we should live at peace with them. We used to go and sit quietly and listen to the prophecies....

I remember when a European came to Karo on a horse, and some of his foot soldiers went into the town. Everyone came out to look at them.... Everyone at Karo ran away—"There's a European, there's a European!"...

At that time Yusufu was the [Fulani] king of Karo. He did not like the Europeans, he did not wish them, he would not sign their treaty. Then he saw that perforce he would have to agree, so he did. The Habe wanted them to come, it was the Fulani who did not like it. When the Europeans came the Habe saw that if you worked for them they paid you for it, they didn't say, like the Fulani, "Commoner, give me this! Commoner, bring me that!" Yes, the Habe wanted them....

Document 4

Source: Royal Niger Company, commissioned by the British government to administer and develop the Niger River delta and surrounding areas, standard form signed by multiple African rulers, 1886

We, the undersigned Chiefs of _____, with the view to the bettering of our country and people, do this day cede to the Royal Niger Company, forever, the whole of our territory extending _____.

We pledge ourselves not to enter into any war with other tribes without the sanction of the said Royal Niger Company....The said Royal Niger Company bind themselves not to interfere with any of the native laws or customs of the country, consistently with the maintenance of order and good government.

The said Royal Niger Company agree to pay native owners of land a reasonable amount for any portion they may require...and to pay the said Chiefs _____ measures native value.

The _____ chiefs...affixed their marks of their own free will and consent.... Done in triplicate at _____, this _____ day, of _____, 188____.

Document 5

Source: Yaa Asantewa, Ashanti queen mother, speech to chiefs, West Africa, 1900

Now I have seen that some of you fear to go forward and fight for our King. If it were in the brave days of old, chiefs would not sit down to see their King taken away without firing a shot. No White man could have dared to speak to chiefs of the Ashanti in the way the British governor spoke to you chiefs this morning. Is it true that the bravery of the Ashanti is no more? I cannot believe it.

Yea, it cannot be! I must say this; if you the men of Ashanti will not go forward, then we will. We the women will. I shall call upon my fellow women. We will fight the White men. We will fight until the last of us falls on the battlefields.

Document 6

Source: Illustration of British soldiers defending against insurgents near Delhi. Created by Janet-Lange, published in *L'Illustration Journal Universel*, Paris, 1857

Document 7

Source: Dadabhai Naoroji, Indian nationalist leader, *The Benefits of British Rule*, 1871

To sum up the whole, the British rule has been: morally, a great blessing; politically, peace and order on one hand, blunders on the other; materially, impoverishment, relieved as far as the railway and other loans go. The natives call the British system "*Sakar ki Churi*," the knife of sugar. That is to say, there is no oppression, it is all smooth and sweet, but it is the knife, notwithstanding. I mention this that you should know these feelings. Our great misfortune is that you do not know our wants. When you will know our real wishes, I have not the least doubt that you would do justice. The genius and spirit of the British people is fair play and justice.

(Answers on pages 357–362.)

Nationalism, Revolution, and Reform

Answers for Chapter 15 are on pages 362–367.

 Key Concept 5.3—The eighteenth century marked the beginning of an intense period of revolution and rebellion against existing governments, leading to the establishment of new nation-states around the world.

I. The rise and diffusion of Enlightenment ideas that questioned established traditions in all areas of life often preceded the revolutions and rebellions against existing governments.

   A. Enlightenment philosophers applied new ways of understanding and empiricist approaches to both the natural world and human relationships, encouraging observation and inference in all spheres of life; they also reexamined the role that religion played in public life, insisting on the importance of reason as opposed to revelation. Other Enlightenment philosophies developed new political ideas about the individual, natural rights, and the social contract.

   B. The ideas of Enlightenment philosophers, as reflected in revolutionary documents—including the American Declaration of Independence, the French Declaration of the Rights of Man and Citizen, and Bolivar's Jamaica Letter—influenced resistance to existing political authority, often in pursuit of independence and democratic ideals.

   C. Enlightenment ideas influenced various reform movements that challenged existing notions of social relations, which contributed to the expansion of rights as seen in expanded suffrage, the abolition of slavery, and/or the end of serfdom.

II. Beginning in the eighteenth century, peoples around the world developed a new sense of commonality based on language, religion, social customs, and territory. These newly imagined national communities linked this identity with the borders of the state, while governments used this idea of nationalism to unite diverse populations. In some cases, nationalists challenged boundaries or sought unification of fragmented regions.

III. Increasing discontent with imperial rule propelled reformist and revolutionary movements.

    A. Subjects challenged the centralized imperial governments.

    B. American colonial subjects led a series of rebellions—including the American Revolution, the Haitian Revolution, and the Latin American independence movements—that facilitated the emergence of independent states in the United States, Haiti, and mainland Latin America.

    C. Slave resistance challenged existing authorities in the Americas.

    D. Increasing questions about political authority and growing nationalism contributed to anticolonial movements.

    E. Some of the rebellions were influenced by diverse religious ideas.

IV. The global spread of European political and social thought and the increasing number of rebellions stimulated new transnational ideologies and solidarities.

    A. Discontent with monarchist and imperial rule encouraged the development of political ideologies, including democracy, liberalism, socialism, and communism.

    B. Demands for women's suffrage and an emergent feminism challenged political and gender hierarchies.

The spread of Enlightenment ideas regarding the relationship between government and the individual, natural rights, and the use of reason when examining the natural world inspired revolutions against existing governments, particularly colonial rulers in the Americas and the French monarchy. The governments that formed in newly independent states in the Americas incorporated some of these ideas. By the end of the time period, the power of monarchies declined greatly as representative forms of government increased. In addition, Enlightenment ideas led to abolitionist movements, the expansion of suffrage, and feminist movements. At the same time, nationalist ideas were occurring that helped to unify multinational empires, but also led to movements among ethnic groups to create their own states by separating from an existing state. Nationalist and Enlightenment ideas inspired anticolonial movements that were largely unsuccessful in achieving independence in this time period in Asia and Africa.

Questions 430–433 refer to the excerpt below.

"1. Men are born and remain free and equal in rights. Social distinctions may be founded only upon the general good.

2. The aim of all political association is the preservation of the natural and imprescriptible rights of man. These rights are liberty, property, security, and resistance to oppression.

3. The principle of all sovereignty resides essentially in the nation. No body nor individual may exercise any authority which does not proceed directly from the nation.

4. Liberty consists in the freedom to do everything which injures no one else; hence the exercise of the natural rights of each man has no limits except those which assure to the other members of the society the enjoyment of the same rights. These limits can only be determined by law.

5. Law can only prohibit such actions as are hurtful to society. Nothing may be prevented which is not forbidden by law, and no one may be forced to do anything not provided for by law."

> Excerpt from the Declaration of the Rights of Man and Citizen,
> approved by the National Assembly of France, August 26, 1789

 Tip: When you see the word "context," try to figure out the following: what was happening in the region where the document was written or a major global trend of the time period. Then determine which relates best to what the document is describing.

430. **The declaration is best understood in the context of which of the following?**

(A) The conquest of France by neighboring powers
(B) The establishment of slavery and serfdom in France
(C) The spread of anticolonial movements
(D) The rise and diffusion of Enlightenment ideas

431. **The passage best illustrates which of the following processes occurring in the Atlantic World in the late eighteenth century?**

(A) Slave resistance challenged existing authorities.
(B) Subjects challenged centralized imperial governments.
(C) Rebellions were influenced by diverse religious ideas.
(D) Authority of rulers became increasingly centralized.

432. Ideas expressed in the declaration would have the most significant influence on which of the following?

    (A) The development of representative governments
    (B) The unification of diverse populations through nationalism
    (C) The rise of communist ideologies
    (D) The increasing influence of religion on political affairs

433. Which of the following groups would most likely <u>disagree</u> with the ideas expressed in the excerpt?

    (A) French landowning elites
    (B) Slaves in French colonies
    (C) European monarchs
    (D) Peasants and serfs

Questions 434–436 refer to the image below.

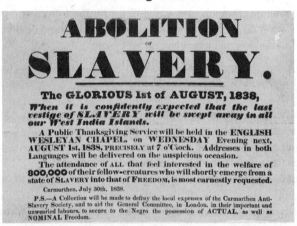

Poster celebrating the abolition of slavery in the British Empire in 1838

434. The poster would be most useful to a historian studying which of the following?

    (A) The economic factors leading to the abolition of slavery
    (B) The influence of Enlightenment ideas on reform movements
    (C) The attitudes of slave owners toward abolition
    (D) The spread of nationalist ideas in Europe

435. Which of the following contributed to the rise of the labor system described in the poster?

(A) The process of industrialization led to increased demand for factory workers.

(B) The colonization of Africa enabled Europeans to enslave natives.

(C) The declining population of Europe resulted in a labor shortage.

(D) The increased demand for cash crops led to the expansion of plantation agriculture.

436. Which of the following factors led to the reform movement shown in the poster?

(A) Slave resistance movements challenged existing authorities in the Americas.

(B) The expansion of suffrage to slaves led to legislation to abolish the practice.

(C) Successful slave rebellions overthrew British rule in the Caribbean.

(D) Nationalist movements developed among slaves in British colonies.

Questions 437–440 refer to the passage below.

"Success will crown our efforts, because the destiny of America has been irrevocably decided; the tie that bound her to Spain has been severed. . . .

We have been harassed by a conduct which has not only deprived us of our rights but has kept us in a sort of permanent infancy with regard to public affairs. If we could at least have managed our domestic affairs and our internal administration, we could have acquainted ourselves with the processes and mechanics of public affairs. . . .

Americans today, and perhaps to a greater extent than ever before, who live within the Spanish system occupy a position in society no better than that of serfs destined for labor, or at best they have no more status than that of mere consumers. Yet even this status is surrounded with galling restrictions, such as being forbidden to grow European crops, or to store products which are royal monopolies, or to establish factories of a type the Peninsula itself does not possess. To this add the exclusive trading privileges, even in articles of prime necessity, and the barriers between American provinces, designed to prevent all exchange of trade, traffic, and understanding. In short, do you wish to know what our future held?—Simply the cultivation of the fields of indigo, grain, coffee, sugar cane, cacao, and cotton; cattle raising on the broad plains; hunting wild game in the jungles; digging in the earth to mine its gold— but even these limitations could never satisfy the greed of Spain."

Simon Bolivar, revolutionary leader, "Letter from Jamaica," 1815

Tip: In addition to underlining main ideas, use the margins to jot down ideas that come into your head as you read the passage or "translate" the document into simpler language.

437. The letter by Bolivar is best seen as evidence for which of the following?

   (A) Ideas promoted by monarchs inspired by Enlightenment ideas
   (B) Governments proposed by American revolutionary leaders
   (C) Grievances of the colonists against the Spanish monarchy
   (D) Results of movements that resisted existing governments

438. Which of the following economic policies utilized by Spain is described by Bolivar in the letter?

   (A) Communism
   (B) Mercantilism
   (C) Capitalism
   (D) Serfdom

439. Based on the passage, Bolivar was most likely influenced by which of the following?

   (A) The spread of Enlightenment ideas advocating political reform
   (B) The growth of abolitionist and feminist movements
   (C) The diffusion of European socialist ideology
   (D) The expansion of universal suffrage movements

440. Which of the following was a result of ideas similar to those expressed in the passage?

   (A) The rise of liberation theology in Latin America
   (B) The creation of constitutional monarchies throughout the Americas
   (C) The reassertion of Spanish imperial rule in Latin America
   (D) The emergence of independent states in Latin America

Questions 441–442 refer to the image below.

**"RIGHT LEG IN THE BOOT AT LAST," POLITICAL
CARTOON ON ITALIAN UNIFICATION, 1860**

RIGHT LEG IN THE BOOT AT LAST.

*The image shows Giuseppe Garibaldi, one of the military leaders of Italian unification, helping
the Italian king with his boot. Garibaldi says, "If it won't go on, sire, try a little more powder."*

441. The cartoon could best be used as evidence for which of the following?

(A) Tactics used by leaders to achieve Italian unification
(B) Relationships between European monarchs and military leaders
(C) Strategies used by Enlightenment philosophers
(D) Reasons for political divisions among Italian states

442. Which of the following ideologies influenced the political change reflected
in the cartoon?

(A) Communism
(B) Conservatism
(C) Nationalism
(D) Mercantilism

Questions 443–445 refer to the following passage.

"We hold these truths to be self-evident, that all men and women are
created equal, that they are endowed by their Creator with certain
inalienable rights, that among these are life, liberty, and the pursuit
of happiness; that to secure these rights governments are instituted,
deriving their just powers from the consent of the governed. Whenever
any form of Government becomes destructive of these ends, it is the
right of those who suffer from it to refuse allegiance to it, and to insist

upon the institution of a new government, laying its foundation on such principles, and organizing its powers in such form as to them shall seem most likely to effect their safety and happiness."

Declaration of Sentiments issued by the Women's Rights Convention held at Seneca Falls, United States, 1848

 Tip: If you compare the wording of this document with the American Declaration of Independence, you will see that they are very similar. That was done intentionally to show the hypocrisy of the lack of rights for women.

443. The passage is best understood in the context of which of the following?

   (A) The spread of communist ideas from Western Europe
   (B) The extension of women's suffrage during the American Revolution
   (C) The continuing presence of women in political affairs
   (D) The rise of feminism that challenged political and gender hierarchies

444. Which of the following most likely influenced the ideas expressed in the passage?

   (A) The growing nationalist ideologies due to common cultural elements
   (B) The ideas of Enlightenment philosophers and revolutionary documents
   (C) The spread of liberal economic policies as a result of industrialization
   (D) The efforts of male politicians to incorporate women into governments

445. The passage best illustrates which of the following?

   (A) The enactment of legislation that immediately transformed gender roles
   (B) The diffusion of political ideologies from East Asia
   (C) The spread of reform movements that challenged existing social relations
   (D) The support of equal gender roles by the government

Questions 446–448 refer to the map below.

INDEPENDENCE MOVEMENTS IN THE WESTERN HEMISPHERE, 1800–1830

446. Which of the following contributed to the changes shown on the map?

(A) Movements using nonviolent forms of resistance

(B) Rebellions led by colonial subjects against imperial rule

(C) Revolts among slaves throughout the region

(D) Ideas among creoles advocating for a classless society

447. The changes on the map are best understood in which of the following contexts?

(A) The diffusion of Enlightenment ideas that influenced resistance to existing political authority.

(B) The spread of ideas regarding emancipation of slaves led to successful uprisings.

(C) The dissemination of industrial technology provided weaponry used for rebellions.

(D) The participation of colonists in imperial bureaucracies inspired independence movements.

448. Which of the following represents a continuity despite the changes shown on the map?

(A) The export of finished goods to former imperial powers

(B) The monopoly on trade by the former imperial power

(C) The control of newly formed governments by monarchs

(D) The persistence of slavery in most newly independent states

Questions 449–453 refer to the passage below.

"The religion of the Hindoos, who form a great part of the natives of India, teaches many things which seem very strange to Englishmen. Among other things they are taught that they will be defiled if they eat any part of a cow. By this defilement they will meet with much contempt from their fellows, and will suffer much after their death in another world. The bulk of the army in India was composed of Hindoos, and it happened that an improved rifle had lately been invented for the use of the soldiers, and that the cartridges used in this rifle required to be greased, in order that they might be rammed down easily into the barrel. The men believed that the grease used was made of the fat of cows, though this was not really the case. There was, therefore, much suspicion and angry feeling among the native soldiers, and when ignorant men are suspicious and angry they are apt to break out into deeds of unreasoning fury. The danger was the greater because a great many of the native princes were also discontented. These princes governed states scattered about over India, though they were not allowed to make war with one another. Many of them had governed very badly, had ruined their subjects by hard taxation, and had spent the money they thus obtained in vicious and riotous living. The English Government in India had interfered with some of these, and had dethroned them, annexing their territories to its own, and ruling the people who had been their subjects by means of its own officers. The consequence was that some of the princes who had been left in possession of authority thought that their turn would come next, and that they too would be dethroned before long. These men were therefore ready to help against the English, if they thought that they had a chance of succeeding.

Gardiner's English History for Schools, account of the Indian Revolt of 1857, found in an English textbook edited for American students, 1881

449. The actions of Indian princes described in the passage are best seen as evidence of which of the following?

(A) The cooperation between native rulers and colonial authorities

(B) The stable positions of colonial governors as a result of imperial policies

(C) The rise of anticolonial movements due to questions about political authority

(D) The economic benefits of cooperation with imperial governments

450. The anger of Indian soldiers described in the passage resulted from which of the following?

(A) Legislation enacted by the British to suppress India's agricultural production

(B) British attitudes of superiority and lack of respect for native religious traditions

(C) Policies which forced natives to adopt Christianity and abandon traditional belief systems

(D) Enlightenment ideas incorporated into colonial governments

451. The presence of the British government in India was the result of which of the following broader historical developments in the period 1750–1900 c.e.?

(A) States with existing colonies strengthened their control over those colonies.

(B) Maritime reconnaissance in the Indian Ocean basin led to the establishment of trading posts.

(C) In some parts of their empires, Europeans established settler colonies.

(D) Industrializing powers practiced economic imperialism and neocolonialism in some areas.

452. Which of the following views would be most useful in evaluating the accuracy of the textbook's account of the Sepoy Mutiny?

(A) An account by a British historian writing around the same time as the textbook was published

(B) An account by a British historian writing in 1857

(C) An account by an Indian historian writing around the same time as the textbook was published

(D) An account by an Indian historian writing in 1857

453. Which of the following early twentieth century developments was an effect of the conflict described in the passage?

(A) The rise of nationalist leaders and groups seeking autonomy from imperial rule

(B) The loosening of economic and political restrictions by imperial rulers

(C) The unification of British and Indian government officials due to transnational movements

(D) The abandonment of resistance movements by colonists

Questions 454–456 refer to the images below.

Image 1

ETCHING OF TRELAWNEY TOWN, THE CHIEF RESIDENCE OF THE MAROONS, CIRCA 1800

The image shows a community of maroons, or runaway slaves, in Jamaica, a British colony.

Image 2

CARTOON TITLED "AUTHENTIC AND IMPARTIAL NARRATIVE OF THE TRAGICAL SCENE WHICH WAS WITNESSED IN SOUTHAMPTON COUNTY," PUBLISHED IN 1831 AFTER NAT TURNER'S REBELLION

The caption states, "The Scenes which the above Plate is designed to represent are— Fig. 1. A Mother intreating for the lives of her Children.—2. Mr Travis, cruelly murdered by his own Slaves.—3. Mr. Barrow, who bravely defended himself until his wife escaped.—4. A comp. of mounted Dragoons in pursuit of the Blacks."

454. Image 1 best reflects which of the following processes in the period 1750–1900 C.E.?

   (A) Plantations were established for the production of cash crops.
   (B) A result of Enlightenment ideas was the emancipation of slaves.
   (C) Slave rebellions were successful in ending the practice of slavery.
   (D) Slave resistance challenged existing authorities in the Americas.

455. Developments such as the one depicted in Image 2 most directly contributed to which of the following?

   (A) Immediate emancipation of slaves throughout the Americas
   (B) Reform movements advocating for the abolition of slavery
   (C) Continuous slave rebellions throughout the American South
   (D) Expansion of suffrage to former slaves

456. Which of the following was most likely the intent of the cartoon?

   (A) To justify the actions of the rebels
   (B) To promote abolitionist movements
   (C) To vilify slaves that engaged in rebellions
   (D) To support slave resistance movements

Questions 457–459 refer to the passage below.

"In republishing at this period the Life of Toussaint Louverture, I am induced to dedicate it to your Imperial Majesty, by feelings which those who know how to appreciate true elevation of character cannot fail to understand.

That illustrious African well deserved the exalted names of Christian, Patriot, and Hero. He was a devout worshipper of his God, and a successful defender of his invaded country. He was the victorious enemy, at once, and the contrast of Napoleon Bonaparte, whose arms he repelled, and whose pride he humbled, not more by the strength of his military genius, than by the moral influence of his amiable and virtuous character: by how many ties, then, of kindred merit and generous sympathy must he not be endeared to the magnanimous Liberator of Europe!

In nothing, however, will your Imperial Majesty more sympathize with the brave Toussaint, than in his attachment to the great cause in which he fell—the cause, not of his country only, but of his race; not merely of St. Domingo, but of the African continent."

James Stephen, British abolitionist, dedication to Tsar Alexander of Russia in his book, *The History of Toussaint Louverture*, 1814

457. Which of the following most likely explains Stephens' attitude toward Toussaint Louverture?

    (A) His audience, the Russian tsar
    (B) His point of view as an abolitionist
    (C) His goal of defeating Napoleon
    (D) His British heritage

458. The author's stance as an abolitionist is likely the result of which of the following?

    (A) The Haitian Revolution
    (B) The independence of North America
    (C) The violence of the Napoleonic wars
    (D) The diffusion of Enlightenment ideas

459. The Haitian Revolution led by Toussaint Louverture is best understood in the context of which of the following?

    (A) The Atlantic Revolutions
    (B) The emergence of racial ideologies
    (C) The Industrial Revolution
    (D) The expansion of the Russian Empire

Short-Answer Questions

Answer all parts of the question that follows.

460. a) Identify ONE way in which ideas developed by Enlightenment philosophers transformed European views on government between 1750 and 1900 C.E.

    b) Explain ONE way in which ideas developed by Enlightenment philosophers continued previous patterns of thinking.

    c) Explain ONE way in which political movements outside of Europe were influenced by Enlightenment ideas from circa 1800 to the present.

Answer all parts of the question that follows.

461. a) Identify ONE way Enlightenment ideas impacted the Haitian Revolution.

    b) Explain ONE difference between the causes of the American Revolution and the Haitian Revolution.

    c) Explain ONE similarity in how Enlightenment ideas affected governments in the United States and Haiti after independence.

Long Essay Questions

462. In the period 1750–1900 C.E., revolution and rebellion began against existing governments, leading to the establishment of new nation-states around the world.

    Develop an argument that evaluates how Enlightenment ideas contributed to revolutions against imperial rule in one or more regions in this time period.

463. In the period 1750–1900 C.E., increasing discontent with imperial rule propelled reformist and revolutionary movements around the world.

    Develop an argument that evaluates the similarities of two reformist and/or revolutionary movements in this period.

Document-Based Question

464. Evaluate the extent to which Enlightenment ideas caused rebellions against existing governments in the period 1750–1900 C.E.

Document 1

Source: John Locke, *Second Treatise on Civil Government*, 1690

"Of the State of Nature"
...(W)e must consider, what state all men are naturally in, and that is, a state of perfect freedom to order their actions, and dispose of their possessions and persons, as they think fit, within the bounds of the law of nature...

There [is] nothing more evident, than that creatures of the same species and rank ...should also be equal one amongst another without subordination or subjection...

"Of the Dissolution of Government"
(W)hen the government is dissolved, the people are at liberty to provide for themselves, by erecting a new legislative, ...for the society can never, ...lose the native and original right it has to preserve itself, which can only be done by a settled legislative, and a fair and impartial execution of the laws made by it. But the state of mankind is not so miserable that they are not capable of using this remedy, ... they have not only a right to get out of [a failed government], but to prevent it.

Document 2

Source: Montesquieu, French Enlightenment philosopher, *The Spirit of the Laws*, 1748

The political liberty of the subject is a tranquility of mind, arising from the opinion each person has of his safety. In order to have this liberty, it is requisite the government be so constituted as one man need not be afraid of another.

When the legislative and executive powers are united in the same person, or in the same body of magistrates, there can be no liberty; Again, there is no liberty, if the power of judging be not separated from the legislative and executive powers. Were it joined with the legislative, the life and liberty of the subject would be exposed to arbitrary control, for the judge would then be the legislator. Were it joined to the executive power, the judge might behave with all the violence of an oppressor.

There would be an end of everything were the same man, or the same body, whether of the nobles or of the people to exercise those three powers that of enacting laws, that of executing the public resolutions, and that of judging the crimes or differences of individuals.

Document 3

Source: Thomas Jefferson, Virginia resident, signed by 56 members of the Continental Congress, Declaration of Independence, 1776

IN CONGRESS, July 4, 1776.
The unanimous Declaration of the thirteen united States of America, We hold these truths to be self-evident, that all men are created equal, that they are endowed by their Creator with certain unalienable Rights, that among these are Life, Liberty and the pursuit of Happiness.—That to secure these rights, Governments are instituted among Men, deriving their just powers from the consent of the governed...

When a long train of abuses and usurpations, pursuing invariably the same Object evinces a design to reduce them under absolute Despotism, it is their right, it is their duty, to throw off such Government, and to provide new Guards for their future security.

Such has been the patient sufferance of these Colonies; and such is now the necessity which constrains them to alter their former Systems of Government. The history of the present King of Great Britain is a history of repeated injuries and usurpations, all having in direct object the establishment of an absolute Tyranny over these States. To prove this, let Facts be submitted to a candid world....

He has refused his Assent to Laws, the most wholesome and necessary for the public good....
For cutting off our Trade with all parts of the world:
For imposing Taxes on us without our Consent:
For depriving us in many cases, of the benefits of Trial by Jury....
For suspending our own Legislatures, and declaring themselves invested with power to legislate for us in all cases whatsoever....

Document 4

Source: National Assembly of France, statement of rights, Declaration of the Rights of Man and Citizen, August 26, 1789

The representatives of the French people, constituted as a National Assembly, and considering that ignorance, neglect, or contempt of the rights of man are the sole causes of public misfortunes and governmental corruption, have resolved to set forth in a solemn declaration the natural, inalienable and sacred rights of man: so that by being constantly present to all the members of the social body this declaration may always remind them of their rights and duties; so that by being liable at every moment to comparison with the aim of any and all political institutions the acts of the legislative and executive powers may be the more fully respected; and so that by being founded henceforward on simple and incontestable principles the demands of the citizens may always tend toward maintaining the constitution and the general welfare.

In consequence, the National Assembly recognizes and declares, in the presence and under the auspices of the Supreme Being, the following rights of man and the citizen:

1. Men are born and remain free and equal in rights. Social distinctions may be based only on common utility.
2. The purpose of all political association is the preservation of the natural and imprescriptible rights of man. These rights are liberty, property, security, and resistance to oppression.
3. The principle of all sovereignty rests essentially in the nation. No body and no individual may exercise authority which does not emanate expressly from the nation. . . .

Document 5

Source: Haitian Constitution of 1801, promulgated on July 8th, 1801 by the Governor General Toussaint Louverture, leader of the slave rebellion against the French government

Art. 3.—There cannot exist slaves on this territory, servitude is therein forever abolished. All men are born, live and die free and French.
Art. 4.—All men, regardless of color, are eligible to all employment. . . .
Art. 5.—The law is the same for all whether in punishment or in protection. . . .

Art. 12.—The Constitution guarantees freedom and individual security. No one shall be arrested unless a formally expressed mandate, issued from a functionary to whom the law grants the right to order arrest and detention in a publicly designated location.
Art. 13.—Property is sacred and inviolable. All people, either by himself, or by his representatives, has the free right to dispose and to administer property that is recognized as belonging to him. Anyone who attempts to deny this right shall become guilty of crime towards society and responsible towards the person troubled in his property. . . .

Document 6

Source: "Washington Crossing the Delaware," Emanuel Leutze, 1851

This image depicts George Washington, American revolutionary leader, crossing the Delaware River to face British troops in battle.

Document 7

Source: Simon Bolivar, South American Revolutionary leader, "Jamaica Letter," 1815

We have been harassed by a conduct which has not only deprived us of our rights but has kept us in a sort of permanent infancy with regard to public affairs. If we could at least have managed our domestic affairs and our internal administration, we could have acquainted ourselves with the processes and mechanics of public affairs. We should also have enjoyed a personal consideration, thereby commanding a certain unconscious respect from the people, which is so necessary to preserve amidst revolutions. That is why I say we have even been deprived of an active tyranny, since we have not been permitted to exercise its functions.

Americans today, and perhaps to a greater extent than ever before, who live within the Spanish system occupy a position in society no better than that of serfs destined for labor, or at best they have no more status than that of mere consumers. Yet even this status is surrounded with galling restrictions, such as being forbidden to grow European crops, or to store products which are royal monopolies, or to establish factories of a type the Peninsula itself does not possess. To this add the exclusive trading privileges, even in articles of prime necessity, and the barriers between American provinces, designed to prevent all exchange of trade, traffic, and under-standing. In short, do you wish to know what our future held?—simply the cultivation of the fields of indigo, grain, coffee, sugar cane, cacao, and cotton; cattle raising on the broad plains; hunting wild game in the jungles; digging in the earth to mine its gold—but even these limitations could never satisfy the greed of Spain.

So negative was our existence that I can find nothing comparable in any other civilized society, examine as I may the entire history of time and the politics of all nations. Is it not an outrage and a violation of human rights to expect a land so splendidly endowed, so vast, rich, and populous, to remain merely passive?

(Answers on pages 362–367.)

Global Migration

Answers for Chapter 16 are on pages 367–370.

Key Concept 5.4—As a result of the emergence of transoceanic empires and a global capitalist economy, migration patterns changed dramatically, and the number of migrants increased significantly.

I.   Migration in many cases was influenced by changes in demography in both industrialized and unindustrialized societies that presented challenges to existing patterns of living.

    A.   Changes in food production and improved medical conditions contributed to a significant global rise in population.

    B.   Because of the nature of the new modes of transportation, both internal and external migrants increasingly relocated to cities. This pattern contributed to the significant global urbanization of the nineteenth century. The new methods of transportation also allowed for many migrants to return, periodically or permanently, to their home societies.

II.   Migrants relocated for a variety of reasons.

    A.   Many individuals chose freely to relocate, often in search of work.

    B.   The new global capitalist economy continued to rely on coerced and semicoerced labor migration, including slavery, Chinese and Indian indentured servitude, and convict labor.

III.   The large-scale nature of migration, especially in the nineteenth century, produced a variety of consequences and reactions to the increasingly diverse societies on the part of migrants and the existing populations.

    A.   Migrants tended to be male, leaving women to take on new roles in the home society that had been formerly occupied by men.

    B.   Migrants often created ethnic enclaves in different parts of the world that helped transplant their culture into new environments and facilitated the development of migrant support networks.

    C.   Receiving societies did not always embrace immigrants, as seen in the various degrees of ethnic and racial prejudice and

the ways states attempted to regulate the increased flow of
people across their borders.

The process of industrialization, new transportation technologies, and global
capitalism contributed to a surge in global migration in this period. Migrants,
whether they were moving within a particular country or between countries,
mainly moved to urban areas for job opportunities. The movement of mainly
men led to changes in family dynamics, and in areas where migrants moved,
ethnic enclaves formed in which migrants maintained cultural elements and
formed networks among people from their home societies. Often, migrants
were not accepted willingly into their new societies, and faced discrimination.

Questions 465–467 refer to the map below.

GLOBAL MIGRATION PATTERNS, CIRCA 1800–1900

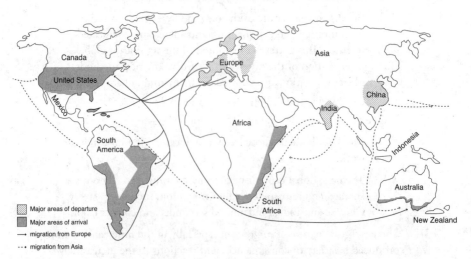

465. The movements depicted on the map most directly emerged from which
of the following developments in the late eighteenth and nineteenth
centuries?

(A) Industrialization improved living conditions for European urban
dwellers.
(B) Global food shortages led to migrations to areas with available
farmland.
(C) Increased food production and the development of new modes of
transportation led to changes.
(D) Enlightenment ideas fostered more representative governments.

466. Which of the following best describes an effect of the patterns shown on the map?

   (A) The spread of communist ideas around the world
   (B) The rise of food production and global population increase
   (C) The universal acceptance of immigrants by receiving societies
   (D) The creation of ethnic enclaves by migrants in new lands

467. The movement of migrants shown on the map was most likely due to which of the following reasons?

   (A) Job opportunities
   (B) Availability of schools
   (C) Political opportunities
   (D) Religious freedom

Questions 468–470 refer to the following sources.

Source 1

FIVE BOYS AT NEW YEAR CELEBRATION, CHINATOWN, NEW YORK CITY, 1911

Source 2

"Is this Chinese immigration desirable? I think not; and, contrary to the expressed opinions of many of the public prints throughout the country, contend that it ought not to be encouraged. It is not desirable, because it is not useful; or, if useful at all, it is so only to themselves—not to us. No reciprocal or mutual benefits are conferred. In what capacity do they contribute to the advancement of American interests? Are they engaged in anything that adds to the general wealth and importance of the country? . . . Under the existing laws of our government, they, as well as all other foreigners, are permitted to work the mines in California as long as they please, and as much as they please, without paying anything for the privilege, except a small tax to the States.... The Chinese are more objectionable than other foreigners, because they refuse to have dealing or intercourse with us; consequently, there is no chance of making any thing of them, either in the way of trade or labor. They are ready to take all they can from us, but are not willing to give anything in return."

Hinton Rowan Helper, American author, *The Land of Gold*, 1855

468. **Source 1 best illustrates which of the following developments?**

(A) The tendency of migrants to completely retain their native cultural traditions in new lands

(B) The formation of ethnic enclaves that facilitated the development of migrant support networks

(C) The creation of syncretic belief systems as a result of new contacts resulting from migration

(D) The universal assimilation of the children of immigrants into the countries they were born in

469. **Attitudes such as the one expressed in Source 2 contributed most directly to which of the following in states receiving immigrants?**

(A) The banning of interregional travel in order to prevent migrants from entering the state

(B) The development of ideologies such as Social Darwinism to facilitate assimilation of migrants

(C) Policies enacted that required migrants to adopt the language and religion of the state

(D) Attempts by states to regulate the increased flow of people across their borders

470. **Which of the following most directly contributed to the demand for labor described in Source 2?**

(A) Increased demand for specialized professionals as a result of industrialization

(B) The decline in population due to more effective forms of birth control

(C) The development of new technologies due to industrialization

(D) Increased agricultural production led to population growth

Questions 471–473 refer to the table below.

SELECTED INTERCONTINENTAL FLOWS OF INDENTURED OR CONTRACT LABOR, NINETEENTH AND EARLY TWENTIETH CENTURY

Origins	Destinations	Totals (rounded)
India to	British Guiana	239,000
	Trinidad	150,000
	Other Caribbean	130,000
	Suriname (Dutch Guiana)	34,000
	Mauritius	455,000
	Fiji	61,000
	South Africa	153,000
China to	Peru	117,000
	Cuba	138,000
	Other Caribbean	24,000
	Hawaii	34,000
Japan to	Hawaii	65,000
	Peru	18,000

Adapted from David Northrup, *Indentured Labor in the Age of Imperialism, 1834-1922*, 1995

 Tip: Although tempting to skip, always read the title of the table, chart, or graph, because it usually provides information that is helpful in answering one or more of the questions.

471. Which of the following best explains the movements shown in the table?

   (A) There was a demand for workers due to the introduction of industrial technology to these regions.
   (B) Indian, Chinese, and Japanese laborers had immunity to tropical diseases.
   (C) Contract laborers were preferred over African slaves as they were less likely to rebel.
   (D) There was a demand for semicoerced labor due to the new global capitalist economy.

472. Which of the following was a consequence of the patterns shown in the table?

   (A) Migrants tended to be male, leaving women to take on new roles in their home societies.
   (B) Population declined severely in India, China, and Japan as families migrated to new regions.
   (C) Migrants completely replaced native workers in the Caribbean and Pacific.
   (D) A syncretic form of Buddhism emerged in the Caribbean and Pacific.

473. Migrants to the areas shown in the table were most likely working to produce which of the following?

    (A) Rubber and oil
    (B) Raw materials and cash crops
    (C) Metals and diamonds
    (D) Textiles and weapons

Questions 474–477 refer to the passage below.

"Atlantic migration in the second half of the nineteenth century took the form of millions of people leaving their European birthplaces in search of better opportunities. The size and the speed of these migratory movements were unprecedented. At the same time, a few powerful governments, mostly in these same European countries, invaded, annexed, and otherwise took control of lands in Asia, Africa, and the world's islands.

The resulting changes were demographic, political, and cultural. The distribution of world population changed, as Europeans filled many spaces in the Americas. The political map of the planet changed, as a small number of great powers took control of large territories. The pattern of the world's languages changed, as migrating families and conquering generals each took their languages to new lands.

This stream of migrants from Europe was not the only great migration of the era. Large numbers of Chinese, Indian, Japanese, and other Asian workers and settlers moved across the Asian landmass, the Indian Ocean, and the Pacific. The more than fifty million Chinese migrants equaled the number of European migrants, and the thirty million Indian migrants were not far behind. Similarly, there was large-scale labor migration within Africa and Latin America in the same period. Overall, the period from 1850 to 1930 was the most intensive era of migration in human history.

Patrick Manning and Tiffany Trimmer,
historians, *Migrations in World History*, 2013

 Tip: Be sure to read carefully! "Contributed to" in this question is asking about causes, whereas in other questions it could be asking about effects, depending on the wording.

474. Which of the following contributed to migrations discussed in the passage?

    (A) Enhancements in urban living conditions and sanitation
    (B) Opportunities for education and possibility of achieving social mobility
    (C) Improved modes of transportation and patterns of urbanization
    (D) Prospects of acquiring land and capital for investment

475. Which of the following supports the authors' assertion that migrations due to conquest changed the patterns of world languages in the period 1850–1930?

    (A) The use of English in North America
    (B) The use of Indian languages in the Caribbean
    (C) The use of English in India
    (D) The use of Chinese in Latin America

476. The migrations discussed in the third paragraph were most likely the result of which of the following?

    (A) The desire for participation in republics and governments
    (B) Demand for skilled labor in factories
    (C) The desire for religious freedom
    (D) Demand for coerced and semicoerced labor

477. Which of the following was an effect of large-scale migrations discussed in the passage?

    (A) The diffusion of East Asian belief systems to new regions
    (B) The adoption of Indian cultural traditions by Africans
    (C) The creation of syncretic forms of Buddhism
    (D) The spread of Enlightenment ideas to the Americas

Questions 478–479 refer to the image below.

COVER OF SHEET MUSIC FOR "WHITE AUSTRALIA," COMPOSED BY AUSTRALIAN MUSICIANS W. E. NAUNTON AND H. J. W. GYLES, 1910

The cover states that "White Australia" is the "Great National Policy Song" and features a white map of Australia and the Australian coat of arms.

While there was not a single policy called "White Australia,"
a series of policies were implemented to prevent Asians,
particularly the Chinese, from immigrating to Australia.

478. The image is best seen as evidence of which of the following?

(A) The use of ideologies, such as White Man's burden, to justify imperialism
(B) Attempts by states to regulate the flow of people across their borders
(C) The sponsorship of the arts by colonial governments
(D) Efforts to promote nationalism and embrace native cultural traditions

479. Which of the following was the most likely purpose of the development of
the song and cover illustration?

(A) To honor native cultural traditions in Australia
(B) To demonstrate the effectiveness of the policy
(C) To criticize British actions in Australia
(D) To glorify the White Australia policy

Questions 480–482 refer to the table below.

ITALIAN EMIGRANTS BY DESTINATION, 1876–1905

Years	Africa	Americas	Asia	Europe	Oceania	Total
1876–1885	39,488	425,588	404	850,219	990	1,314,689
1886–1895	31,082	1,386,057	1,516	970,133	2,261	2,391,049
1896–1905	82,107	2,340,519	3,108	1,890,943	5,748	4,322,425
Total	152,677	4,150,164	5,028	3,711,295	8,999	8,028,163

Source: *Un Secolo di Emigrazione Italiana, 1876–1976, 1978*, p. 545

480. Italian migration shown in the table was most directly enabled by which of
the following?

(A) Decreased global integration and communication
(B) More legal restrictions on immigration around the world
(C) Technological developments in transportation
(D) Improvements in manufacturing techniques

481. Which of the following best explains the patterns shown in the table?

(A) The availability of economic opportunities in the Americas and Europe
(B) The outbreak of global conflict in the last decade of the nineteenth
century
(C) The sponsorship of voyages by governments in the Americas and Europe
(D) The resistance to foreign immigrants by governments in Asia and Oceania

482. **Which of the following best describes a likely effect of the patterns shown in the table?**

(A) Italian migrants abandoned cultural elements from their home societies.

(B) Italian migrants formed ethnic enclaves to transplant their culture into new environments.

(C) Italian migrants created a syncretic form of Christianity in their new society.

(D) Italian migrants rejected all cultural elements of the regions they migrated to.

Questions 483–485 refer to the editorial below.

"A clause was introduced at the public meeting setting forth the necessity of an 'importation of foreign labor' for the exigencies of our tropical industry, more especially of the sugar enterprise; unfortunately that clause was struck out by the Town Council.

Next year, the quantity of labor that will be required to bring to a profitable result the large and increasing sugar cultivation now going on will be great beyond the possibility of its being supplied by our own natives, no matter how vigorous and how successful may be the measures of Government in the meantime for the better development of native industry. Every succeeding year, the demand for labor will increase in an almost geometrical ratio. In the island of Mauritius, there are not more than 60,000 acres under sugar cultivation, and for this small area—producing however, upwards of 100,000 tons of sugar annually—not fewer than 60,000 laborers are required."

> Editorial in the *Natal Mercury*, Itongati, South Africa, on the
> visit of Sir George Grey, British colonial governor, June 6, 1855

483. **Which of the following best explains the labor shortage as described in the editorial?**

(A) The decline in native populations due to food shortages

(B) The migration of Mauritians to Europe to perform factory labor

(C) The spread of epidemic diseases due to contact between the British and Mauritians

(D) The abolition of slavery and increased global demand for raw materials

484. **Which of the following was the most likely purpose of the editorial?**

(A) To criticize the laziness of native laborers in the sugar industry

(B) To persuade the colonial governor to approve the clause to introduce foreign labor

(C) To demonstrate the importance of sugar cultivation in Britain's economy

(D) To convince the colonial governor to invest in factories in South Africa

485. The increased demand for laborers as described in the editorial was typically fulfilled by which of the following?

   (A) The migration of coerced and semicoerced laborers from China and India

   (B) The forced migration of West African slaves to plantations in Mauritius

   (C) The migration of European farmers displaced by the introduction of machines

   (D) The importation of chattel slaves from India by British colonists in South Africa

Questions 486–487 refer to the graph below.

GLOBAL POPULATION, 1750–1900

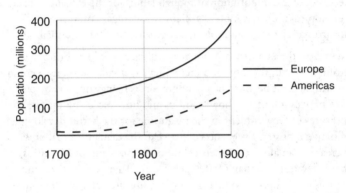

486. Which of the following best explains the trend shown on the graph?

   (A) Vaccination campaigns and the end of famines

   (B) The eradication of epidemic diseases due to medical innovations

   (C) Improved medical conditions and increased food production

   (D) Longer life spans due to measures to reduce environmental pollution

487. By 1900, the change illustrated on the graph had which of the following effects?

   (A) The creation of new languages

   (B) New forms of governance

   (C) Changes in religious traditions

   (D) Shifts in migration patterns

Questions 488–491 refer to the cartoon below.

POLITICAL CARTOON TITLED "THE UNRESTRICTED DUMPING GROUND," UNITED STATES, LOUIS DALRYMPLE, 1903

The cartoon shows rats representing immigrants labeled "socialist, Mafia, anarchist" arriving "direct from the slums of Europe daily."

488. **The cartoon best illustrates which of the following?**

(A) The forced removal of undesired groups by European governments

(B) Ethnic and racial prejudice against immigrants in receiving societies

(C) The adoption of European ideologies by Americans as a result of increased contact

(D) Discrimination against immigrants in receiving societies, which was uncommon

489. **Which of the following can be inferred about the purpose of the cartoon?**

(A) To promote policies restricting immigration

(B) To demonstrate the benefits of immigration

(C) To denounce Marxist ideologies

(D) To demonstrate the need for unskilled laborers

490. **Which of the following contributed to the situation illustrated in the cartoon?**

(A) Enlightenment ideas were incorporated into the government of the United States.

(B) Revolutions in Europe prompted mass migration overseas.

(C) Relocation was fueled by the desire for economic opportunities.

(D) Industrialization in the United States fueled demand for skilled laborers.

491. **Attitudes similar to the viewpoint expressed in the cartoon contributed most directly to which of the following?**

(A) Legislation embracing socialist and anarchist ideologies

(B) The implementation of regulations to exclude immigrants

(C) Increased tensions between the United States and European nations

(D) The forced removal of European migrants from American cities.

Questions 492–494 refer to the passage below.

"Brazil had promoted immigration during the closing decades of the nineteenth century as a replacement for the African slave labor that it finally abolished in 1888. But, as in Argentina, it was European immigration that its coffee planters had subsidized, in return for contract labor on their plantations. From 1880 to 1900, 1.6 million Europeans arrived in Brazil, half of them from Italy and most of the rest from Iberia. But Brazilian plantation owners, used to slave labor, treated their European workers like slaves, and the Italian and Spanish governments responded by forbidding new emigration, while many of the earlier immigrants left the plantations as soon as they could. This created a rural labor shortage that Brazil's planters and the government they dominated thought they would once again fill with nonwhite workers. They considered the importation of Chinese coolie labor, but rejected it on racial grounds. Japanese were also racially problematic in a country whose racial policy was to whiten the population through miscegenation, but Brazil's economy depended on its coffee exports, the biggest in the world, and Brazilian coffee planters needed labor."

> Peter Winn, historian, "South America: Land of
> Immigrants and Emigrants—Italian and Japanese
> Migration to Argentina and Brazil—and Back," 2008

492. **Which of the following contributed to the Brazilian immigration policies described in the passage?**

    (A) The desire to maintain a Brazilian identity
    (B) Revolts by Brazilian coffee planters
    (C) Epidemic diseases spread by migrants
    (D) Enlightenment ideas that inspired reform

493. **Which of the following enabled the movement of Japanese migrants to Brazil in this era?**

    (A) Japanese sponsorship of overseas travel
    (B) Political ideologies embracing diversity
    (C) New navigational technologies
    (D) The development of steamships

494. **Which of the following most likely resulted from the migration described in the passage?**

    (A) The development of a syncretic language
    (B) The mechanization of the coffee industry
    (C) The widespread adoption of Buddhism by Brazilians
    (D) The creation of support networks among Japanese migrants

Short-Answer Questions

Answer all parts of the question that follows.

495. a) Identify ONE way that the movement of migrants in the period 1750–1900 C.E. illustrates a continuity of previous patterns of interregional movement.

b) Explain ONE change in migration patterns in the Western Hemisphere between 1500 and 1900 C.E.

c) Explain ONE cultural change that occurred as a result of long distance migrations between 1750 and 1900 C.E.

Use the following image to answer all parts of the question that follows.

"THE HYPHENATED AMERICAN," CARTOON PUBLISHED IN *PUCK* MAGAZINE, UNITED STATES, 1899

In the cartoon, Uncle Sam sees hyphenated Americans and asks, "Why should I let these freaks cast whole ballots when they are only half Americans?"

496. a) Identify ONE change in migration patterns between 1500 and 1900 that led to attitudes similar to those expressed in the cartoon.

b) Explain ONE way the cartoon illustrates a continuity in the attitudes toward immigrants between 1800 and 2001 C.E.

c) Explain ONE economic change that led to new migration patterns in the period 1750–1900 C.E.

Long Essay Questions

497. In the period 1750–1900, the large-scale nature of migration produced a variety of consequences and reactions to the increasingly diverse societies on the part of migrants and the existing populations.

    Develop an argument that evaluates the effects of long-distance migrations on one or more receiving societies in this period.

498. In the period 1750–1900, migration was influenced by changes in demographics in both industrialized and unindustrialized societies that presented challenges to existing patterns of living.

    Develop an argument that evaluates the factors that led migrants to relocate in this period.

(Answers on pages 367–370.)

PERIOD 6 (c. 1900 TO THE PRESENT)
Accelerating Global Change and Realignments

Science and the Environment

Answers for Chapter 17 are on pages 371–374.

Key Concept 6.1—Rapid advances in science altered the understanding of the universe and the natural world and led to advances in communication, transportation, industry, agriculture, and medicine.

I.   Researchers made rapid advances in science that spread throughout the world, assisted by the development of new technology.

    A.   New modes of communication—including the Internet, radio communication, and cellular communication—and transportation reduced the problem of geographic distance.

    B.   The Green Revolution and commercial agriculture increased productivity and sustained the earth's growing population as it spread chemically and genetically enhanced forms of agriculture.

    C.   Medical innovations, such as vaccines and antibiotics, increased the ability of humans to survive and live longer lives.

    D.   Energy technologies including the use of oil and nuclear power raised productivity and increased the production of material goods.

II. During a period of unprecedented global population expansion, humans fundamentally changed their relationship with the environment.

    A.   As human activity contributed to deforestation, desertification, and increased consumption of the world's supply of fresh water and clean air, humans competed over these and other resources more intensely than ever before.

    B.   The release of greenhouse gases and other pollutants into the atmosphere contributed to debates about the nature and causes of climate change.

III. Disease, scientific innovations, and conflict led to demographic shifts.

    A.   Diseases associated with poverty persisted, while other diseases emerged as new epidemics and threats to human survival. In addition, increased longevity led to higher incidence of certain diseases.

B. More effective forms of birth control gave women greater control over fertility and transformed sexual practices.

C. New military technology and new tactics and the waging of "total war" led to increased levels of wartime casualties.

The growth of scientific knowledge and technological innovations led to major changes in communication, transportation, farming, and medicine that transformed human society both positively and negatively. Population growth strained resources and negatively impacted the environment, while new military technologies led to devastating conflicts with unprecedented casualty rates. However, medical advances allowed for longer life spans and new energy technologies increased the availability of consumer goods.

Questions 499–501 refer to the graph below.

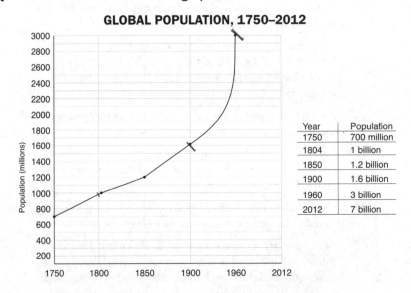

GLOBAL POPULATION, 1750–2012

Year	Population
1750	700 million
1804	1 billion
1850	1.2 billion
1900	1.6 billion
1960	3 billion
2012	7 billion

 Tip: Examine the graph carefully, and draw lines between the dates asked about in the questions (i.e., 1800, 1900) so that you can focus on the trend in the smaller window of time.

499. Which of the following best explains the change in population from 1800–1900 C.E.?

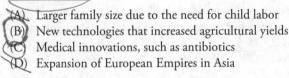

(A) Larger family size due to the need for child labor
(B) New technologies that increased agricultural yields
(C) Medical innovations, such as antibiotics
(D) Expansion of European Empires in Asia

500. Which of the following explains the change in population from 1900–2012 C.E.?

   (A) New methods of communication and transportation
   (B) Lack of effective forms of birth control
   (C) Medical innovations that led to longer life spans
   (D) Programs promoting childbirth in fascist states

501. Which of the following was a consequence of the trend shown on the graph?

   (A) Increased competition for resources such as water
   (B) Vaccines and antibiotics that increased longevity rates
   (C) Increased child mortality rates
   (D) Depletion of cash crops and manufactured goods

Questions 502–504 refer to the passage below.

"The Green Revolution was based on the assumption that technology is a superior substitute for nature, and hence a means of producing limitless growth, unconstrained by nature's limits. However the assumption of nature as a source of scarcity, and technology as a source of abundance, leads to the creation of technologies which create new scarcities in nature through ecological destruction. The reduction in availability of fertile land and genetic diversity of crops as a result of the Green Revolution practices indicates that at the ecological level, the Green Revolution produced scarcity, not abundance."

> Vandana Shiva, scientist, *The Violence of the Green Revolution: Third World Agriculture, Ecology, and Politics*, 2016

502. Technological innovations referred to in the passage most directly led to which of the following?

   (A) The end of poverty and famine
   (B) Higher incidence of epidemic disease
   (C) Increased agricultural yields
   (D) New energy technologies

503. The environmental impact of the Green Revolution as discussed in the passage is most similar to the impact of which of the following?

   (A) The plantation system on the Caribbean
   (B) The Grand Canal on China
   (C) The Columbian Exchange on Europe
   (D) The rise of serfdom on Russia

504. Based on the passage, it can be inferred that Shiva might also support which of the following assertions?

(A) Sustaining the expanding global population is more important than environmental issues.

(B) Technological innovations should not occur at the expense of the environment.

(C) Depletion of resources can be effectively remedied by the use of technology.

(D) Ecological destruction cannot be addressed with scientific advances.

Questions 505–506 refer to the chart below.

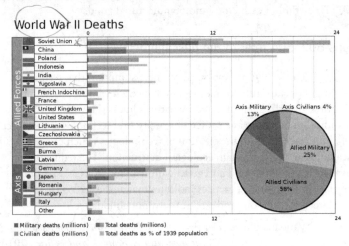

Source: The Shadowed at English Wikipedia [CC BY-JA 3.0]
(http://creativecommons.org/licenses/by-sa/3.0)

505. Which of the following factors led to civilian deaths shown in the graph?

(A) The waging of "total war"

(B) The use of nuclear weapons

(C) Compulsory military service

(D) New modes of communication

506. Which of the following contributed to high death rates in Eastern Europe and Russia shown on the graph?

(A) The outbreak of civil war within these countries due to opposition to the war

(B) The development of a nuclear arms race between the Allied powers

(C) The rise of extremist groups that led to the annihilation of ethnic and religious groups

(D) The use of submarines and naval blockades that led to mass famine

Questions 507–510 refer to the passage below.

"Twenty years ago, the first genetically modified (GM) crops were planted in the USA, alongside dazzling promises about this new technology. Two decades on, the promises are getting bigger and bigger, but GM crops are not delivering any of them. Not only was this technology supposed to make food and agriculture systems simpler, safer and more efficient, but GM crops are increasingly being touted as the key to 'feeding the world' and 'fighting climate change.' The promises may be growing, but the popularity of GM crops is not…

Why have GM crops failed to be the popular success the industry claims them to be? As the promises have expanded, so too has the evidence that GM crops are ill adapted to the challenges facing global food and agriculture systems. These promises have proved to be myths: some of these benefits have failed to materialize outside the lab, and others have unraveled when faced with the real-world complexities of agricultural ecosystems, and the real-world needs of farmers. In reality, GM crops have reinforced the broken model of industrial agriculture, with its biodiversity-reducing monocultures, its huge carbon footprint, its economic pressures on small-scale farmers, and its failure to deliver safe, healthy and nutritious food to those who need it."

Greenpeace International, "Twenty Years of Failure: Why GM
Crops Have Failed to Deliver on Their Promises," 2015

507. **The passage is a reaction to which of the following developments?**

(A) The end of the Cold War
(B) The Green Revolution
(C) The rise of the European Union
(D) New international organizations

508. **Based on the passage, it can be inferred that the organization might also support which of the following assertions?**

(A) Government intervention in farming will lead to better alternatives to genetically modified crops.
(B) The rise of multinational corporations in food production will be beneficial to the environment.
(C) Scientific advances will eventually lead to a solution for global poverty and famine relief.
(D) The release of pollutants into the atmosphere has contributed to climate change.

509. The passage reflects which of the following developments in the twentieth century?

   (A) The rise of groups that protested the environmental consequences of global integration
   (B) The spread of free-market economic principles that led to regional trade agreements
   (C) The growth of religious movements to redefine the relationship between the individual and state
   (D) Transnational ideological movements that sought to unite people across national boundaries

510. The title of the article best suggests that the author is responding to the arguments of which of the following?

   (A) Anti-imperialist leaders
   (B) Conservative nationalists
   (C) Supporters of commercial agriculture
   (D) Opponents of industrial agriculture

Questions 511–512 refer to the graph below.

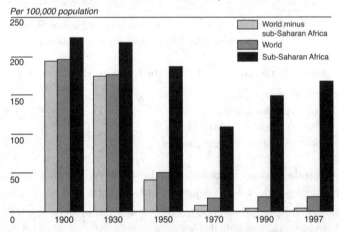

MALARIA MORTALITY RATES, 1900–1997

511. The difference in mortality rates of sub-Saharan Africa and the world without sub-Saharan Africa shown on the graph best illustrates which of the following?

   (A) The lack of effective treatments for diseases like malaria
   (B) The increase in epidemic diseases due to improved transportation
   (C) The eradication of malaria outside of sub-Saharan Africa
   (D) The persistence of diseases associated with poverty

512. The overall trend shown on the graph is a result of which of the following?

(A) Epidemic diseases
(B) The Green Revolution
(C) Medical innovations
(D) Increased food supply

Questions 513–515 refer to the passage below.

"Ecological degradation is today most catastrophic in Third World countries. Developed countries cannot face the unpleasant fact that the environmental problems in the Third World are also problems for developed countries. One important cause of environmental crisis in the Third World lies in the political and economic structure of North-South trade. Developing countries produce mainly raw materials and monocultural products for export to developed countries . . . In modern agriculture human beings are forced to create the early stages of ecological succession artificially . . . We attempt to increase the weights of plants by the use of fertilizers and the improvement of plant breeding. Then, a special group of herbivora becomes more and more dominant. The frequent occurrence of harmful insects is due in part to the intensive use of chemical elements. In traditional agriculture, matter and energy within a particular area circulated in ways such that little waste matter was produced. In modern agriculture, however, most matter and energy are introduced from outside the land under cultivation."

Mario Giampietro and Kozo Mayumi, ecological economists,
"Another View of Development, Ecological
Degradation, and North-South Trade," 1998

513. Which of the following best supports the authors' assertion that environmental degradation is most catastrophic in Third World countries?

(A) The exports produced contribute to deforestation and soil depletion.
(B) The reliance on imported manufactured goods led to economic stagnation.
(C) The use of alternative energy technologies by Third World nations.
(D) The use of fertilizers increased agricultural yields.

514. Which of the following resulted from ecological devastation described in the passage?

(A) The Green Revolution increased agricultural productivity.
(B) The abandonment of monoculture in developing nations.
(C) Human competition over the world's supply of fresh water and clean air.
(D) Population decline due to climate change.

515. Based on the passage, it can be inferred that the authors might also support which of the following assertions?

   (A) The rise of transnational corporations contributed to the economic decline of the Global South.
   (B) The release of greenhouse gases and other pollutants contributed to climate change.
   (C) New modes of communication had a devastating impact on the environment.
   (D) Innovations in technology have been more beneficial to the environment than harmful.

Questions 516–518 refer to the graph below.

LIFE EXPECTANCY AT BIRTH BY REGION, 1950–2050

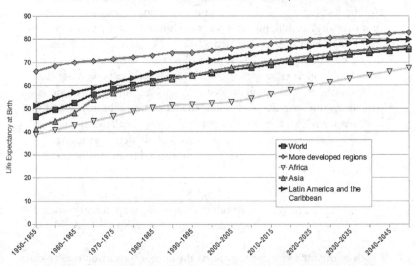

Source: UN World Population Prospects, 2008, RC Ragun (*http://creativecommons.org/licenses/*)

516. The trend shown on the graph illustrates which of the following?

   (A) Fewer outbreaks of epidemics have occurred due to medical innovations.
   (B) Less developed regions have failed to benefit from medical innovations.
   (C) Life expectancy for Africans and Asians has remained stable.
   (D) Medical innovations of the twentieth century led to increased longevity.

517. Which of the following is an effect of the trend shown on the graph?

   (A) The persistence of diseases associated with poverty
   (B) Higher incidence of diseases such as Alzheimer's and heart disease
   (C) The faster spread of epidemic diseases, such as AIDS and Ebola
   (D) The decline in birth rates due to more effective forms of birth control

518. The trend shown on the graph is most similar to patterns of which of the following?

(A) Europe from 1750 to 1900
(B) The Americas from 1492 to 1750
(C) Africa from 1750 to 1900
(D) South Asia from 1450 to 1750

Questions 519–522 refer to the passage below.

"International trade is at the heart of globalization. The tremendous expansion of global trade over the last few decades has driven economic growth in many developing countries, while providing more diverse and less expensive products to consumers in the developed world. At the same time, it has created dramatic upheaval, as workers in poor countries have moved to cities in search of new jobs, while some in wealthier nations have lost jobs that have moved overseas. The 2007 Pew Global poll shows that, all things considered, people consistently endorse international trade. Sizeable majorities in all 47 countries said growing trade ties between countries are having a positive impact on their country. In 9 countries, at least 90 percent of those surveyed took this position…

Furthermore, people generally say they are willing to sacrifice economic growth to secure a clean environment. In 46 of the 47 countries surveyed by Pew in 2007, majorities agreed with the statement 'Protecting the environment should be given priority, even if it causes slower economic growth and some loss of jobs.' In rich and poor nations alike, there is a consensus that damaging the environment is too high a price to pay for economic expansion."

Andrew Kohut and Richard Wike, directors of the
Pew Research Center, "Assessing Globalization:
Benefits and Drawbacks of Trade and Integration," 2008

519. Which of the following contributed to the expansion of global trade described in the passage?

(A) The invention of machines powered by fossil fuels
(B) The formation of international organizations to maintain world peace
(C) Free-market economic policies and economic liberalization
(D) Greater agricultural productivity due to the Green Revolution

520. **Which of the following factors contributed to environmental concerns referred to in the passage?**

    (A) The Internet and cellular communication led to environmental degradation.

    (B) The increase in agricultural yields occurred due to the Green Revolution.

    (C) The use of petroleum and nuclear power led to lower prices of consumer goods.

    (D) The release of greenhouse gases led to debates about the nature of climate change.

521. **Which of the following most directly resulted from economic changes referred to in the passage?**

    (A) The rise of regional trade agreements designed to protect national economies

    (B) Movements that protested the inequalities created by global economic integration

    (C) The development of religious fundamentalist movements

    (D) Movements that resisted the greater attainment of economic opportunities

522. **The process of globalization described in the passage was accelerated by which of the following developments of the twentieth century?**

    (A) Changing economic institutions, such as the World Trade Organization

    (B) The rivalry among global superpowers that emerged following World War II

    (C) Urbanization that expanded the availability of unskilled laborers

    (D) The use of more effective forms of birth control

Questions 523–525 refer to the graph below.

WHEAT YIELDS IN SELECTED COUNTRIES, 1950–2004

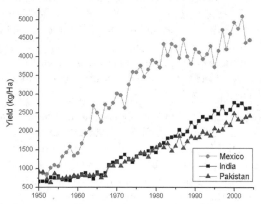

Source: *World Health*, May–June 1991, World Health Organization

523. The trend shown on the graph is most directly due to which of the following?

(A) The redistribution of land to create a more equitable social system
(B) The spread of chemically and genetically modified forms of agriculture
(C) The increased use of fossil fuels and nuclear power for energy
(D) The control of farm production by the governments of these nations

524. Which of the following most directly resulted from the trend shown on the graph?

(A) Increased agricultural production led to the eradication of poverty in these nations.
(B) Increased yields in these nations led to economic collapse in other wheat producing nations.
(C) Increased population led to longer life spans and fewer epidemics.
(D) Increased population led to competition for resources more intensely than before.

525. The trend shown on the graph is most similar to which of the following?

(A) Sub-Saharan Africa in the period 1450–1750
(B) Europe in the period 600–1450 c.e.
(C) China in the period 600–1450 c.e.
(D) India in the period 1750–1900 c.e.

Questions 526–528 refer to the passage below.

"The highest prevalence rates of diabetes are to be found in develop-ing nations. In extreme cases one-third or more of the adult popula-tion suffers from this disease, and one-tenth is not unusual in urban areas of the developing world. Diabetes can no longer be considered a disease of affluent nations alone; it has become a global problem, a major epidemic of the late twentieth century, and one which shows no sign of abating…

Diabetes has a strong genetic component, but it also stems from social, economic, behavioural and environmental factors. There may be fundamental differences between developed and developing coun-tries in this respect, but there is also a predictable pattern of health change in most populations where infectious diseases tend to decline as economic conditions improve and noncommunicable diseases become major causes of disease and death. In some cases, high rates of infections and noncommunicable diseases coexist, leading to the so-called 'double burden.'"

> Hilary King, responsible for the World Health Organization
> activities concerning diabetes, "WHO and Diabetes," 1991

 Tip: The World Health Organization is an agency of the United Nations that seeks to improve public health through international cooperation.

526. Which of the following best explains the increase in diabetes discussed in the passage?

(A) Changing lifestyles led to increased consumption of foods high in fat and sugar.

(B) Medical innovations that decreased infectious diseases inadvertently increased diabetes rates.

(C) Improved economic conditions led to increased strains on the environment.

(D) Longer life spans led to increased populations that strained resources for diabetes prevention.

527. The creation of the organization responsible for the information in the passage best reflects which of the following developments of the twentieth century?

(A) The development of regional cooperation initiatives

(B) The emergence of new institutions of global association

(C) The increasing independence of individual states

(D) The interdependence of humans and the environment

528. Which of the following <u>refutes</u> the author's claim that infectious diseases have declined?

   (A) The development of medical innovations, such as vaccines and antibiotics
   (B) The increased prevalence of heart disease and higher cancer rates
   (C) The persistence of diseases associated with poverty, such as malaria
   (D) The emergence of new epidemics, such as HIV/AIDS and Ebola

Short-Answer Questions

Use the graph below to answer all parts of the question that follows.

PEOPLE OF THE WORLD—FROM 1000 C.E. TO THE PRESENT

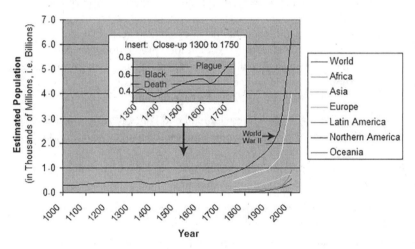

529. a) Identify ONE cause of the change to the pattern of the graph between 1900 and the present.

   b) Explain ONE change in the relationship between humans and the environment as a result of the trend shown on the graph.

   c) Explain ONE continuity in the relationship between humans and the environment from 1000 c.e. to the present.

Use the following article to answer all parts of the question that follows.

   "The Green Revolution also contributed to better nutrition by raising incomes and reducing prices, which permitted people to consume more calories and a more diversified diet. Big increases occurred in per capita consumption of vegetable oils, fruits, vegetables, and livestock products in Asia..."

Critics of the Green Revolution argued that owners of large farms were the main adopters of the new technologies because of their better access to irrigation water, fertilizers, seeds, and credit. Small farmers were either unaffected or harmed because the Green Revolution resulted in lower product prices, higher input prices, and efforts by landlords to increase rents or force tenants off the land. Critics also argued that the Green Revolution encouraged unnecessary mechanization, thereby pushing down rural wages and employment. Although a number of village and household studies conducted soon after the release of Green Revolution technologies lent some support to early critics, more recent evidence shows mixed outcomes. Small farmers did lag behind large farmers in adopting Green Revolution technologies, yet many of them eventually did so. Many of these small-farm adopters benefited from increased production, greater employment opportunities, and higher wages in the agricultural and nonfarm sectors. Moreover, most smallholders were able to keep their land and experienced significant increases in total production. In some cases, small farmers and landless laborers actually ended up gaining proportionally more income than larger farmers, resulting in a net improvement in the distribution of village income."

> International Food Policy Research Institute,
> "Green Revolution: Blessing or Curse?," 2002

530. a) Identify ONE reason why the institute may have been evaluating the effects of the Green Revolution at this time.

b) Explain ONE specific example from the period 1750–1900 C.E. that had similar effects as the Green Revolution.

c) Explain ONE difference between the impact of the Green Revolution and the Neolithic Revolution.

Tip: Questions on secondary sources are evaluating the skill of historical interpretation, and will often ask for evidence that supports or refutes a claim, or relates to a similar event.

Long Essay Question

531. In the period 1900–2001, disease, scientific innovations, and conflict led to demographic shifts.

Develop an argument that evaluates how scientific innovations led to demographic shifts in this period.

(Answers on pages 371–374.)

nflicts and sequences

CHAPTER

18

n pages 374–379.

Key Concept 6.2—Peoples and states around the world challenged the existing political and social order in varying ways, leading to unprecedented worldwide conflicts.

I. Europe dominated the global political order at the beginning of the twentieth century, but both land-based and transoceanic empires gave way to new forms of transregional political organizations by the century's end.

   A. The older land-based Ottoman, Russian, and Qing Empires collapsed due to a combination of internal and external factors.

   B. Between the two world wars, European imperial states often maintained control over their colonies and in some cases gained additional territories.

   C. After the end of World War II, some colonies negotiated their independence, while other colonies achieved independence through armed struggle.

II. Emerging ideologies of anti-imperialism contributed to the dissolution of empires and the restructuring of states.

   A. Nationalist leaders in Asia and Africa sought varying degrees of autonomy within or independence from imperial rule.

   B. Regional, religious, and ethnic movements challenged both colonial rule and inherited imperial boundaries.

   C. Transnational movements sought to unite people across national boundaries.

   D. The Mexican Revolution arose in opposition to neocolonialism and economic imperialism, and movements to redistribute land and resources developed within states in Africa, Asia, and Latin America, sometimes advocating communism or socialism.

   E. In many parts of the world, religious movements sought to redefine the relationship between the individual and the state.

III. Political changes were accompanied by major demographic and social consequences.

A. The redrawing of old colonial boundaries led to conflict as well as population displacement and/or resettlements, such as the partitioning of India and Pakistan and population displacements following the creation of the state of Israel.

B. The migration of former colonial subjects to imperial metropoles (the former colonizing country, usually in the major cities) maintained cultural and economic ties between the colony and the metropole even after the dissolution of empires.

C. The rise of extremist groups in power led to the annihilation of specific populations, notably in the Holocaust during World War II, and to other atrocities, acts of genocide, or ethnic violence.

IV. Military conflicts occurred on an unprecedented global scale.

A. World War I and World War II were the first total wars. Governments used a variety of strategies, including political propaganda, art, media, and intensified forms of nationalism, to mobilize populations (both in the home countries and the colonies or former colonies) for the purpose of waging war. Governments used ideologies, including fascism and communism, to mobilize all of their states' resources for war and, in the case of totalitarian states, to direct many aspects of daily life during the course of the conflicts and beyond.

B. The sources of global conflict in the first half of the century varied and included imperialist expansion by European powers and Japan, competition for resources, the economic crisis engendered by the Great Depression, and the rise of fascist and totalitarian regimes to positions of power.

C. The global balance of economic and political power shifted after the end of World War II and rapidly evolved into the Cold War. The democracy of the United States and the communist Soviet Union emerged as superpowers, which led to ideological conflict between capitalism and communism across the globe. This conflict extended beyond its basic ideological origins to have profound effects on economic, political, social, and cultural aspects of global events.

D. The Cold War produced new military alliances, including NATO and the Warsaw Pact, and promoted proxy wars between and within postcolonial states in Latin America, Africa, and Asia.

E. Expansions in U.S. military spending and technological development, the Soviet invasion of Afghanistan, and economic weaknesses in communist countries led to the end of the Cold War and the collapse of the Soviet Union.

V. Although conflict dominated much of the twentieth century, many individuals and groups—including states—opposed this trend. Some individuals and groups, however, intensified the conflicts.

A. Groups and individuals challenged the many wars of the century, and some, such as Mohandas Gandhi, Martin Luther King Jr., and Nelson Mandela, promoted the practice of nonviolence as a way to bring about political change.

B. Groups and individuals, including the Non-Aligned Movement, opposed and promoted alternatives to the existing economic, political, and social orders.

C. Militaries and militarized states often responded to the proliferation of conflicts in ways that further intensified conflict.

D. Some movements used violence against civilians to achieve political aims.

While the West dominated the nineteenth century due to industrialization and imperialism, the beginning of the twentieth century saw the end of land empires and the world wars, which devastated Europe and contributed to nationalist movements on the part of colonists. Independence from European control was achieved using violent and nonviolent methods, and resulted in major demographic, social, and economic changes. In the aftermath of World War II, the Cold War between the United States and the Soviet Union had global repercussions, including the creation of alliances, proxy wars, and the collapse of most communist governments.

Questions 532–535 refer to the images below.

Image 1

CANADIAN POSTER, "VICTORY BONDS WILL HELP STOP THIS. KULTUR VS. HUMANITY," 1918

In the image, a Canadian soldier is holding a drowned Red Cross worker, referring to the sinking of the Canadian Red Cross ship Llandovery Castle by a German submarine.

Image 2

AMERICAN POSTER, "WHEN YOU RIDE ALONE YOU RIDE WITH HITLER! JOIN A CAR-SHARING CLUB TODAY!," EARLY 1940s

In the image, a man is driving a car with the outline of Adolf Hitler in the passenger seat.

532. **Image 1 best illustrates which of the following?**

    (A) The importance of naval battles in ending the war
    (B) Increased levels of wartime casualties due to the waging of "total war"
    (C) The use of fascist ideologies to mobilize resources for war
    (D) Diminished importance of military strategies in warfare

533. **The conflict referred to in Image 2 was a result of which of the following developments in the first half of the twentieth century?**

    (A) The collapse of the land-based Ottoman and Qing Empires
    (B) The complete dissolution of European transoceanic empires
    (C) The global economic crisis engendered by the Great Depression
    (D) The emergence of the United States and the Soviet Union as superpowers

534. **The images would be most useful to a historian studying which of the following?**

    (A) The use of propaganda to mobilize populations to support the war effort
    (B) The factors contributing to the start of global military conflicts
    (C) The response of civilians to propaganda campaigns
    (D) The impact of industrialization on global military conflicts

535. **Which of the following was created as a direct reaction to the conflicts shown in the images?**

    (A) Groups that promoted alternatives to the existing order, such as the Non-Aligned Movement
    (B) The formation of military alliances, including NATO and the Warsaw Pact
    (C) Movements that used violence against civilians to achieve political aims, such as Al-Qaeda
    (D) International organizations to facilitate international cooperation, such as the United Nations

Questions 536–538 refer to the following document.

"The Declaration of the French Revolution made in 1791 on the Rights of Man and the Citizen states 'all men are born free and with equal rights, and must always remain free and have equal rights.' Those are undeniable truths. Nevertheless, for more than eighty years, the French imperialists, abusing the standard of Liberty, Equality, and Fraternity, have violated our Fatherland and oppressed our fellow-citizens. They have acted contrary to the ideals of humanity and justice. They have enforced inhuman laws; they have set up three distinct political regimes in the North, the Center, and the South of Vietnam in order to wreck our national unity and prevent our people from being united."

> Ho Chi Minh, Prime Minister and President of North Vietnam, Vietnamese Declaration of Independence, 1945

536. **The views in this document are best seen as evidence of which of the following?**

(A) The rise of nationalist leaders and parties that challenged imperial rule

(B) The rejection of Enlightenment ideas by nationalist leaders

(C) The influence of communist ideologies on Asian nationalist leaders

(D) The development of religious movements that challenged imperial rule

537. **Ho Chi Minh's attitude toward the French as described in this document is most likely the result of which of the following?**

(A) The granting of rights to the Vietnamese people based on Enlightenment ideas

(B) The establishment of Vietnam as a settler colony for the French

(C) The policies implemented by the French that granted autonomy to the Vietnamese

(D) The subjugation of the Vietnamese by the French during colonial rule

538. **A historian researching twentieth century nationalist movements would most likely find the document useful as a source of information for which of the following?**

(A) The impact of the Cold War on independence movements

(B) Justifications for anti-imperial movements by nationalist leaders

(C) The impact of ideologies, such as fascism, on nationalist movements

(D) Reasons for cooperation with European colonial rulers

Questions 539–541 refer to the map that follows.

POPULATION MOVEMENTS IN SOUTH ASIA, 1947–1948

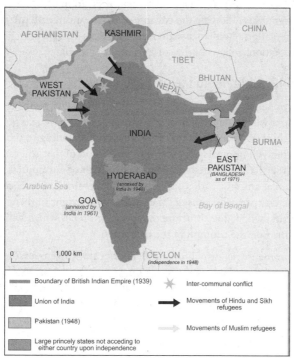

539. The developments depicted on the map most directly emerged from which of the following developments in the early twentieth century?

(A) The end of British policies promoting cooperation between Hindus and Muslims

(B) The desire by nationalist leaders to make an independent India a Hindu theocracy

(C) British colonial policies that furthered existing religious tensions in the region

(D) Mughal policies that were viewed as intolerant by the Hindu majority

540. The movements shown on the map reflect which of the following world historical processes?

(A) The migration of former colonial subjects to cities in the former colonizing country

(B) The development of ethnic enclaves as these migrants moved for work opportunities

(C) The migration patterns associated with male seasonal laborers

(D) Population resettlement caused by redrawing former colonial boundaries

541. The circumstances surrounding migrations shown on the map are most similar to which of the following?

(A) Population displacements following the creation of Israel
(B) Migrations following the collapse of communism in Eastern Europe
(C) Population resettlements after the American Civil War
(D) Migrations following the collapse of the Ottoman Empire

Questions 542–544 refer to the passage below.

"We invoke, we give notice: that [regarding] the fields, timber, and water which the landlords, scientists, or bosses have usurped, the pueblos or citizens who have the titles corresponding to those properties will immediately enter into possession of that real estate of which they have been despoiled by the bad faith of our oppressors, maintain at any cost with arms in hand the mentioned possession; and the usurpers who consider themselves with a right to them [those properties] will deduce it before the special tribunals which will be established on the triumph of the revolution.

...the immense majority of Mexican *pueblos* and citizens are owners of no more than the land they walk on, suffering the horrors of poverty without being able to improve their social condition in any way or to dedicate themselves to Industry or Agriculture, because lands, timber, and water are monopolized in a few hands."

Emiliano Zapata, Mexican revolutionary, *Plan of Ayala*, 1911

542. The outbreak of the revolution Zapata participated in was a result of which of the following?

(A) Communist policies in which the Mexican government controlled all land and businesses
(B) Neocolonialism and economic imperialism by the United States and European powers
(C) Imperial rule by the Spanish as a result of the conquest of the Aztec Empire
(D) Religious groups that wished to implement social reforms

543. Ideas such as those expressed by Zapata would have the most significant influence on which of the following?

(A) Religious movements that embraced liberation theology
(B) Political movements that rejected Enlightenment ideas regarding natural rights
(C) Land reform movements in response to unequal distribution of land and resources
(D) Religious movements that sought to redefine the relationship between the individual and state

544. **Which of the following best describes a similarity between the Mexican Revolution of 1910 and the Russian Revolution of 1917?**

 (A) Both were prompted by the desire to overthrow autocratic monarchs.

 (B) Both gained the support of bureaucrats within the existing governments.

 (C) Both were initiated in response to invasions by foreign powers.

 (D) Both gained the support of peasants with the promise of land reform.

Questions 545–548 refer to the two sources below.

Source 1

> "I do not believe that Soviet Russia desires war. What they desire is the fruits of war and the indefinite expansion of their power and doctrines. But what we have to consider here today while time remains, is the permanent prevention of war and the establishment of conditions of freedom and democracy as rapidly as possible in all countries. Our difficulties and dangers will not be removed by closing our eyes to them. They will not be removed by mere waiting to see what happens; nor will they be removed by a policy of appeasement."

> Winston Churchill, British Prime Minister,
> "Iron Curtain" speech, 1946

Source 2

> "Mr. Churchill begins to set war loose by a racial theory, maintaining that only nations speaking the English language are fully valuable nations, called upon to decide the destinies of the entire world. In substance, Mr. Churchill and his friends in England and the United States present nations not speaking the English language with something like an ultimatum: 'Recognize our lordship voluntarily and then all will be well. In the contrary case, war is inevitable.'"

Joseph Stalin, Soviet Premier, "Answer to *Pravda** Correspondent," 1946

*Pravda was the official newspaper of the Soviet Communist Party.

545. **The two sources are best understood in the context of which of the following?**

 (A) The shifting balance of economic and political power in the aftermath of World War II

 (B) The increase in tensions between world powers during the Great Depression

 (C) The conflicting goals of Britain and the Soviet Union before World War I

 (D) The competition between European powers for control of overseas colonies

546. Based on <u>Source 1</u>, which of the following was the likely purpose of Churchill's speech?

(A) To demonstrate the threats of communist ideology to Britain's working class.

(B) To warn Britain's allies of the inevitability of war with the Soviet Union

(C) To encourage immediate action in response to increasing Soviet influence

(D) To advocate for cooperation with the Soviets in order to spread democratic principles

547. Which of the following groups would most likely agree with Stalin's views expressed in <u>Source 2</u>?

(A) Members of the Non-Aligned Movement

(B) NATO member states

(C) Founders of the United Nations

(D) Nationalist leaders in Asia and Africa

548. The tensions between the leaders as reflected in the sources most directly led to which of the following?

(A) The declaration of war by Great Britain against the Soviet Union

(B) The outbreak of proxy wars in Asia and new military alliances

(C) The independence of colonies in Africa through armed struggle

(D) The collapse of communist governments in Eastern Europe

Questions 549–551 refer to the map below.

MILITARY ALLIANCES AND POLITICAL MOVEMENTS, CIRCA 1955

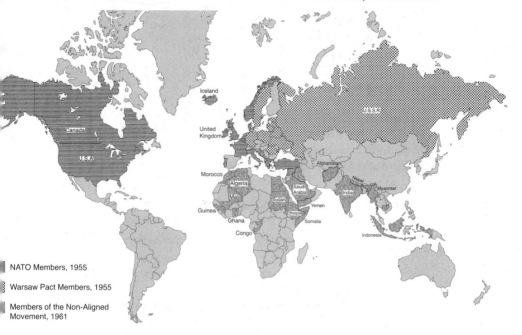

NATO Members, 1955

Warsaw Pact Members, 1955

Members of the Non-Aligned
Movement, 1961

549. The military alliances shown on the map were developed as a result of which of the following?

(A) The economic crisis engendered by the Great Depression
(B) Religious and ethnic movements that challenged colonial rule
(C) The ideological struggle between communist and capitalist powers
(D) Extremist movements that annihilated specific populations

Tip: All of these choices represent events of the twentieth century and are directly from the key concepts, so they all may sound correct, but remember to focus on the question: the cause of the military alliances.

550. The Non-Aligned Movement shown on the map developed for which of the following reasons?

(A) To create a military alliance to counter NATO and the Warsaw Pact
(B) To oppose the existing global political and economic order
(C) To unite colonies in fighting for independence from imperial rulers
(D) To remove economic barriers and promote free trade

551. **Which of the following was the most direct effect of the alliances shown on the map?**

    (A) The development of environmental organizations
    (B) Declaration of war between the superpowers
    (C) The formation of regional trade agreements
    (D) Proxy wars in Latin America, Africa, and Asia

Questions 552–555 refer to the passage below.

"For centuries, Europeans dominated the African continent. The white man arrogated to himself the right to rule and to be obeyed by the non-white; his mission, he claimed, was to 'civilise' Africa. Under this cloak, the Europeans robbed the continent of vast riches and inflicted unimaginable suffering on the African people...

It is clear that we must find an African solution to our problems, and that this can only be found in African unity. Divided we are weak; united, Africa could become one of the greatest forces for good in the world."

Kwame Nkrumah, Ghanaian nationalist, "I Speak of Freedom," 1961

552. **The passage by Nkrumah is best understood in the context of which of the following?**

    (A) The spread of communist ideologies
    (B) Emerging ideologies of anti-imperialism
    (C) The diffusion of industrial technologies
    (D) New economic policies imposed by Europeans

553. **The views in the passage best illustrate which of the following processes?**

    (A) The development of transnational movements to unite people across national boundaries
    (B) The rise of religious movements to redefine the relationship between individuals and the state
    (C) The shift in the global balance of power from Europe to Africa and Asia
    (D) The complete end of European influence on the African economy

554. **Which of the following best explains European actions described in the first paragraph?**

    (A) The continued practice of slavery and serfdom
    (B) The desire to spread Enlightenment ideas
    (C) The demand for African manufactured goods
    (D) The use of racial ideologies to justify imperialism

555. The solution to Africa's problems that was proposed in the passage was mostly hindered by which of the following?

   (A) Arguments over the use of free-market policies and participation in the United Nations
   (B) European legal systems that continued after African nations achieved autonomy
   (C) Ethnic and tribal disputes resulting from artificial boundaries created by Europeans
   (D) Rebellions against imperial rule that weakened nationalist ideologies

Questions 556–558 refer to the image below.

PROPAGANDA POSTER, "THE WOMAN WHO VOTES HAS OUTDONE THE MAN WHO DIDN'T!," EARLY 1950s

The poster was from a series published by the United States Information Agency and printed in multiple languages (including Bikol, Burmese, Cebuano, Chinese, French, Hiligaynon, Iloko, Indonesian, Japanese, Khmer, Korean, Lao, Malay, Pampango, Panagasinan, Tagalog, Tamil, Thai, and Vietnamese) for distribution to countries throughout Asia.

556. The distribution of the poster is best understood in which of the following contexts?

   (A) The struggle between the United States and the Soviet Union to spread their ideologies
   (B) The abolition of women's suffrage by governments in Asia
   (C) The collapse of communism at the end of the Cold War
   (D) The decline of land-based empires due to internal factors

557. Which of the following best describes the likely intent of the poster?

(A) To promote traditional gender roles in Asian societies
(B) To build support for communist ideologies promoting gender equality
(C) To encourage women to participate in the democratic process
(D) To build support for the mobilization of women in the world wars

558. The action shown in the poster was the result of which of the following?

(A) The spread of free-market economies throughout Asia
(B) The challenging of traditional gender roles due to rights-based discourses
(C) The continuation of nineteenth century political policies regarding suffrage
(D) The abolition of Enlightenment values by communist governments

Questions 559–561 refer to the passage below.

"A country's national policy can be defined as militaristic if there is 'an excessive reliance on the use, or threat, of force as a legitimate means of pursuing foreign policy goals.' Application of this particular version of the definition depends on a definition of 'excessive,' which in turn is essentially a value judgment. There was certainly a greater propensity for global involvement during the Cold War; by that measure, the United States was clearly more militaristic. Yet military intervention was not new to the American republic, as Central Americans, Mexicans, and Native Americans can attest. Between 1891 and 1933, there were more than 30 foreign military interventions. In the case of many of the smaller interventions as well as the Army's frontier wars, however, most of the nation was not affected on the same scale as was the case during the Cold War. While isolationism did not die out as completely as had been assumed, the Cold War did bring with it a propensity for global intervention that would not have been conceivable in an earlier era. A tentative conclusion of an increased level of militarism under the national policy definition can then be justified."

Hubert van Tuyll, historian, "Militarism, the
United States, and the Cold War," 1994

559. The author's argument regarding the effects of the Cold War on the United States' foreign policy is likely based on which of the following?

(A) The involvement in global conflicts to combat fascism and Japanese expansion
(B) United States' policies toward newly independent states in Latin America
(C) The participation in international organizations and regional agreements by the United States
(D) United States' involvement in proxy wars and the arms race with the Soviet Union

560. Which of the following would most directly <u>challenge</u> the author's argument that the United States became more militaristic during the Cold War?

    (A) Policies of peaceful coexistence and cultural exchanges with the Soviet Union

    (B) United States' actions in response to the Soviet invasion of Afghanistan

    (C) The formation of the North Atlantic Treaty Organization (NATO)

    (D) The increasing global influence of American popular culture

561. Which of the following most directly led to the end of the Cold War and collapse of the Soviet Union?

    (A) War between the Soviet Union and Eastern European satellite nations

    (B) Economic weaknesses in communist countries and the Soviet invasion of Afghanistan

    (C) Soviet failure to introduce free-market policies and greater political freedoms

    (D) Intervention by the Soviet Union on the Korean peninsula and Vietnam

Short-Answer Questions

Use the following two images to answer all parts of the question that follows.

<u>Image 1</u>

**BRITISH IMPERIAL MARITIME LEAGUE,
"WOMEN OF BRITAIN SAY 'GO!,'" POSTER, 1914**

The poster shows women watching soldiers march away.

Image 2

"ARE WE AFRAID? NO!," POSTER, 1915

This postcard uses the Union Flag and the icon of the Bulldog to show Britain, Australia, Canada, India, New Zealand, and South Africa standing united against a common threat.

562. a) Identify ONE common historical process in the twentieth century that is reflected in both images.

b) Explain ONE difference in the targeted audience of the posters.

c) Explain ONE way in which images such as these can be seen as an example of the political uses of art in the twentieth century.

Answer all parts of the question that follows.

563. a) Identify ONE way in which military conflicts led to demographic changes in the twentieth century.

b) Explain ONE way in which military conflicts in the twentieth century represent a continuity with previous patterns of interaction in world history.

c) Explain ONE way in which military conflicts in the twentieth century influenced changes in the global political order.

Long Essay Questions

564. In the period 1900–2001 C.E., challenges to the prevailing political order led to military struggles around the world.

Develop an argument that evaluates how changes in the global balance of power led to one or more regional or global military conflicts during this time period.

565. In the period 1900–2001 C.E., emerging ideologies of anti-imperialism contributed to the dissolution of empires and the restructuring of states.

Develop an argument that evaluates how one or more empires changed in response to emerging ideologies of anti-imperialism during this time period.

Document-Based Question

566. Evaluate the extent to which the international situation following World War I contributed to World War II.

Document 1

Source: John Maynard Keynes, English Economist, *The Economic Consequences of the Peace*, 1920

The Treaty includes no provisions for the economic rehabilitation of Europe—nothing to make the defeated Central Empires into good neighbors, nothing to stabilize the new States of Europe, nothing to reclaim Russia; nor does it promote in any way a compact of economic solidarity amongst the Allies themselves; no arrangement was reached at Paris for restoring the disordered finances of France and Italy, or to adjust the systems of the Old World and the New ...

Europe consists of the densest aggregation of population in the history of the world. This population is accustomed to a relatively high standard of life, in which, even now, some sections of it anticipate improvement rather than deterioration. In relation to other continents Europe is not self-sufficient; in particular it cannot feed itself. Internally the population is not evenly distributed, but much of it is crowded into a relatively small number of dense industrial centers ...

The danger confronting us, therefore, is the rapid depression of the standard of life of the European populations to a point which will mean actual starvation for some (a point already reached in Russia and approximately reached in Austria). Men will not always die quietly. For starvation, which brings to some lethargy and a helpless despair, drives other temperaments to the nervous instability of hysteria and to a mad despair. And these in their distress may overturn the remnants of organization, and submerge civilization itself in their attempts to satisfy desperately the over-whelming needs of the individual. This is the danger against which all our resources and courage and idealism must now co-operate.

Document 2

Source: Excerpt from the Washington Naval Treaty between the United States of America, the British Empire, France, Italy, and Japan. Signed in Washington, February 6, 1922

Article VII
The total tonnage for aircraft carriers of each of the Contracting Powers shall not exceed in standard displacement, for the United States 135,000 tons (137,160 metric tons); for the British Empire 135,000 tons (137,160 metric tons); for France 60,000 tons (60,960 metric tons); for Italy 60,000 tons (60,960 metric tons); for Japan 81,000 tons (82,296 metric tons).

Document 3

Source: Benito Mussolini, Italian government publication, "Fascism: Doctrine and Institutions," 1935

Anti-individualistic, the Fascist conception of life stresses the importance of the State and accepts the individual only in so far as his interests coincide with those of the State, which stands for the conscience and the universal, will of man as a historic entity. It is opposed to classical liberalism which arose as a reaction to absolutism and exhausted its historical function when the State became the expression of the conscience and will of the people. Liberalism denied the State in the name of the individual; Fascism reasserts the rights of the State as expressing the real essence of the individual ... The Fascist conception of the State is all embracing; outside of it no human or spiritual values can exist, much less have value. Thus understood, Fascism, is totalitarian, and the Fascist State—a synthesis and a unit inclusive of all values—interprets, develops, and potentates the whole life of a people ...

Fascism does not, generally speaking, believe in the possibility or utility of perpetual peace. It therefore discards pacifism as a cloak for cowardly supine renunciation in contradistinction to self-sacrifice. War alone keys up all human energies to their maximum tension and sets the seal of nobility on those peoples who have the courage to face it. All other tests are substitutes which never place a man face to face with himself before the alternative of life or death.

Document 4

Source: Agreement concluded at Munich, September 29, 1938, between Germany, Great Britain, France, and Italy, commonly referred to as the Munich Pact. It followed the German invasion of the Sudeten region of Czechoslovakia.

GERMANY, the United Kingdom, France and Italy, taking into consideration the agreement, which has been already reached in principle for the cession to Germany of the Sudeten German territory, have agreed on the following terms and conditions governing the said cession and the measures consequent thereon, and by this agreement they each hold themselves responsible for the steps necessary to secure its fulfilment: ...

(4) The occupation by stages of the predominantly German territory by German troops will begin on 1st October ...

(8) The Czechoslovak Government will within a period of four weeks from the date of this agreement release from their military and police forces any Sudeten Germans who may wish to be released, and the Czechoslovak Government will within the same period release Sudeten German prisoners who are serving terms of imprisonment for political offences ...

Document 5

Source: Adolf Hitler, Speech of April 12, 1921

"After the War, production had begun again and it was thought that better times were coming. Frederick the Great after the Seven Years War had, as the result of superhuman efforts, left Prussia without a penny of debt: at the end of the World War, Germany was burdened with her own debt of some 7 or 8 milliards of marks and beyond that was faced with the debts of "the rest of the world"—'the so-called reparations.' The product of Germany's work thus belonged, not to the nation, but to her foreign creditors....Therefore, in the economic sphere, November 1918 was in truth no achievement, but it was the beginning of our collapse...

Then some one has said: 'Since the Revolution the people has gained *Rights*. The people governs.' Strange! The people has now been ruling three years and no one has in practice once asked its opinion. Treaties were signed which will hold us down for centuries: and who has signed the treaties? The people? No! Governments which one fine day presented themselves as Governments. And at their election the people had nothing to do save to consider the question: there they are already, whether I elect them or not. If we elect them, then they are there through our election. But since we are a self-governing people, we must elect the folk in order that they may be elected to govern us."

Document 6

Source: *Washington Evening Star*, "It's a Good Act but It's Hard on the Spectators," August 20, 1939

IT'S A GOOD ACT BUT IT'S HARD ON THE SPECTATORS —

The cartoon was published after Adolf Hitler put new demands on Poland to give the city of Danzig to Germany. Hitler is balancing the world on the tip of a rifle as nervous representatives from the United States, Great Britain, and France watch.

Document 7

Source: Selected articles from the Treaty of Versailles, developed by main victors of World War I, 1919

80. Germany will respect the independence of Austria.

81. Germany recognizes the complete independence of Czechoslovakia.

87. Germany recognizes the complete independence of Poland.

119. Germany surrenders all her rights and titles over her overseas countries.

159. The German military forces shall be demobilized and reduced not to exceed 100,000 men.

181. The German navy must not exceed 6 battleships, 6 light cruisers, 12 destroyers, and 12 torpedo boats. No submarines are to be included.

198. The Armed Forces of Germany must not include any military or naval air forces.

231. Germany and her Allies accept the responsibility for causing all the loss and damage to the Allied Powers.

233. Germany will pay for all damages done to the civilian population and property of the Allied Governments.

428. To guarantee the execution of the Treaty, the German territory situated to the west of the Rhine River will be occupied by Allied troops for fifteen years.

431. The occupation forces will be withdrawn as soon as Germany complies with the Treaty.

(Answers on pages 374–379.)

Key Concept 6.3—The role of the state in the domestic economy varied, and new institutions of global association emerged and continued to develop throughout the century.

I. States responded in a variety of ways to the economic challenges of the twentieth century.

    A. In communist states, such as the Soviet Union and China, governments controlled their national economies, often through repressive policies and with negative repercussions for their populations.

    B. Following World War I and the onset of the Great Depression, governments began to take a more active role in economic life.

    C. In newly independent states after World War II, governments often took on a strong role in guiding economic life to promote development.

    D. In a trend accelerated by the end of the Cold War, many governments encouraged free-market economic policies and promoted economic liberalization in the late twentieth century.

    E. In the late twentieth century, revolutions in information and communications technology led to the growth of knowledge economies in some regions, while industrial production and manufacturing were increasingly situated in developing economies including the Pacific Rim and Latin America.

II. States, communities, and individuals became increasingly interdependent, a process facilitated by the growth of institutions of global governance.

    A. New international organizations were formed to maintain world peace and to facilitate international cooperation.

    B. Changing economic institutions sought to spread the principles and practices associated with free-market economics throughout the world.

    C. Movements throughout the world protested the inequality of environmental and economic consequences of global integration.

III. People conceptualized society and culture in new ways; rights-based discourses challenged old assumptions about race, class, gender, and religion. In much of the world, access to education, as well as participation in new political and professional roles, became more inclusive in terms of these factors.

IV. Political and social changes of the twentieth century led to changes in the arts and literature. In the second half of the century, popular and consumer culture became global.

The extent of government involvement in economic affairs varied across the twentieth century. Generally, governments became more active in the economy during the Great Depression and the world wars, but tended to move toward free-market policies at the end of the century. The rise of new international organizations and trade agreements led to economic integration, a process commonly referred to as globalization. Due to increased communication and new forms of media, popular culture became more global. The promotion of human rights led to more inclusive legal systems, and greater participation in the economy and society by groups that were previously marginalized based on religion, race, gender, or class.

Questions 567–570 refer to the following passage.

"Imperialism as an international phenomenon means, for example, the unfavorable flow of capital to nations with more developed productive forces from the 'underdeveloped' nations, thereby drawing the latter into the world market, into the unequal exchange between 'raw materials' and 'finished products' which works to the disadvantage of those nations whose productive forces are 'underdeveloped…'

…the reproduction of capitalist production relations and productive forces on a world scale, also therefore reproduces class struggle on a world scale. At the time it gives rise to an inter-related international hierarchy of national entities. This is because capitalism develops unevenly—in some countries productive forces are developing, in others the development of the productive forces is blocked. These developments are determined by the character of the production relations and the differing places and roles assigned to the various national entities by the structure of the hierarchy. This international hierarchy is dominated by a hegemonic power, whose economic, political and ideological strength and influence are decisive for the maintenance and control of the world system."

Paul Costello, Marxist author, "World Imperialism and Marxist Theory: On the International Line of the Communist Movement," 1979

Source: Encyclopedia of Anti-Revisionism online *www.marxists.org/history/erol/periodicals/ TheoreticalReview/19790901.htm*

567. **Which of the following best describes the cause of the economic developments described in the first paragraph of the passage?**

(A) Lack of production of finished goods in Africa and Asia as a result of a small class of artisans

(B) Decreased availability of capital among European investors due to industrialization

(C) Increased demand for natural resources and cash crops by industrial powers

(D) Lack of economic development in Africa and Asia due to decentralized governments

568. **The passage is best understood in the context of which of the following?**

(A) The rivalry of superpowers during the Cold War

(B) The establishment of postwar international organizations

(C) The outbreak of violence among social classes in Western states

(D) The free-market economic reforms implemented in communist states

569. **Which of the following best supports the author's assertion that underdeveloped nations are at a disadvantage?**

(A) Rapid economic growth in regions that industrialized in the postwar period

(B) The lack of involvement by these nations in global trade

(C) Economic growth in Asia as a result of free-trade policies

(D) Economic dependency of newly independent states on their former mother country

570. **Which of the following challenges the author's assertion that the international hierarchy is dominated by hegemonic powers?**

(A) The rise of international organizations to facilitate international cooperation

(B) The formation of NATO and the Warsaw Pact

(C) The organization of movements to protest economic inequalities

(D) The spread of multinational corporations

Questions 571–574 refer to the following two images.

Image 1

SOVIET POSTER, BY YAKOV GUMINER, 1931

*The text reads, "The arithmetic of an industrial-financial counter-plan:
2 + 2 plus the enthusiasm of the workers = 5."*

Image 2

MAO ZEDONG SHAKES HANDS WITH
PEOPLE'S COMMUNE WORKERS, 1959

*The image appeared in a book issued by the government of China to celebrate
the 10th anniversary of the founding of the People's Republic of China.*

Tip: Read carefully, as this question is asking what led to the establishment of the Soviet Union, which was the Russian Revolution.

571. Which of the following directly enabled the establishment of the government that produced Image 1?

(A) The failure of the existing monarchy to abolish serfdom and other forms of coerced labor

(B) Redrawn national boundaries as a result of peace treaties at the end of World War I

(C) Increased rebellion by ethnic minorities due to imperial expansion in the nineteenth century

(D) Discontent with the monarchy and financial pressures of the First World War

572. The ideology reflected in Image 2 was most directly the result of which of the following developments of the nineteenth century?

(A) Demands for women's suffrage and emancipation of coerced laborers

(B) Enlightenment ideas that challenged monarchies and denounced global capitalism

(C) Growing discontent with existing forms of government and unequal distribution of wealth

(D) Rebellions against imperial rule that led to the formation of autonomous states in Asia

573. The images reflect which of the following responses to economic challenges of the twentieth century?

(A) Governments controlled national economies in communist states through repressive policies.

(B) Governments often took on a strong role in guiding economic life in newly independent states.

(C) Governments expanded free-market economic policies and economic liberalization.

(D) Governments began to take a more active role in economic life as a result of the Great Depression.

574. Which of the following best describes the likely intent of the posters?

(A) To promote participation in international organizations and trade agreements

(B) To build support for centrally directed economic programs in these nations

(C) To promote resistance to the prevailing political order and offer a more attractive alternative

(D) To build support for anti-imperialist movements in Asia and Africa

Tip: The question below is a general question that refers to artwork used for propaganda purposes.

575. Artworks with a purpose similar to those in the images were used for all of the following EXCEPT to

(A) encourage citizens in these nations to adopt Western popular culture
(B) mobilize support for proxy wars that arose during the Cold War
(C) promote support for alliances, such as the Warsaw Pact
(D) demonize capitalist countries and economic policies

Questions 576–579 refer to the passage below.

[Line 1] "Whereas recognition of the inherent dignity and of the equal and inalienable rights of all members of the human family is the foundation of freedom, justice and peace in the world,

[Line 2] Whereas disregard and contempt for human rights have resulted in barbarous acts which have outraged the conscience of mankind, and the advent of a world in which human beings shall enjoy freedom of speech and belief and freedom from fear and want has been proclaimed as the highest aspiration of the common people,

[Line 3] Whereas it is essential, if man is not to be compelled to have recourse, as a last resort, to rebellion against tyranny and oppression, that human rights should be protected by the rule of law....

[Line 4] Now, Therefore THE GENERAL ASSEMBLY proclaims THIS UNIVERSAL DECLARATION OF HUMAN RIGHTS as a common standard of achievement for all peoples and all nations, to the end that every individual and every organ of society, keeping this Declaration constantly in mind, shall strive by teaching and education to promote respect for these rights and freedoms and by progressive measures, national and international, to secure their universal and effective recognition and observance, both among the peoples of Member States themselves and among the peoples of territories under their jurisdiction."

Preamble to "Universal Declaration of Human Rights,"
adopted by the General Assembly of the United Nations, 1948

576. The ideas referred to in <u>Line 1</u> are most directly the result of which of the following?

(A) Atlantic Revolutions
(B) The Enlightenment
(C) The Cold War
(D) The Renaissance

577. The barbarous acts referred to in <u>Line 2</u> are best understood in the context of which of the following?

    (A) Imperial expansion by European powers

    (B) The spread of communism during the Cold War

    (C) The annihilation of specific populations during the world wars

    (D) Coerced labor systems and resistance to imperial rule

578. The passage best illustrates which of the following processes that occurred in the twentieth century?

    (A) The desire of international organizations to impose policies on member nations

    (B) New ideas about the role of citizens in the political process and governmental decision-making

    (C) The formulation of alternative visions of society in response to the spread of global capitalism

    (D) New conceptualizations about race, class, gender, and religion that challenged traditions

579. Which of the following resulted from ideas similar to those expressed in the passage?

    (A) Increased participation in political and professional roles by groups that were previously marginalized

    (B) The justification for violent rebellions against neocolonialist policies in Africa and Latin America

    (C) Increased intervention by governments in national economies and international trade policies

    (D) The abolition of women's suffrage and emancipation of coerced laborers on Caribbean plantations

Questions 580–582 refer to the graph below.

**ECONOMIC GROWTH IN THE "ASIAN TIGERS," 1960–2014
WITH PROJECTIONS THROUGH 2020**

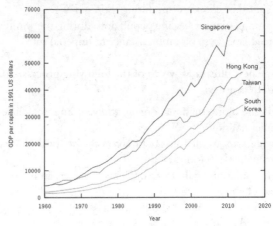

Source: *www.commons.wikimedia.org/wiki/File:Four_tigers_GDP-per-capita.svg#filelink.* Author: Kanguole.

580. **The graph best illustrates which of the following economic changes in the late twentieth century?**

   (A) The shift in industrial production from China and Japan to Singapore, Hong Kong, and South Korea

   (B) The decline in consumption by the United States and the new role of Asian consumerism

   (C) The shift in manufacturing from Europe and the United States to the Pacific Rim

   (D) The decline in European participation in the global economy as a result of self-sufficiency

581. **The changes shown on the graph are most likely due to which of the following?**

   (A) New international organizations that were formed to maintain world peace

   (B) New economic institutions and regional trade agreements

   (C) Movements that protested economic consequences of global integration

   (D) Greater control of governments in national economies through regulations

582. **The trend shown on the graph is most similar to which of the following?**

   (A) Western Europe in the twentieth century

   (B) Sub-Saharan Africa in the twentieth century

   (C) India and China in the nineteenth century

   (D) Western Europe in the nineteenth century

Questions 583–586 refer to the passage below.

"As well as being associated with America, Coca-Cola also encapsulates the trend toward a single global marketplace: in a word, globalization. Believers in globalization argue that abolishing trade barriers, tariffs, and other obstacles to free and unfettered international commerce is the best way to improve the fortunes of rich and poor countries alike... Opponents of globalization complain that such practices are exploitative, since they create low-wage, low-status jobs; multinational companies are also able to exploit looser labor and environmental regulations by shifting jobs overseas... An oft-heard complaint, as companies spread their tentacles around the world and compete on a global playing field, is that globalization is merely a form of imperialism. Antiglobalization activists argue that the world's only superpower, the United States, is intent on invading the rest of the world not with soldiers and bombs, but with its culture, companies, and brands, chief among them Microsoft, McDonald's, and Coca-Cola."

Tom Standage, journalist, *A History of the World in 6 Glasses*, 2006

583. The process of globalization as described in the passage is the result of which of the following?

(A) New modes of communication and transportation that reduced the problem of geographic distance

(B) Medical innovations that increased the ability of humans to survive and live longer lives

(C) The control of national economies by governments through repressive policies

(D) Changes in literature and the arts that promoted the return to cultural traditions

584. Which of the following developments of the late twentieth century best supports the complaints of those who oppose globalization as described in the passage?

(A) Many governments encouraged free-market economic policies and promoted economic liberalization following the end of the Cold War.

(B) Revolutions in information and communications technology led to the growth of knowledge economies in some regions.

(C) Industrial production and manufacturing were increasingly situated in developing economies including the Pacific Rim and Latin America.

(D) Changing economic institutions sought to spread the principles and practices associated with free-market economics throughout the world.

585. Which of the following occurred as a reaction to the developments described in the passage?

   (A) New international organizations were formed to maintain world peace and to facilitate international cooperation.

   (B) Rights-based discourses challenged old assumptions about race, class, gender, and religion.

   (C) Changing economic institutions sought to spread the principles and practices associated with free-market economics throughout the world.

   (D) Movements throughout the world protested the inequality of environmental and economic consequences of global integration.

586. Which of the following occurred in the late twentieth century as a result of global economic integration?

   (A) Access to education became more inclusive globally.

   (B) Popular and consumer culture became global.

   (C) International organizations maintained world peace.

   (D) Regional customs were completely replaced by American culture.

Questions 587–589 refer to the image below.

EARTH DAY CARTOON, R. J. MATSON, 2009

587. The cartoon best illustrates which of the following twentieth-century processes?

   (A) Regional trade agreements that were promoted free-trade policies

   (B) Movements that protested the environmental consequences of global integration

   (C) New international organizations that were formed to maintain world peace and international cooperation

   (D) Expansion of European empires that led to the expansion of market economies globally

588. The conditions depicted on the right side of the cartoon are in large part the result of which of the following?

(A) Mobilization of resources due to the outbreak of global conflict

(B) Protectionist economic policies that restricted imports during the Great Depression

(C) Cold War rivalries that led to the increased production of consumer goods

(D) Communication and transportation technologies that promoted economic integration

589. Which of the following best describes the likely purpose of the cartoon?

(A) To demonstrate the benefits of alternative transportation methods

(B) To illustrate the effectiveness of environmental movements

(C) To show the hypocrisy of some who celebrate Earth Day

(D) To promote legislation designed to improve the environment

Questions 590–591 refer to the map below.

EUROPEAN UNION MAP

The map shows original members of the European Union (EU) when it formed in 1993, as well as nations admitted in 2007. The EU was created to reduce trade barriers among member nations.

590. The formation of the organization shown on the map best illustrates which of the following processes of the twentieth century?

(A) Regional trade agreements that reflected the spread of free-market principles and practices

(B) Movements that promoted regional trade and rejected participation in global trade

(C) Economic nationalism and government intervention in national economies

(D) Military alliances created in response to the rivalries that developed during the Cold War

591. Which of the following best explains the reason why nations of Eastern Europe were admitted later than the original members shown on the map?

(A) The continued control of those nations by the Soviet Union
(B) The collapse of communism and the end of the Cold War
(C) The resistance by fascist governments in those nations
(D) The onset of the Great Depression and the world wars

Questions 592–594 refer to the passage below.

"WE THE PEOPLES OF THE UNITED NATIONS DETERMINED

- to save succeeding generations from the scourge of war, which twice in our lifetime has brought untold sorrow to mankind, and
- to reaffirm faith in fundamental human rights, in the dignity and worth of the human person, in the equal rights of men and women and of nations large and small, and
- to establish conditions under which justice and respect for the obligations arising from treaties and other sources of international law can be maintained, and
- to promote social progress and better standards of life in larger freedom,

AND FOR THESE ENDS

- to practice tolerance and live together in peace with one another as good neighbours, and
- to unite our strength to maintain international peace and security, and
- to ensure, by the acceptance of principles and the institution of methods, that armed force shall not be used, save in the common interest, and
- to employ international machinery for the promotion of the economic and social advancement of all peoples..."

> Preamble to the United Nations Charter,
> signed by original member nations in 1945

592. The passage best illustrates which of the following processes of the twentieth century?

(A) The growth of institutions of global governance
(B) The spread of free-market economies
(C) The tensions between capitalist and communist powers
(D) The rise of regional trade agreements

593. The creation of the organization discussed in the passage is best understood in the context of which of the following?

    (A) The support for economic cooperation as a result of the Great Depression
    (B) The desire to prevent global conflict following World War I
    (C) The rivalry between the superpowers at the onset of the Cold War
    (D) The desire for international cooperation in the aftermath of World War II

594. Which of the following most directly <u>challenged</u> the principles set forth in the document in the late twentieth century?

    (A) Neocolonialism in Latin America that led to civil wars
    (B) Rebellions by groups seeking independence from imperial rulers
    (C) Conflicts between nations for control of resources, such as oil
    (D) Military alliances designed to prevent conflict

Questions 595–596 refer to the image below.

POSTER PROMOTING THE WINTER OLYMPICS IN LAKE PLACID, 1936

595. The participation in the event illustrated in the poster by most nations in the twentieth century illustrates which of the following?

    (A) Increasing cooperation and global interdependence
    (B) Increasing nationalism and economic self-sufficiency
    (C) Declining cooperation and increase in global conflict
    (D) Decreasing global integration and lack of diplomacy

596. Participation in the event illustrated in the poster contributed to which of the following?

   (A) The increased emphasis on athletics over politics
   (B) The globalization of popular culture
   (C) Decreased rivalries among nations
   (D) A decline in military conflicts

Short-Answer Questions

Answer all parts of the question that follows.

597. a) Identify ONE economic challenge of the twentieth century that led governments to take a more active role in economic life.

   b) Explain ONE difference between economic policies of communist states and newly independent states following World War II.

   c) Explain ONE similarity in the economic policies of governments in the period following the end of the Cold War.

Answer all parts of the question that follows.

598. a) Identify ONE reason why states have become increasingly interdependent in the twentieth century.

   b) Explain ONE change in the role of government in economic affairs in the period between 1900 and the present.

   c) Explain ONE continuity in economic patterns in the period between 1900 and the present.

Long Essay Questions

599. In the period 1900–2001, states responded in a variety of ways to economic challenges of the twentieth century.

   Develop an argument that evaluates how one or more states responded to economic challenges in this period.

600. In the period 1900–2001, people conceptualized society and culture in new ways; rights-based discourses challenged old assumptions about race, class, gender, and religion.

   Develop an argument that evaluates how rights-based discourses in one or more nations challenged previous assumptions about race, class, gender, or religion in this period.

(Answers on pages 379–383.)

ANSWERS

Note: Full Answers Explained with detailed explanations why the incorrect answers are wrong can be found at *www.barronsbooks.com/ap/docs/h72bdc/QA1125.pdf* or by using the QR code below.

CHAPTER 1: THE PEOPLING OF THE EARTH AND THE PALEOLITHIC AGE

1. **(B)** As shown on the map, our earliest human ancestors originated in Eastern Africa 3.6 million years ago. From there, a gradual migration occurred throughout Afro-Eurasia, then eventually to Oceania, and lastly to the Americas.

2. **(C)** Early humans often migrated when resources were limited or to follow herds.

3. **(B)** As humans migrated to a variety of climatic regions, they adapted to local environments through the development of a variety of technologies. For example, they harnessed fire, built homes with hearths, created textiles with pelts, and dug ice cellars into the permafrost for the storage of meats.

4. **(D)** Paleolithic people were nomadic due to their need to follow food sources. The people migrated seasonally to follow the animals they hunted.

5. **(A)** In the Paleolithic Age, or Old Stone Age, humans developed stone tools as shown in the image.

6. **(D)** Cave paintings of the Paleolithic Age, as shown in Image 2, often depicted animals and humans hunting. Some historians hypothesize that cave art had religious meaning, while others feel that it was used to plan hunts.

7. **(A)** The stone tools and cave paintings show that early humans used the materials and animals around them to survive.

8. **(C)** The authors claim that cultural transmission, or the transfer of knowledge, was responsible for the consistent supply of stone tools.

9. **(B)** Migrations occurred as resources became scarce, such as berries and edible plants, and to follow animals for hunting.

10. **(D)** As the passage indicates, humans were able to adapt to varied environments.

11. **(C)** In order to carve this sculpture out of stone, tools were necessary.

12. **(A)** Art often reflects the values of societies. Historians believe that figurines like the one shown are of fertility goddesses due to the emphasis on the reproductive parts of the female body.

13. **(B)** The author argues that "traditions, habits, and customs...were considered to be proven means of keeping small groups of people alive." In other words, they helped early humans sustain or preserve themselves.

14. **(D)** Foragers were superstitious due to the precarious, or dangerous, relationship with their surroundings.

15. **(C)** The various nomadic clans developed individual ideas about supernatural forces. Although these clans may have shared ideas with one another, organized belief systems did not develop.

CHAPTER 2: THE NEOLITHIC REVOLUTION AND EARLY AGRICULTURAL SOCIETIES

16. **(C)** The warming temperatures at the end of the last Ice Age led to a decline in Ice Age animals that were being hunted to extinction. Additionally, warming temperatures allowed for longer growing seasons that facilitated the expansion of agriculture.

17. **(A)** The question basically asks which was not an effect of the adoption of agriculture. Agriculture required an increase in cooperation among community members to clear land and to establish the irrigation systems necessary to domesticate crops successfully.

18. **(B)** The map demonstrates that a wide variety of crops were domesticated in various regions throughout the world.

19. **(D)** Some environments, such as the Eurasian steppe, were not conducive to the domestication of crops. Instead, these environments were more suitable to grazing domesticated animals. Those who move from place to place while grazing domesticated animals are known as pastoralists.

20. **(A)** A surplus of agriculture is necessary before settlements with larger populations can develop.

21. **(C)** Although a high degree of social stratification (as seen in later civilizations like that in Mesopotamia and Egypt) did not exist, varying home sizes may have reflected the development of early social classes.

22. **(C)** The agricultural surplus that made settlements like that shown in Image 2 possible also allowed for job specialization as some people had the ability to adopt occupations other than farming. Excavations at many Neolithic sites including Catalhöyük show evidence of jewelry production as well as pottery, basket, and textile production.

23. **(B)** The passage describes how the composition of the land determined the role of women. For example, in tropical climates, women helped with slash-

and-burn agriculture, so they had a higher status than in areas where farming was male dominated.

24. **(A)** As human populations have continued to grow, more land has been cleared for agriculture to support the larger populations. This negatively impacts the environment and contributes to less biodiversity.

25. **(D)** The passage describes how the rise of sedentary agriculture with animal-drawn plows led to fewer female cultivators.

26. **(B)** The passage discusses how the gods provided water for orchards and cattle, showing the link between farming and religion.

27. **(C)** The passage mentions the inundation, which is another term for flooding. Additionally, early civilizations that were heavily reliant on agriculture had a close but risky relationship with their surroundings.

28. **(A)** Both farming and herding societies had more dependable food sources (crops and animals), which enabled their populations to grow.

29. **(D)** The passage describes how environmental factors, such as flooding, impacted the view of the gods.

30. **(C)** The passage discusses the rise of villages and civilizations, which required cooperation to develop irrigation systems and clear land.

CHAPTER 3: THE RISE AND INTERACTIONS OF EARLY AGRICULTURAL, PASTORAL, AND URBAN SOCIETIES

31. **(A)** The passage shows that punishments varied depending on one's social class, indicating inequalities.

32. **(B)** The law code reflects the social distinctions that developed due to the rise of specialized jobs.

33. **(D)** Many rulers of early states claimed to be semidivine or protected by the gods.

34. **(C)** The carving shows a procession or parade of palace officials, which displays their power.

35. **(C)** The carving shows chariots, which was a new form of transportation first thought to be used by the Hittites when conquering Mesopotamia.

36. **(A)** Image 1 shows strong government, while Image 2 shows technological innovation.

37. **(D)** The passage demonstrates the Zhou dynasty's use of the concept of Mandate of Heaven, which claims that power is derived from the gods.

38. **(B)** Early states' authority depended on military power and support. Without support from the military, rulers of those early states could be overthrown. This is particularly true not only of China but of Mesopotamia as well.

39. **(C)** The passage indicates that the Zhou dynasty successfully overthrew the Shang dynasty. This led to the assumption that the Zhou had greater access to resources (including military resources) that gave them the advantage.

40. **(A)** The passage describes the concept of Mandate of Heaven. In this idea, the ruler who does not rule well and fulfill one's duties may be overthrown and a new ruler can claim the Mandate of Heaven.

41. **(A)** Bantu migrations were sparked by population growth, resulting in the need for more suitable farmland. Indo-European migrations were sparked by the need for more available pastureland.

42. **(B)** Both the Bantu and Indo-European migrations spread language and knowledge of ironwork to their respective regions.

43. **(D)** Egyptian pyramids reflected religious belief in the afterlife and were tombs for pharaohs.

44. **(B)** Throughout history, states have used large building projects (monumental architecture) to display their wealth and power, as this ziggurat did in Mesopotamia.

45. **(A)** In order to construct these buildings, labor had to be mobilized by the state.

46. **(a)** An acceptable response provides specific details on an economic change that occurred. An example of a specific response could include how "The Neolithic Revolution led to the development of private property, such as land and animal herds, due to the sedentary lifestyle." Other examples include the development of specialized jobs, such as artisans, priests, and rulers, and the division of labor among genders, leading to the rise of patriarchy.
    (b) An acceptable response explains a reason why an economic change occurred as a result of the Neolithic Revolution. A specific response could include how "Farmers settled in one place due to the need to stay with their crops and domesticated animals, so private ownership of land developed." Other examples include that food surpluses allowed some to specialize in a particular trade, such as pottery or metallurgy, rather than having every member of society producing his or her own food, or farming and herding was more physically taxing than hunting and gathering, so men tended to play a greater role in farm production, leading to patriarchal gender roles.
    (c) An acceptable response explains a continuity in lifestyles despite all the changes that occurred with the Neolithic Revolution. For example, a specific response could be how "Some people continued a nomadic way of life and gained food through hunting and gathering." Other examples include that there was a strong reliance on the environment for food production, and a lack of scientific knowledge prevented major technological adaptations to the environment, or religious beliefs concerning fertility were important due to the dependence on animal and soil fertility.

47. **(a)** An acceptable response explains a specific way pastoral and agricultural societies interacted, such as the transfer of weapon technologies from pastoralists to settled farmers, the trade of handicrafts from farmers to herders, or the conquest of settled societies by pastoralists.
(b) An acceptable response should include a specific similarity. For example, "Both pastoral and agricultural societies relied on animals and plants to provide sustenance, although the ways the societies obtained them differed." Other acceptable responses are that both societies cooperated with members of an extended family in order to get food for consumption or that the surrounding environment determined the plants and animals the societies could use.
(c) An acceptable response should provide a specific difference. For example, "Pastoral societies were nomadic and migrated, while agricultural societies were sedentary." Other differences are that pastoralists often lived in more arid regions, while farmers settled in areas where they could access water for irrigation, such as river valleys. Pastoralists often did not have food surpluses due to the need to maintain the herd, while cultivators were able to harvest and store or barter extra crops. Agriculturalists were more susceptible to the spread of diseases, while pastoralists were less susceptible.

48. **(a)** An acceptable response should not simply state a change as a result of the Neolithic Revolution (as in question 46, part a). Instead, the response must also link the change to the rise of civilizations. For example, "The adoption of agriculture led to larger populations that required organization and the eventual development of civilizations." Other acceptable responses could include that the development of private property led to disputes over land and attacks from nomadic groups, which led to civilizations with legal codes to address these issues.
(b) A good response should include a specific reason. For example, "Early civilizations developed in river valleys due to access to water for irrigation of crops as well as for bathing and transportation." Other reasons could include that flooding of the rivers contributed to soil fertility, which added to surpluses.
(c) A good response shows continuity throughout the entire period from circa 8000 B.C.E. (the Neolithic Revolution) to circa 600 B.C.E. (when classical civilizations and major world religions developed). Examples include the presence of nomadic societies despite the shift to agriculture by some, early agricultural centers that relied on mainly the same crops throughout the period, religious beliefs that were mainly polytheistic with nature gods, and the organization of farmers into villages and cities rather than highly centralized empires.

CHAPTER 4: THE DEVELOPMENT AND CODIFICATION OF RELIGIOUS TRADITIONS

49. **(A)** Confucianism emphasizes the importance of education for government officials rather than inherited positions based on social status, as reflected in the civil service examination system.

50. **(C)** The imperial examination system was first implemented during the Han dynasty in order to recruit officials based on their capabilities rather than on their family connections.

51. **(D)** The passage discusses proper behavior, including performing rituals, correct conduct, and education.

52. **(B)** Hinduism rejects the concept of social mobility through education. Instead, Hinduism promotes the idea of clear social distinctions through the caste system.

53. **(A)** The Hindu concept of karma, or the impact of one's actions on the fate of his/her soul, developed in the Vedic Age and influenced later South Asian belief systems.

54. **(B)** The edicts promoted the idea that all religions could be practiced because Ashoka, who converted to Buddhism, ruled over a mainly Hindu India and did not want to alienate his subjects.

55. **(C)** Most often long-standing religious traditions impact the law codes of empires because legal systems tend to reflect existing values rather than implement new values.

56. **(D)** Buddhism originated in South Asia and spread to China via the Silk Road trade networks.

57. **(C)** The caption notes that this Buddhist statue was commissioned or sponsored by the Indian King Ashoka, most likely to promote himself as a devout Buddhist.

58. **(B)** Throughout history, art and architecture have been products of their creators, who are shaped by cultural values such as religions.

59. **(A)** The passage illustrates the use of military force, shown when the Assyrians killed (slew) and hung rebels. The passage also shows diplomacy because some were pardoned and asked to pay tribute.

60. **(C)** The passage indicates that those who did not rebel were not killed although royal tribute was imposed upon them.

61. **(C)** The Assyrians were one of several groups that conquered Jewish populations, driving them out of their homeland and leading to the diaspora, or dispersal, of Jewish communities.

62. **(B)** The Bhagavad Gita is a Hindu holy text and Hinduism is the oldest major belief system in South Asia. Hinduism is based on indigenous and Aryan beliefs, such as dharma and reincarnation of the soul.

63. **(B)** The passage refers to duty, or dharma, several times. It also mentions an indestructible self in each person's body, referring to reincarnation.

64. **(A)** This passage mentions the idea that the self or soul is indestructible. The passage also implies that, for this reason, one should not grieve the death of his/her body.

65. **(D)** Buddhism rejects the caste system. Instead, Buddhism advocates the concept that anyone can attain enlightenment and end the cycle of rebirth.

66. **(C)** The map shows that Christianity spread in the Mediterranean basin while Buddhism spread via the Silk Road.

67. **(A)** In the first few centuries of Christianity's existence, Roman authorities persecuted Christian missionaries, saints, and their followers. Despite this, the faith spread due to its message of acceptance and spiritual equality.

68. **(B)** As Buddhism spread to various parts of Asia, the practices of the religion blended with native beliefs. This is known as syncretism.

69. **(A)** The Ten Commandments provided basic guidelines for Judaism, and the Old Testament of the Christian Bible is the holy text of Judaism.

70. **(C)** Many of the world's religions were founded during this era and provided guidelines for their followers.

71. **(A)** Islam drew upon the beliefs of Judaism and Christianity, and Islam developed in the early seventh century.

72. **(D)** This Daoist temple, built into a mountainside, reflects traditional Chinese architecture, which uses Daoist principles such as symmetry.

73. **(B)** Daoism rejects strong government and calls for an "unobtrusive" government.

74. **(C)** Buddhist, Daoist, and Confucian values diffused from China to Japan during period 3.

75. **(A)** The last line of the passage discusses how Indian and native traditions combined.

76. **(D)** The passage discusses how rulers of Southeast Asia linked themselves to gods and goddesses to legitimize their rule.

77. **(B)** It shows that the native Animist beliefs of Southeast Asians were being practiced by nonelites.

78. **(B)** The direct links between South and Southeast Asia would have developed due to sea trade in the Indian Ocean basin.

79. **(a)** An acceptable response provides a specific link between Hinduism and the rise of Buddhism. For example, "The founder of Buddhism, Siddhartha Gautama, was a Hindu prince who embraced the Hindu concepts of reincarnation, karma, and dharma when developing the core set of beliefs of the religion."

(b) An acceptable response states a detailed similarity in the beliefs of both Hinduism and Buddhism, not just in describing both religions. For example, both have a goal of ending the cycle of rebirth (*moksha* in Hinduism and nirvana in Buddhism). They both teach that one's karma is the result of one's actions and that each individual has a duty to fulfill, or dharma.

(c) An acceptable response provides a clear difference between Hinduism and Buddhism. Examples can include Hinduism having a caste system, and Buddhism rejecting caste and propagating the idea that anyone can achieve enlightenment. Hinduism is monistic in nature, while the original form of Buddhism is nontheistic. Hinduism teaches that past lives influence one's fate. However, Buddhism teaches that an individual's ability to achieve enlightenment and salvation is not dependent on his/her social status or past lives.

80. (a) An acceptable response states a specific cultural change. Examples include the increased value placed on education due to the Confucian idea that education makes a gentleman, the emphasis on family relationships, and the concept of filial piety.

(b) An acceptable response includes a change that links Confucianism to ideas about government. Examples include the implementation of the civil service exam to recruit knowledgeable bureaucrats and the idea that the ruler must act as a role model but, in return, the people must obey.

(c) An acceptable continuity must have occurred for much of Chinese history through 600 C.E. and should identify principles from ancient China that influenced new belief systems, such as ancestor veneration and the concept of Mandate of Heaven.

81. This LEQ question focuses on the reasoning skill of change and continuity over time. It examines the link between religion and government. The essay should include a thesis that makes a claim outlining at least two major changes. You may choose only one example on which to focus. However, a stronger essay should show a complex understanding of the issue. One of the ways to do so is to include a variety of examples as evidence to show nuances. One point is earned for providing examples relevant to the question. A second point is earned for supporting an argument in response to the question. In order to earn the second point, the essay should clearly link the evidence back to the claims made in the thesis. Two of the examples that would work best for this question are the influence of Hinduism in the Mauryan and Gupta Empires of India and the influence of Confucianism in the Han dynasty. The Indian empires changed when the government embraced Hindu principles that reinforced the caste system. Legal codes were based on Hindu concepts, which continued earlier traditions regarding gender roles and the nature of the caste system. The introduction of Confucianism in China provided the basis for the civil service system to select bureaucrats. It also reinforced the existing concept of Mandate of Heaven by ensuring that the ruler act as a role model or be overthrown. The key concept is the idea that belief

systems reflected existing social and gender structures (continuity) and that governments embraced aspects of belief systems that reinforced their rule or made it easier to govern (change). Contextualization must be explained for each region used. For example, Confucianism rose during the Warring States period to find the best way to create an orderly society. The Han dynasty embraced Confucianism once the Qin dynasty unified the various warring states. The tradition of the civil service exam was continued by most dynasties because it limited the influence of noble families. In addition to a thesis, contextualization and specific evidence-analysis is needed. One point is earned for explaining the reasons for the changes. For example, one point can be earned for stating that as a result of Hindu beliefs that reinforced the caste system, the Gupta government ensured social stability. A second point can be earned if the essay demonstrates historical complexity, which could be earned by explaining continuities or by making connections across history. For example, a pattern throughout history is that rebellions occurred among the lower classes because of resentment of their position in society. However, the beliefs of karma and dharma redirected blame for social inequalities from the government to one's actions in a past life. This is one of the reasons why governments embraced these belief systems.

82. This essay is assessing the skill of comparison and is focused on the similarities between two belief systems. To earn the contextualization point, the essay should discuss how the transformation of river valley civilizations into larger empires and greater trade connections via the Silk Road and Indian Ocean trade networks led to the spread of ideas. The historical development for the religions to be examined can be described as well. This would be the rise of Christianity in the Roman Empire or the rise of Confucianism and Daoism during the Warring States period.

For this question, choose two belief systems that originated in the same region—such as Hinduism and Buddhism, Judaism and Christianity, or Confucianism and Daoism. Explain similarities and the greater historical context. The thesis statement should identify two to three major similarities. Throughout the essay, evidence must be used to support the argument. The reasoning skill of comparison must be demonstrated throughout the essay, which identifies and explains the similarities and the reasons for them. Examples of a thesis that makes a claim could be that Hinduism and Buddhism were similar in their beliefs in reincarnation, the goal of the end of the cycle of rebirth, and the concepts of karma and dharma. However, they differed in the way they believed one could achieve salvation. Examples of major similarities between Judaism and Christianity could include the ethical code embodied in the Ten Commandments and the roles of Abraham and Moses as prophets from God. A reason for this similarity could be that Christianity drew upon Jewish traditions due to their common place of origin and Jesus's Jewish upbringing. To show historical complexity, differences can be explained or how the similarities identified in the essay result from similar circumstances. A major difference could include the belief of Christians that Jesus of Nazareth was the Messiah as opposed to the Jewish belief that the Messiah has yet to arrive.

> **Note:** Full Answers Explained with detailed explanations why the incorrect answers are wrong can be found at *www.barronsbooks.com/ap/docs/h72bdc/QA1125.pdf* or by using the QR code below.
>
>

CHAPTER 5: THE DEVELOPMENT OF STATES AND EMPIRES

83. **(C)** The passage discusses both the political roles of the consuls, such as managing magistrates, interacting with the senate, and calling general assemblies, as well as the military role, such as preparing for war.

84. **(A)** The passage shows how consuls used institutions, the senate in this case, to manage the empire.

85. **(D)** Roman consuls were most like the absolute monarchs of the early modern period of Europe in that both groups managed political and military affairs.

86. **(B)** As the Roman Empire expanded, spending for defense and administration increased. This led to increased taxation and economic difficulties for the empire's citizens.

87. **(D)** The Great Wall connected walled cities to defend against borderland nomadic tribes.

88. **(C)** The Han dynasty replaced the Qin dynasty and united the areas formerly under Qin rule with areas south and west.

89. **(A)** The Han used the civil service exam to ensure that bureaucrats who carried out the emperor's policies were educated.

90. **(B)** The Persians used the Royal Road to improve communication. They also developed a bureaucracy with satraps ruling as governors to administer the expansive empire.

91. **(C)** The Persians developed a bureaucracy in order to administer the empire. The empire was divided into districts called satrapies that were governed by satraps who each ruled individual regions and reported back to the emperor.

92. **(C)** Urban areas typically develop as centers of commerce and government due to the concentration of people and resources in one area.

93. **(D)** The Roman Empire expanded rapidly in the Mediterranean region, which greatly increased the empire's population and thus the number of citizens of military age.

94. **(A)** The statistics show that the population was increasing, which was due to expansion through a strong military. This caused the Roman government to raise taxes, which put a strain on the lower classes and created a large gap between the rich and the poor.

95. **(B)** Like the Romans, the Ottomans expanded rapidly by conquering groups on their borders in the Mediterranean basin using a strong army and navy. This expansion led to a larger population within the empire.

96. **(C)** The passages emphasize the different areas of the city that various castes (Kshatrya, Vaisya, Sudra, Bráhmans) lived in, while Buddhism promotes spiritual equality and the idea that anyone can achieve salvation.

97. **(D)** The second passage shows patriarchal values in that women have to wait for fairly long periods of time for their husbands to return, depending on their caste.

98. **(A)** The passages show that the treatise determined where members of each caste lived in the fort as well as rules regarding marriage relationships.

99. **(A)** Ashoka was known for displaying edicts throughout the empire on large stone pillars that showed the influence of his Buddhist faith.

100. **(B)** The image shows the king being depicted as powerful.

101. **(C)** Cities usually serve these purposes because people are concentrated in one area, which is helpful in running a government, conducting business, and performing rituals.

102. **(D)** It is thought that Mayan city-states may have strained resources to the point where the environment could not support a large population. Alternatively, it may have declined due to warfare among competing city-states.

103. **(C)** Nomadic invaders often attacked Roman cities, which were centers of trade and seats of government. Invaders could pillage and loot these cities.

104. **(A)** The Roman Empire declined due to tensions between social classes because high taxation was needed to fund the military and bureaucracy.

105. **(C)** Invasions caused urban decline, leading to the rise of feudalism as people fled to the countryside. In addition, the Byzantine Empire ruled the area for another millennium.

106. **(B)** The passage states that war captives in Rome were "sold off to private bidders," whereas in the Han, war captives were "turned into forced laborers or drafted into the military."

107. **(D)** The passage focuses on slavery and labor systems, which is one of the main avenues of food production.

108. **(A)** Slaves were brought from Africa and sold at auction to provide labor on plantations in the Americas.

109. **(C)** The civil service exam was implemented to ensure that bureaucrats were educated and capable. Since the positions were earned rather than inherited through family, they served to limit the influence of large landowning families.

110. **(C)** The passage is claiming that government officials ("generals and soldiers and lordlings of prominent offices in the city") are collecting taxes (exactions) above what is owed, are taking oxen, and are disturbing their livelihood, showing the weakening of government.

111. **(B)** The passage shows that a bureaucracy was in place, although it was corrupt.

112. **(A)** Corruption eroded faith in the government and rebellions occurred in response to ineffective rulers.

113. **(a)** A good response includes at least one new technique and the empire that employed it. Examples could include the satrap system in Persia that used satraps, or governors, to manage regions of the empire; the civil service examination system in Han China to choose bureaucrats who had the required knowledge of governance and Confucian values; or the Twelve Tables of Roman law that outlined the legal system for the republic.
     (b) A good response should identify a similarity among two specific empires. For example, Roman, Han, and Persian bureaucracies were used to manage their large empires (choose two of the three empires); the use of defensive walls to protect the empire, such as Hadrian's Wall in the Roman Empire and the Great Wall of China in the Han; or the use of roads to improve communication in the Han, Roman, and Persian Empires (again, choose two of the three empires).
     (c) A good response should explain a difference between two empires, not simply a unique aspect of one empire. Examples include the Han civil service exam that limited the influence of landowning families, while the Roman government officials, including senators, were mostly from wealthy families; or the use of a state religion by Roman emperors to justify their rule, as opposed to the Han emperor's worship of traditional gods but not claiming divinity.

114. **(a)** A good response includes a specific change that caused an empire to decline. Examples include the difficulty that the Roman, Gupta, and Han Empires faced in defending their borders from nomadic tribes; the loss of faith in the government in the Roman Empire due to corruption; and peasant rebellions due to unequal land distribution in the Han dynasty.
     (b) A good response explains how a change led to the fall. For example, the difficulties faced by the Roman and Han dynasties in protecting their borders enabled nomadic invaders to raid cities, causing discontent and loss of faith in the political system and the eventual collapse of the government. Another reason could be that peasant rebellions in the Han were a signal that

the emperor had lost the Mandate of Heaven, which justified the overthrow of his rule.

(c) A good response identifies a continuity despite the changes outlined above. For example, despite the collapse of the Han dynasty, Confucian values remained the core principles guiding family relationships or how the caste system that shaped the social hierarchy in classical India remained despite the collapse of centralized imperial rule.

115. This LEQ question focuses on the reasoning skill of causation, particularly the causes of the expansion of empires. The essay should include a thesis that makes a claim outlining the major causes and makes a judgment as to what contributed most to the success of the empire. The thesis must be specific. For example, "Empires in the period from 600 B.C.E. to 600 C.E., such as the Roman and Persian Empires, used large militaries, complex bureaucracies, and religious ideas to govern." You may choose one example on which to focus. However, a stronger essay would show a complex understanding of the issue. One of the ways to do this is to use a variety of examples as evidence. For example, if focusing on the Roman Empire, the causes of expansion could include the organized military that took advantage of the power vacuum that resulted from the collapse of the Hellenistic empires; the use of a bureaucracy to manage the vast empire; the construction of infrastructure, such as roads and aqueducts; or incorporating conquered groups into the empire and granting them citizenship. Historical context could include the rise of the Roman Republic. This rise includes expansion of Roman imperial rule in the eastern Mediterranean as a result of the conquest of Greek city-states. It also includes disintegration of the Persian Empire following the death of Alexander the Great, which enabled Roman expansion. The evidence provided in the essay must discuss how the developments helped the empire govern. For analysis, the essay should discuss why each development was necessary or how it helped the government overcome a challenge. To demonstrate historical complexity, the methods of various empires could be compared or the reasons why the methods of governments differed could be discussed. The essay could also make connections to later empires and the methods those empires used.

116. This essay question focuses on the skill of causation. The essay should explain how challenges led to the fall of one or more empires. For contextualization, the broader picture should be explained, such as what things enabled these empires to rise to power or how nomads were attracted to the wealth of empires and then later threatened them with attacks on their borders. The essay may focus on one empire and use it as a case study for imperial decline or could examine several empires. If examining the decline of the Roman Empire, specific evidence should include the political reasons such as corruption among bureaucrats and fights over succession. Also a discussion of social tensions can be included, such as resentment of the large slave class by small landowning peasants, or economic issues such as military

and administrative expenses that led to high taxation. This contributed to anger among the lower classes and loss of loyalty. To demonstrate historical reasoning, the evidence provided must link back to the question by clearly explaining what the challenge was and why that caused the empire to decline. An example of historical complexity would be to explain how two or more empires can be compared, or how the fall of the empires led to new states developing in these regions—reconstituted states. For example, the Eastern Roman Empire was able to survive despite the fall of the Western Roman Empire. Additionally, the Byzantine Empire incorporated some Roman values, such as legal principles, while developing innovative techniques.

CHAPTER 6: EMERGENCE OF INTERREGIONAL NETWORKS OF COMMUNICATION AND EXCHANGE

117. **(C)** In this period, the domestication of the camel enabled caravans to travel longer distances with their goods.

118. **(B)** The map shows the extension of trade across regions (transregional), which contributed to larger networks of exchange as various regional networks became connected.

119. **(A)** Islam spread to sub-Saharan Africa via trans-Saharan routes due to trade connections between Berber merchants, many of whom adopted Islam, and merchants of both Ghana and Mali.

120. **(D)** The introduction of new crops to the Middle East led to the need for irrigation systems, such as *qanats*.

121. **(A)** Water wheels were constructed to bring water to higher elevations. Water wheels were developed to adapt to the dry climate.

122. **(C)** The two images show technologies that provided water to crops. Both of these technologies developed due to the introduction of rice and cotton to the Middle East.

123. **(C)** Technologies such as the compass enabled merchants to travel long distances.

124. **(B)** Diseases spread via trade routes and greatly impacted cities since people were concentrated in cities. The spread of pathogens further weakened the Roman and Han Empires by lowering their populations.

125. **(A)** The Han dynasty fell in 220 C.E. and the Roman Empire fell in 476 C.E., so they were on the decline in this time frame, which led to decreased trade as wealth and their economies declined.

126. **(B)** The map shows both land and sea routes that connected the Han and Roman Empires.

127. **(D)** The image shows that the caves were built into the existing hillside, most likely using locally available materials.

128. **(D)** Religions often change as they spread because they tend to blend with existing beliefs. The Chinese depiction of Buddha shown in the statue is different from an Indian depiction, which would portray the Buddha as more serious in facial expression and more slender in build. This is due to the use of an image of an existing Chinese deity by Buddhist missionaries to gain converts.

129. **(C)** Christianity spread along trade routes. Christian merchants may have settled in this trading city and maintained their beliefs.

130. **(A)** The Mediterranean region has natural harbors and a variety of resources due to the wealth and diversity of the Roman Empire.

131. **(B)** Christianity originated in modern-day Israel in the Middle East, and Christian missionaries took advantage of Mediterranean routes to spread the faith.

132. **(C)** Both overland routes and sea routes existed throughout Eurasia.

133. **(A)** Merchants traveling in the Indian Ocean learned the monsoon wind patterns to determine the best times of the year to travel in each direction.

134. **(D)** Trading connections between India and Southeast Asia led to the spread of both Hinduism and Buddhism.

135. **(C)** Merchants throughout history have been responsible for transmitting cultural traditions, such as language, religion, and food to new areas. Merchants bring those elements with them as they travel.

136. **(A)** Advances in technology enabled merchants to travel longer distances, which extended the trade networks and integrated more groups and goods.

137. **(B)** The Silk Road linked previously disconnected areas, leading to the spread of disease to groups that did not have immunity to the pathogens.

138. **(B)** The Han dynasty was relatively stable and had a surplus at this time, which explains the increase in population.

139. **(C)** Toward the end of the Roman Empire, invasions by Germanic tribes and the Huns ravaged cities and led to population decline.

140. **(A)** The declining population led to economic difficulties in both empires as labor shortages occurred.

141. **(C)** Bentley claims that "demographic collapse aggravated social and economic difficulties."

142. **(D)** The populations of cities declined drastically because diseases spread rapidly. This occurred due to the close contact of people living within cities.

143. **(B)** The Mongols helped to revive Silk Road trade by protecting trade and by decreasing risks to merchants since they controlled the entire length.

144. **(C)** The passage shows how the practice of Buddhism varied depending on who was practicing it and where it was being practiced. The author refers to different sects and how Indian beliefs spread to Central Asia.

145. **(A)** The passage refers to the Hinayana or Theravada sect of Buddhism as well as varied practices among commoners and monks in Central Asia.

146. **(D)** Religious pilgrims often used existing trade routes since there were services available for travelers and knowledge of the physical area.

147. **(a)** A good response should provide a specific effect of trade, ideally on a particular region. Some examples include the spread of Buddhism from India to China and eventually to Korea and Japan due to Silk Road trade, the spread of Confucian values to Southeast Asia, and the spread of Christianity to trading cities on the Silk Road.
     (b) A good response highlights a similarity in the causes of the rise of these trade routes. For example, both were aided by the adoption of new technologies that allowed merchants to engage in long-distance travel, such as the knowledge of monsoon winds and the use of pack animals.
     (c) A good response notes a distinction between impact of the Silk Road and Indian Ocean trade. For example, the Silk Road facilitated the spread of Buddhism from South to East Asia. In contrast, Indian Ocean trade contributed to the spread of Hinduism and Buddhism to Southeast Asia. Another example is that the Silk Road contributed to the spread of disease, which led to the decline of the Roman and Han Empires. The Indian Ocean trade routes, however, did not spread pathogens as rapidly, nor did the spread of disease contribute to the decline of empires in the region.

148. **(a)** A good response clearly states a specific change that occurred within this period. For example, Silk Road trade declined as the Han and Roman Empires declined. Silk Road trade fell because uncertain political times weakened the economies of these empires, which lowered the demand for luxury goods that were mainly traded long distances.
     (b) A good response discusses a specific link between the growth of interregional trade and economic growth within empires. For example, participation in the Silk Road trade networks integrated the Han dynasty into existing trade routes. This increased demand for the production of luxuries such as silk and porcelain and therefore strengthened China's economy. Increased trade increased tax revenues.
     (c) A good response provides a social or cultural continuity that remained for most of the time period. For example, the caste system dominated Indian society regardless of the new ideas that were introduced and despite the rise and fall of the Mauryan and Gupta Empires. In addition, Confucianism guided relationships and family life through and after the collapse of the Qin and Han dynasties.

149. This essay is assessing the historical reasoning skill of change and continuity over time. A good response examines the technological factors that contributed to the growth of long-distance trade in this period and makes a judgment as to which factor had the greatest impact. For example, the domestication of pack animals, such as camels and horses, enabled merchants to travel longer

distances with more goods. This led to the greater availability of goods, particularly luxuries. As a result, Silk Road networks developed, which led to the spread of Christianity and Buddhism. In the Indian Ocean basin, increased understanding of monsoon wind patterns allowed merchants to avoid becoming stranded in ports overseas and allowed the merchants to undertake voyages at times that would allow them to maximize their time away. Discussing empires that rose up in this period and generated wealth provides relevant context. This includes the expansion of the Roman and Han Empires. Historical complexity could be addressed through the examination of continuities, such as the trade of luxury goods since they would be the most profitable.

150. This question is assessing the skill of causation. A good response makes a claim that discusses the effects of the expansion of empires on trade while providing specific historical evidence to justify the assertion. Contextualization could describe the reasons for the expansion of empires and how stable governments both led to wealth and increased the demand for luxuries. The thesis should clearly identify two to three ways the growth of empires, such as Roman and Han, impacted trade. Specific evidence could include how the rise of Silk Road trade between the Roman and Han Empires led to the spread of Buddhism from South Asia to China because the Silk Road enabled missionaries to travel. In addition, the growth of Mediterranean trade spread Christianity throughout the Roman Empire despite persecution of Christians by the government. Another example of an effect is that increased contact between groups of people led to the spread of pathogens that eventually contributed to the decline of the Han and Roman Empires. The spread of crops from South Asia to the Middle East led to new farming techniques and increased yields led to population growth. For historical complexity, examining the effects of the decline of empires on trade routes and the long-term effects of the decline could be addressed.

CHAPTER 7: EXPANSION AND INTENSIFICATION OF COMMUNICATION AND EXCHANGE NETWORKS

151. **(B)** In the period 600–1450 c.e., trade intensified due to the rise of credit, bills of exchange, checks, banking houses, and paper money. All of these facilitated commerce and decreased the risks associated with carrying gold and silver.

152. **(A)** The development and spread of technologies, such as the compass and astrolabe, and the improvement of ship design enabled merchants to travel long distances by sea.

153. **(C)** Crops and diseases spread at the end of the classical period and throughout the postclassical era.

154. **(D)** Indian Ocean basin trade was mainly conducted by Arab Muslim merchants who retained their religion when they traveled to different cities

and sometimes settled in new regions. Diasporic communities are those that are dispersed from their original homeland.

155. **(B)** Trade contacts led to the spread of knowledge among cultures.

156. **(C)** The passage refers to humiliations faced by Christians which resulted from the Crusades, since Christians attempted to take back holy sites from Muslim control.

157. **(D)** The description of the beauty and workmanship, as well as the use of gold and marble, in this place where Muslims believe Muhammad (referred to in the passage as "the Prophet") ascended into heaven, shows the mosque's importance in the religion.

158. **(A)** Several travelers in this period documented their journeys, such as Marco Polo, Ibn Battuta, and Xuanzang.

159. **(A)** The Chinese government sponsored the construction of the Grand Canal. The goal was to improve trade between the northern and southern regions of China since most of China's rivers flowed from west to east.

160. **(B)** Both the Grand Canal and Incan roads facilitated trade within the empires by connecting various regions.

161. **(D)** Zhouzhang's location on the Grand Canal enabled residents to import goods from other cities and regions. The Grand Canal even indirectly connected the city to the Silk Road.

162. **(A)** The Grand Canal connected Beijing in the north with the rice-growing regions in the south. This allowed for increased commerce and for taxes, in the form of rice, to be sent to the capital.

163. **(C)** The Bantu were farmers who spread knowledge of cultivation and iron metallurgy as they migrated and settled in new areas.

164. **(C)** As Polynesian migrants settled in islands across Oceania (the Pacific region), they brought new plants and domesticated animals with them, spreading knowledge.

165. **(D)** Camel caravans and the establishment of routes through the desert enabled merchants to travel longer distances.

166. **(A)** More contact through trade exposed more people to Islam. Additionally, merchants of West Africa often converted to improve trading relationships with Muslims of North Africa.

167. **(C)** Both sides agreed to allow access to merchants from the other region and provide legal protection.

168. **(A)** The Hanseatic League was a trading organization of northern Europe that led to increased commerce in the region.

169. **(B)** Trade goes beyond the exchange of goods because it usually leads to the spread of knowledge, religion, and technology.

170. **(B)** As empires expanded, more people were brought into trade networks, which led to increased volume of trade and a greater variety of goods.

171. **(D)** The Caliphate and Delhi Sultanate were Muslim-ruled empires that conquered the areas shown. The Delhi Sultanate established control in northern India in areas where missionaries had worked to gain converts.

172. **(C)** Use of the compass improved travel and the establishment of caravanserai, or rest houses, improved conditions for merchants.

173. **(A)** Contact among new groups of people led to the exchange of plants and diseases.

174. **(C)** The bubonic plague or Black Death spread along the Silk Road in this period, leading to the loss of approximately one-third of Europe's population.

175. **(C)** The passage indicates that the spread of disease was "revealing the judgments of God." In other words, it was a punishment from God.

176. **(D)** The sudden death of roughly one-third of the population led to fewer workers, so the survivors were able to negotiate for lower dues or move off of manors to take city jobs, which weakened serfdom.

177. **(A)** The author describes how nomads in Central and East Asia "did not attempt to displace existing cultural establishments or to impose foreign values."

178. **(C)** As the Turks conquered Anatolia, which is modern-day Turkey, they imposed their language on the region.

179. **(D)** The Ottoman Empire was founded by nomadic Turks led by Osman the Great. They conquered the Anatolian Peninsula and the remains of the Byzantine Empire.

180. **(B)** Nomadic expansion, especially that of the Mongols, increased trade connections. This occurred because the nomads controlled the entire length of the Silk Road, making it safer to travel.

181. **(a)** A good response provides a specific piece of information and relates it back to the author's argument. The concept of southernization is the idea that the Southern hemisphere became integrated through trade. Examples of evidence to support this could include the spread of Islam from the Middle East to South and Southeast Asia due to the establishment of diasporic communities by Arab merchants; the diffusion of Chinese goods throughout the Indian Ocean basin, such as silk, porcelain, and iron tools; and the wealth of the Swahili city-states in Eastern Africa due to their role as intermediaries in trade between the Indian Ocean and the interior of Africa.
(b) A good response must explain how the process of southernization paved the way for westernization in later periods. For example, when Europeans arrived in the Indian Ocean basin beginning in the fifteenth century, European trading companies were able to expand by using routes and ports that were well established. These companies served as transporters of goods that had already

been in production by local merchants. This helped fuel industrialization that led to Western imperialism. Another example could be that Europeans used silver from the Americas to inject themselves into the existing spice trade. Europeans also used gunpowder technologies to establish trading posts and colonies that contributed to expansion in the nineteenth century.

(c) A good response explains how the Crusades helped bring Europe into existing trading networks. For example, due to increased contact between Europeans and Arabs, Europeans gained exposure to Asian goods that were not common in Western Europe since the fall of the Roman Empire and the rise of feudalism. This led to increased trade and cultural diffusion. It also spread technologies to Western Europe, such as the compass and medical knowledge.

182. (a) A good response shows understanding of the reasons for expansion of trade that led to the flourishing of trading cities and caravanserai, which served as rest stops for merchant caravans. For example, trade routes connected larger empires and more people, which contributed to a greater volume of trade. Also, the expansion of the Mongol Empire facilitated trade by protecting trade routes.

(b) A good response identifies a pattern of trade in this era. For example, throughout this period, the goods traded by merchants who utilized the caravanserai were mainly luxury items—such as silk, porcelain, ivory, and spices. This was due to the expense of trading across long distances.

(c) A good response explains the increase in trade that resulted from Mongol expansion. For example, the Mongols controlled the Silk Road trading networks, which made it safer for merchants to travel longer distances. In addition, the Mongols had a courier system that improved communication.

183. This question is assessing the skill of change and continuity over time. A strong thesis identifies at least two changes in trade networks as a result of technologies and commercial practices. For example, "In the period 600–1450, improved ship designs and navigational tools increased the reach of Indian Ocean trade, while the development of money economies intensified trade networks across Afro-Eurasia." Contextualization could discuss the revival of empires after the fall of classical empires. Contextualization could also discuss the rise of Islam, which provided a common cultural background for merchants, particularly in the Indian Ocean basin. In the essay, specific evidence must be used to support the argument and the reasons why these changes occurred must be explained. For example, the increased knowledge of the patterns of the monsoon winds contributed to more reliable transportation in the Indian Ocean because merchants would not be as concerned with becoming stranded overseas. Other evidence includes how new tools, such as the compass and astrolabe, made voyages more accurate and therefore less risky. Another change that could be described would be in commercial practices, such as the extension of credit and the use of currencies, which made trade less risky. For historical complexity, a

discussion of continuities could be included, such as the use of existing ports to transport luxuries and the continued connections between Indian Ocean trade and the Silk Road.

184. This essay question assesses the skill of causation. A strong thesis would make a claim regarding two or three effects of the growth of empires on trade networks. Contextualization could discuss the causes of the revival of empires after the fall of the classical empires before 600 C.E.; mentioning technological developments that contributed to merchants' ability to travel longer distances could also work. Effects could include the support of trade through imperial economic policies, how the increased wealth and stability of new empires led to greater demand for goods, and commercial growth due to state practices. One example of state practices that could be used is how the rise of the Mongol Empire in the twelfth and thirteenth centuries led to the revival of Silk Road trade. Another example includes the establishment of the Islamic Caliphates, which promoted trade and led to the spread of Islam as Arab merchants set out for new ports. Examples of how the wealth and stability of empires enabled trade to thrive could include the diffusion of technologies such as the spread of the compass from China, and the spread of the number system and concept of zero from India. To demonstrate historical complexity, continuities could be discussed, such as using the knowledge of monsoon wind patterns to plan travel; the transport of mainly luxury goods, such as silk, porcelain, tea, and spices; and the spread of belief systems, such as Buddhism and Islam.

185. This DBQ is assessing the skill of comparison and your ability to create an argument using historical evidence. An acceptable thesis makes a claim that identifies differences in attitudes of these groups toward their respective religions. For example, Christians mainly faced persecution as the faith spread through the Roman Empire, whereas West African kingdoms embraced Islam. The broader context for Christianity could include the idea that the Roman state religion claimed divinity of the emperor, which Christians rejected due to their monotheistic beliefs. For West Africa, a description of how the trans-Saharan trade networks linked West Africans to Muslim merchants could be included. Evidence from at least six documents should be used to prove the claim made in the thesis. For three of the documents, the essay must address the significance of the point of view, purpose, historical situation/context, and/or the audience. For example, document 4 was written by a bishop after Constantine's death. So the author is likely emphasizing Constantine's devotion to God and connections to priests to enhance his own authority. Evidence beyond the documents must also be provided but cannot be the same evidence used for contextualization. For example, the end of persecution of the Christians and the establishment of Christianity as the official religion of the empire can be elaborated on, or the reasons for the conversion to Islam by West African kings could be discussed. An explanation of change over time could be used to demonstrate complexity. For example, persecution

of Christians continued while the Roman Empire was thriving. Then the religion came to be embraced as the empire was on the decline. Similarities to demonstrate historical complexity could explain how leaders eventually embraced these new monotheistic faiths with the adoption of Christianity by Constantine and the pilgrimage to Mecca by Mansa Musa.

CHAPTER 8: INTERACTIONS AMONG NEW AND RECONSTITUTED STATES

186. **(C)** The introduction of the law code claims that God is overseeing the success of the empire. This code is essentially streamlining and reordering Roman laws, both of which are used to "prove" that Justinian is the legitimate ruler of the Byzantine Empire.

187. **(B)** This legal code drew upon Roman law but was adapted to suit Justinian's philosophy of rule.

188. **(A)** Feudal Europe consisted of many weak kingdoms that lacked bureaucracies and legal codes, whereas the Byzantine Empire was centralized.

189. **(D)** The Byzantine Empire was the surviving eastern half of the Roman Empire, which had been split in an attempt to save the empire.

190. **(B)** This is the first time period in which the Koreans paid tribute to the Chinese emperor as a sign of respect.

191. **(C)** The diplomatic missions to China resulted in the Japanese adoption of Buddhism, Neoconfucianism, technologies, and architectural styles.

192. **(D)** The Tang dynasty's participation in Silk Road trade led to the spread of ideas between China and the Abbasid Caliphate of the Middle East, such as medical knowledge and tools for navigation.

193. **(A)** The purpose of Zheng He's voyages was to establish trade relations. The presence of the mural shows that his arrival had a lasting impact.

194. **(D)** Chinese voyages resulted in the spread of knowledge into Southeast Asia.

195. **(B)** The lack of the presence of the Chinese navy enabled European merchants to establish trading posts throughout the Indian Ocean basin.

196. **(C)** The passage discusses the idea of filial piety, or respect for elders. It also discusses the idea that the ruler and other superiors should act as role models for the people.

197. **(B)** The passage shows the influence of Neoconfucianism, which is a combination of traditional Chinese beliefs.

198. **(A)** The Mongols invaded China and dismantled many Chinese traditions during the Yuan dynasty, such as the civil service system.

199. **(D)** The Crusades led to increased contact between Christians and Muslims as crusaders traveled to the Holy Land.

200. **(C)** While Western Europe was in the Dark Ages, Muslims were experiencing a Golden Age with advances in medicine. Increased contact between these groups led to the transfer of knowledge.

201. **(B)** The passage describes how the Incan government redistributed food and supplies to those in need, which indicates that the government was centralized.

202. **(A)** The Spanish conquistador was an outsider, so the author may not have fully understood the government system.

203. **(C)** The Spanish took advantage of a civil war that broke out among the Inca. The Spanish conquered the Incan Empire and colonized the area.

204. **(D)** The *daimyo* and nobles in Japan and Europe, respectively, were the landowners in each society, and they are the upper class.

205. **(A)** The fall of the Roman Empire due to Germanic invasions led people to flee the cities and to agree to provide service to a landowner in exchange for protection.

206. **(C)** The Meiji Restoration in the late nineteenth century led to the end of the feudal system and the establishment of a centralized government under the rule of the emperor.

207. **(B)** The khanates were ruled by individual khans, or rulers, once the empire was split.

208. **(B)** The Mongols were able to conquer such a large area due to strategies employed by their cavalry and their access to gunpowder from the Tang dynasty.

209. **(A)** The Mongol Empire controlled the Silk Road, which increased trade and the spread of ideas. Under Mongol control, the Silk Road became a much safer route to travel than it had been previously.

210. **(C)** The image shows a lord, which shows the expansion of imperial states from the previous rule of the Olmecs.

211. **(D)** Art is often commissioned by the elites in a given society to promote themselves, and this vessel depicts a lord.

212. **(A)** The Maya were decentralized, comprised of city-states. (Note that this may seem contradictory to question 210. However, that question asks about the Americas in general, while this specifically asks about the Maya.)

213. **(B)** Cambodia is in Southeast Asia, and this image shows a temple that was originally devoted to a Hindu god but eventually became a Buddhist temple.

214. **(D)** Indian Ocean trade contributed to the spread of the South Asian belief systems of Hinduism and Buddhism.

215. **(A)** Hinduism and Buddhism developed in South Asia, modern-day India, while this image shows that these religions were practiced in Southeast Asia.

216. **(a)** A good response identifies a specific change that resulted from increased contact between the Chinese navy and ports in the Indian Ocean basin. For example, the voyages established new trade relationships between Chinese merchants and merchants in the ports that were visited. These relationships lasted beyond the voyages and expanded commerce in the region. Another change that resulted was how the Chinese government projected military authority to new areas such as South Asia and East Africa through the use of a large navy.

     (b) A good response explains a continuity in the Indian Ocean basin, such as the trade in specific luxury goods like spices from Southeast Asia and cotton from India; the diffusion of Islam through merchant and missionary activity; and the dominance of Arab merchants in conducting trade.

     (c) A good response clearly states a long-term impact of the decision to end the voyages on China. For example, the lack of the presence of the Chinese navy in the Indian Ocean basin enabled European merchants to expand their influence in the region. It created competition for private Chinese merchants. Another impact was that the rise of European maritime empires eventually fueled industrialization and economic imperialism in China in the nineteenth century.

217. **(a)** A good response includes similarities such as the use of bureaucracies by the Chinese and Byzantine Empires, legal codes developed in the Byzantine Empire and Caliphates, and the use of religious authority to govern in the Caliphates and Byzantine Empire.

     (b) A good response explains a reason why multiple empires used these techniques. For example, bureaucracies were used by China and the Byzantine Empire because they were reconstituted states that drew upon previous traditions. Bureaucracies were an effective way to manage a vast empire.

     (c) A good response explains the varying government structures of two regions. For example, Western Europe was decentralized with small kingdoms that used feudalism to define roles of the nobility and serfs. In contrast, the Caliphates were centralized under one ruler who claimed political and military authority. Another example could include the Swahili city-states of East Africa, which were governed independently and controlled the surrounding countryside. In contrast, the kingdoms of Ghana and Mali in West Africa used tax revenues to expand their military and protect trade routes and gold mines.

218. This question assesses the skill of causation. For this question, focusing on one empire may be best or on two that are similar. A strong thesis identifies at least two ways one or more states governed in this period. For example, "In the period from 600 to 1450, new states such as the Tang and Song dynasties and the Byzantine Empire built upon previous administrative techniques but implemented new ideas in law codes and the use of religion to govern." Contextualization could include a description of the decline of classical civilizations that preceded these, such as the Han dynasty and Roman

Empire, and the reasons for the resurgence of these empires. Evidence used to support the claim could be how empires drew upon previous techniques and can include the use of Roman laws to create Justinian's Code in the Byzantine Empire, the revival of the civil service system in China, and the bureaucratic structure of the Han dynasty. Examples of the use of religion to govern could include how the Byzantine ruler claimed authority over the patriarch (religious leader) of Constantinople, and the Chinese emperor claiming the Mandate of Heaven and embracing the Confucian Five Relationships to ensure obedience to his rule. To show analysis and reasoning, the essay could discuss how both areas borrowed ideas from previous government to establish their rule and learned from the mistakes of the fallen empires. To show historical complexity, the essay can examine changes that occurred in governments as the period progressed. These include the establishment of tributary relationships by the Chinese, the decline of the Byzantine due to threats from the Caliphates, and the sacking of Constantinople by Crusaders.

219. A strong essay identifies at least three major causes of the rise and fall of cities as linked to the rise of empires. One cause that may be included is the pattern of urbanization during the Sui, Tang, and Song dynasties due to government support of the economy and the construction of the Grand Canal. Another cause that may be discussed is the revival of trading cities across Central Asia due to trade under the Mongol Empire. A third cause of urban revival is agricultural expansion resulting from new technologies in Western Europe during the High Middle Ages. This also led to population growth. Contextualization would explain the circumstances surrounding the rise of empires following the fall of the Roman, Han, Persian, and Gupta Empires in the classical period. A strong essay would explain the links between the reconstitution of several empires and include specific examples that led to the growth of cities for each.

220. This DBQ is assessing the skill of causation and one's ability to construct an argument using historical evidence. An acceptable thesis would make a claim such as, "Imperial rulers in the period from 600 to 1450 tended to support trade and commercial activity as long as they could benefit." Although most of the documents seem to show more positive attitudes toward trade, one must account for different policies to show historical complexity. Contextualization could provide evidence regarding the development of these empires or their role in trade networks. For example, an explanation of the revival of centralized dynasties in China and expansion of the tributary system would help explain the tax reforms discussed in document 1 and the support of merchants by the government demonstrated in document 2. For three documents, the significance of the source's audience, purpose, point of view, or historical situation must be explained. For example, document 6 should take into account that the ruler wants to attract merchants to his kingdom in order to collect the tax, equal to one thirtieth of the profit. If previous policies were in place in which the entire cargo was seized,

merchants would likely avoid trading in this state. Specific evidence regarding the link between government and commerce must be included and must go beyond paraphrasing the source. Outside knowledge could include promotion of trade by the Mongol Empire, which helped revive Silk Road trade and led to cultural diffusion. To demonstrate historical complexity, a comparison of the documents could show an understanding of the patterns of history.

CHAPTER 9: INCREASED ECONOMIC PRODUCTIVITY AND ITS CONSEQUENCES

221. **(C)** The Mexica, or Aztecs, built causeways to connect their capital, Tenochtitlan, to the mainland and used *chinampas*, or floating gardens, to create more land for farming.

222. **(B)** Cities flourished as centers of trade and because of agricultural innovations, like *chinampas*, that increased yields and supported a growing population.

223. **(A)** The Mexica were militaristic and conquered surrounding groups forcing them to pay tribute in the form of goods or people.

224. **(D)** Cities tend to have multiple roles, including seats of government, trading hubs, and religious centers because there is a large concentration of people.

225. **(D)** The passage is an agreement between a serf and a lord in which the serf is pledging to provide service in exchange for protection (guardianship), food, and clothing.

226. **(A)** Serfs often rebelled when payments to the noble were deemed unfair.

227. **(C)** This system developed as Western Europe faced invasions by Germanic tribes, Muslims, and Vikings in this period. Since invaders targeted cities because they are ideal for pillaging, many people fled to the countryside and sought protection and a place to work and live.

228. **(B)** As trade increased in this period, the demand for luxury goods like silk increased.

229. **(D)** In this era demand for coal and iron increased and the passage discusses "black stones," which are in abundance in China.

230. **(C)** Marco Polo traveled to China in the thirteenth century, which was the height of the Mongol Empire. Since that empire controlled the Silk Road, trade and travel increased and there were fewer risks than before.

231. **(A)** Sugar and cotton, like other crops, spread from East and South Asia to the Middle East via trade routes.

232. **(C)** Crop production increased in many regions due to technological innovations, such as multiple cropping and using manure to improve soil conditions as described in the passage.

233. **(B)** As production increased, various types of labor were used, such as slavery and free peasant labor.

234. **(D)** As the demand for cash crops such as cotton and sugar increased, Europeans established plantations in areas with tropical climates that could support these crops, such as the Caribbean.

235. **(B)** This law was issued shortly after the Black Death spread through Europe, which is referred to as "that pestilence." Because of the labor shortages that resulted due to the death toll, the remaining workers demanded higher pay.

236. **(A)** The king is calling for the return to previous salary levels because workers were demanding high wages. Workers' demands strained the nobility, who likely put pressure onto the king to address the issue.

237. **(C)** Due to the sudden loss of a large segment of the population, tools and machines were invented to replace human labor.

238. **(D)** Innovations such as swamp draining and terracing, as well as the introduction of champa rice from Southeast Asia, led to increased population since food production expanded.

239. **(C)** In this period, urbanization occurred as trade intensified and population increased.

240. **(B)** Patriarchy was a continuity in most regions. In addition, the social hierarchy did not change much in the face of population increases.

241. **(A)** *Tale of Genji* was the world's first novel and was written by a woman, which shows that there were some literate Japanese women. The popularity of *Tale of Genji* meant that female writers were not taboo.

242. **(D)** China had more defined gender roles than Japan. Chinese women rarely received an education.

243. **(B)** Like in other regions, innovations in agriculture, such as the heavy plow and three-field system, led to population growth.

244. **(C)** Famine did not occur with population growth because food production expanded to meet the needs of the population.

245. **(A)** The Green Revolution of the late twentieth century was caused by new agricultural methods, like in Europe at the time shown on the graph, and caused rapid population growth.

246. **(D)** The Black Death in the mid-fourteenth century led to a rapid drop in population.

247. **(C)** The expansion of empires integrated more people into trading networks. This gave people access to more goods and expanded the demand for both luxuries and consumer goods.

248. **(B)** As production and trade increased, cities grew because they served as centers of commerce.

249. **(A)** When India was a British colony, manufactured goods were sold to the colony. This is similar to the way that manufactured goods were sold to China's tributaries in Southeast Asia.

250. **(D)** Neoconfucian values spread as trade occurred between China and Southeast Asia.

251. **(a)** A good response explains how the fall of the Roman Empire contributed to the rise of serfdom as people fled cities and gave up freedoms to a landowner in exchange for a plot of land and protection.
     (b) A good response explains a commonality among slaves and serfs. The response must be beyond the idea that they were both forced laborers. For example, both mainly performed manual labor on farms or acted as household servants. Both could be traded or sold as property.
     (c) A good response explains a distinction between slaves and serfs. For example, serfs originally entered into agreements with nobles (although the status became hereditary). In contrast, slaves in this era were usually prisoners of war or debt slaves and were sold against their will. Another difference is the idea that serfs were bound to the land they worked on rather than the property of an owner. In contrast, slaves were considered to be the property of the owner and could be transferred off the land.

252. **(a)** A good response explains how agricultural production expanded in volume, providing food surpluses and larger-scale production of cash crops, such as cotton and sugar.
     (b) A good response explains how new technologies contributed to increased agricultural production, such as terrace farming by the Inca, the three-yield system in Europe, the draining of swamps in China, or the development of chinampas by the Aztecs (Mexica).
     (c) A good response identifies a specific continuity. One example is the focus on the production of food crops rather than cash crops to support a growing population. Another example is agricultural labor consisting of a variety of free peasants and coerced labor.

253. This question is assessing the skill of change and continuity over time. A strong essay discusses in depth at least two major changes in social structures. Contextualization could explain changes in governments that led to new forms of coerced labor, such as the decentralized nature of Western Europe as a result of the fall of the Roman Empire or the centralization of China under the Tang and Song dynasties. One change could be the increasing complexity of social hierarchies as the expansion of trade led to increased specialization and a growing role for merchants. Another change could be the expansion of coerced labor as population growth occurred. A complex argument would examine varying attitudes among civilizations. For example, Confucian beliefs held that merchants were parasites that profited from the work of others, so merchants in China were looked down upon when compared to merchants in other regions. Continuities that could be explained would be how in most societies, rulers and landowning elites continued to dominate

the social hierarchy, while unskilled laborers comprised the lowest class. Coerced laborers had less status than free peasants.

254. This essay question assesses the skill of change and continuity over time. A strong essay examines at least two major changes in labor systems, such as the development of serfdom in Japan and Western Europe, and the implementation of the Incan *mit'a* system. Contextualization should discuss the reasons why these labor systems developed at the time. Examples include the rise of feudalism in Japan as a result of warfare and the development of manorialism in Western Europe in the aftermath of the fall of the Roman Empire and in the face of invasions. Specific changes should be addressed. One example is the change from a mainly free peasantry in the Roman Empire to the binding of the serfs to the land as a result of the rise of the manor system. Another example is the rise of the *mit'a* system in the Inca Empire to redistribute agricultural surplus throughout the empire. To show complexity, continuities could include the persistence of slavery from the classical period and the role of the free peasantry, with China serving as a strong example.

Note: Full Answers Explained with detailed explanations why the incorrect answers are wrong can be found at *www.barronsbooks.com/ap/docs/h72bdc/QA1125.pdf* or by using the QR code below.

CHAPTER 10: GLOBALIZING NETWORKS OF COMMUNICATION AND EXCHANGE

255. **(A)** European involvement in Asian trade was due to maritime reconnaissance, which is another term for exploration.

256. **(C)** Europeans had a large role in the global circulation of silver because they brought it from its source (Latin America) to China.

257. **(D)** Due to the silver trade, Europeans set up trading posts in the Indian Ocean basin in order to get the goods they desired. As a result, Europeans became intermediaries in global trade.

258. **(B)** Missionaries, such as the Jesuits, traveled to Asia to spread Christianity in this period.

259. **(B)** The Atlantic system included the exchange of cash crops (sugar, coffee, tobacco, cotton) grown on plantations with slave labor.

260. **(C)** The clearing of land for plantations and the continued planting of the same crop had negative effects on the environment.

261. **(A)** Slave rebellions occurred because slaves did not merely accept their status.

262. **(A)** The arrival of the British in North America was possibly due to the availability of tools for navigation, such as the astrolabe and compass, and to improved cartography (mapmaking).

263. **(D)** Once European monarchs heard of Columbus's claiming of land on behalf of Spain, they often sponsored voyages in order to claim land for themselves.

264. **(C)** Improved ship designs led to the discovery and conquest of the Americas. This caused trade to be truly global and led to mercantilist policies.

265. **(A)** The compass was invented in China but was adopted by merchants in the Indian Ocean basin in the previous time period and spread to Europeans as a result of the contact with Arabs during the Crusades.

266. **(B)** Exploration was facilitated by improvements in existing navigational technologies.

267. **(C)** Most European trade was conducted by privately owned joint-stock companies.

268. **(A)** European governments taxed trade and used the income to commission paintings, theater, and monumental architecture.

269. **(B)** Existing religions, such as Christianity and Buddhism, spread through missionaries and merchants.

270. **(D)** The European conquest of the Americas integrated that region into the global economy for the first time.

271. **(C)** In this period, European imperial powers developed mercantilist economic systems. In these systems, Europeans manufactured products from raw materials that were extracted from their colonies.

272. **(A)** Joint-stock companies were mainly used in this period to finance overseas trading expeditions.

273. **(B)** Access to silver deposits in the Americas enabled Europeans to buy Asian luxuries.

274. **(C)** Enlightenment ideas led to revolutions in the nineteenth century that disrupted trade.

275. **(D)** Food crops from the Americas, such as potatoes and maize, led to better diets and thus a population increase.

276. **(C)** The African slave trade was occurring, which is also referred to as a diaspora because Africans were dispersed throughout the Americas. This caused Africa to have less of an increase in population compared to India and China.

277. **(B)** In the mid-seventeenth century, the Ming dynasty was weakening. It was conquered by the Manchus, who established the Qing dynasty. The war and famine from this change resulted in many deaths.

278. **(A)** Contact between the indigenous peoples of the Americas and the Europeans led to a dramatic population decline among the Amerindians due to their lack of immunity.

279. **(D)** The author was likely describing the natives as primitives who would make good servants. He wanted to show the king and queen of Spain, who sponsored his voyage, how their investment would pay off.

280. **(C)** The author most likely noted that the natives did not have weapons because he wanted to conquer them and profit from their labor.

281. **(B)** As a result of Columbus's voyage, Europeans migrated to the Americas, conquered the natives, and imported slaves to work on plantations.

282. **(C)** Las Casas's role as a missionary led him to feel sympathetic toward the natives since he worked closely with them and was trying to spread Christian ideas.

283. **(C)** Spanish cruelty and disease led to population decline, which then led to a labor shortage and the importation of African slaves to the Americas.

284. **(A)** The Spanish viewed the natives as barbarians due to the natives' polytheistic religion, lack of advanced weapons, and cultural traditions that the Spanish did not understand, so the Spanish felt conquest was justified.

285. **(A)** The Enlightenment ideas of liberty and equality led to the questioning of slavery and the eventual emancipation of slaves in the mid-nineteenth century.

286. **(a)** and **(b)** Strong responses should describe two specific pieces of evidence that support the authors' claim that the role of Europeans was as middlemen in the silver trade. Examples include the use of silver to purchase goods throughout trading posts in the Indian Ocean, the transportation of silver from the Americas to the Philippines to buy goods from China, the role of silver as a new global currency, the role of the Dutch in the spice trade, and the establishment of trading posts by the Portuguese in the Indian Ocean basin and coastal West Africa. The response should not simply summarize the author's claim.
     (c) A good response includes evidence that refutes the claim that silver flowed from west to east. China's demand for silver as a payment for goods such as silk, porcelain, and tea would be included. The response should also include the transport of silver from mines in Peru and Mexico to the Philippines and the lack of demand for European goods by Asian markets that led to trade deficits or an unfavorable balance of trade.

287. **(a)** A good response clearly describes demographic (population) changes that occurred as a result of the contact between the Eastern and Western

Hemispheres following Columbus's initial voyage. Examples include the decline of native populations as a result of diseases; the increase in populations in Afro-Eurasia as a result of new food crops from the Americas; the mixing of European, American, and European populations in the New World; the creation of mestizo and mulatto populations in the Americas; and/or the increased presence of European peoples in the Americas.

(b) A good response explaining environmental changes could include deforestation and soil depletion due to the clearing of land for plantation agriculture, the introduction of new species of plants, such as wheat and rice, and animals, such as horses, cattle, and pigs, into the ecosystems of the Americas and the Old World, the mining boom due to the demand for silver, and/or monoculture on plantations.

(c) A good response explains specific economic changes. It could include the rise of triangular trade/the Atlantic trading system, the global silver trade, the trade of cash crops grown in the Americas across the Atlantic, the rise of mercantilist policies as European powers colonized the Americas, and the integration of the Americas into global trade.

288. This question assesses the skill of change and continuity over time. A strong thesis identifies at least two major changes that occurred in one or more regions. Contextualization could discuss any of the following: European motivations for exploration; access to new navigational tools, knowledge of winds and currents, and adaptations to technologies gained from Arab merchants through the Crusades; the sponsorship of voyages of exploration by European powers due to the desire to profit from Asian trade; and the desire to circumvent the Ottoman middlemen to seek a direct route to Asia. Changes in the Americas can include the introduction of pathogens that devastated native populations due to lack of immunity; the introduction of European animals, such as horses, pigs, and cattle, that led to new lifestyles and diets; and the introduction of crops such as sugarcane that led to the clearing of land for plantations and soil depletion due to the continued cultivation of one crop in the same area (monoculture). Changes can also include the rise of mixed-race populations due to European settlement and the introduction of African slaves as a result of the demand for labor on plantations. Changes in Europe could include the introduction of new crops from the Americas that led to more nutritious diets and growing populations, such as beans and potatoes, and the introduction of corn that could be used to feed livestock. A complex argument could examine continuities, such as the agricultural practices of Native Americans who lived outside of the tropical areas, the continued cultivation of traditional crops in the Americas, and the continued importance of wheat in European diets despite the introduction of new crops.

289. The skill assessed in this question is change and continuity over time. A strong thesis identifies at least two major changes in trade networks due to the rise of truly global trade following the European "discovery" of the Americas. Contextualization could include an explanation of European

motivations for exploration; the inclusion of the Americas in global trade due to the extraction of silver; the rise of trans-Atlantic trade due to the establishment of plantations in the Caribbean and Brazil; and the voyage of Vasco da Gama and Portuguese expansion in the Indian Ocean basin. Changes could include the shift from the dominance of Arab merchants in the Indian Ocean basin due to the new role of Europeans as middlemen in trade, the establishment of trading posts by Europeans, the colonization of Indonesia by the Dutch and the Philippines by the Spanish, the widespread use of silver from the Americas as a global currency, and the spread of Christianity as a result of missionary activity. Changes in Silk Road trade could include the decline in volume due to the rise of direct sea routes from Europe to Asia and the increased risk of overland travel in Central Asia due to the fall of the Mongol Empire. To show complexity, continuities could be examined. Examples include the presence of Arab, Indian, and African merchants; the production of goods by local artisans and peasants; the dominance of Islam in the Indian Ocean basin, and the luxury goods traded (silk, porcelain, tea, spices, ivory).

290. The skill assessed in this DBQ essay is change and continuity over time. However, if the essay addressed effects of the conquest and colonization by the Spanish, that would be acceptable as long as it discussed changes resulting from the Columbian Exchange. A strong thesis describes at least two major changes as a result of European arrival on the Americas, such as the subjugation of Native Americans (documents 1, 2, 7), violent conquests of the Aztec and Incan Empires (documents 3, 4, 5), and the introduction of European cultural elements (documents 4, 6). Contextualization could include an explanation of the factors leading to European arrival in the Americas, such as the desire for trade routes and Columbus's miscalculation of the circumference of the earth which led him to sail west; the characteristics of the existing native empires; and the motivations of Spanish settlers after initial contact. For three of the documents, explaining the significance of the historical situation, audience, purpose, and/or point of view is required. For example, in document 7, the Spanish monk clearly feels sympathetic toward the natives based on his description of the labor. He even calls the Indians "poor fellows," which is likely due to his position as a monk and his close relationship with the natives when attempting to convert them. Outside evidence that would add to the essay's argument could include the religious beliefs of the Aztecs, which would provide context for documents 4 and 6, or the establishment of a hierarchy based on race, known as the *castas* system. To demonstrate historical complexity, the essay may compare the documents. For example, similarities could include the lack of trust Native Americans and the Spanish had for one another, the violence that broke out due to resentments toward the other side, and the lack of understanding of cultures. Differences could include the initial reaction of the Aztecs welcoming Cortés and how they treated him with respect, as opposed to the general disregard for the

natives that the Spanish accounts illustrate. A complex argument would note relationships among the documents, such as the reason for the varying accounts of documents 4 and 5.

CHAPTER 11: NEW FORMS OF SOCIAL ORGANIZATION AND MODES OF PRODUCTION

291. **(C)** Most African slaves were used for labor on plantations for the production of cash crops, such as sugar.

292. **(A)** More men than women were taken in the Atlantic slave trade, resulting in areas of West Africa that had significantly more women than men. Some results of this gender imbalance were polygamy due to less available male partners and women in leadership roles.

293. **(D)** The slave trade led to the spread of Christianity as slaves converted and as syncretism occurred as African religious traditions, such as Vodun, merged with Christian religious traditions in the Americas.

294. **(B)** Prior to the Atlantic slave trade, slaves were transported via the trans-Saharan routes to the Mediterranean basin and others were brought to East African coastal cities to be transported in the Indian Ocean basin trade networks.

295. **(D)** The passage describes Equiano's tribe in West Africa in terms of defense from attacks and roles of slaves.

296. **(B)** Prior to the Atlantic slave trade, which arose in the sixteenth century, African slaves were transported within sub-Saharan Africa and in the Indian Ocean basin trade networks.

297. **(A)** Slave raids increased greatly due to the trans-Atlantic slave trade in which Europeans brought manufactured goods to coastal tribes in exchange for slaves, who were captured by Africans.

298. **(A)** The Columbian Exchange included the transfer of plants from the Americas, such as beans, potatoes, and corn. This led to more varied and nutritious diets throughout Eurasia.

299. **(C)** Although sub-Saharan Africa was introduced to new crops that contributed to population growth, millions of slaves were removed each century. This explains why the population in sub-Saharan Africa did not grow as quickly as in Europe.

300. **(B)** As the population grew, peasants and artisans had to increase yields to meet greater demand.

301. **(A)** Since the author was a Spanish monk most likely there to convert natives, Espinosa likely felt sympathetic toward the natives because he worked closely with them.

302. **(C)** The demand for silver increased because having available silver enabled Europeans to participate in trade in China. Europeans had very few products

that China did not already produce. European merchants who wanted Chinese luxury goods had to pay for them in silver.

303. **(B)** The author is a monk who was working with the natives to convert them. He used phrases like "poor fellows" and called the labor "evil."

304. **(D)** The *mita* system was an example of coerced labor used in mines in the Spanish colonies.

305. **(B)** During the Little Ice Age, global cooling occurred. This led to the abandonment of farms in Northern Europe due to the shorter growing season, ports freezing over, and the inability to grow certain crops in cooler climates.

306. **(A)** Global cooling during the Little Ice Age led to changes in farming. These included the cultivation of potatoes because they thrive in cool climates and the abandonment of farms in Northern Europe.

307. **(B)** Indentured servitude was considered to be coerced labor even though the servant agreed to the contract. While in service, the servants were strictly controlled by their master.

308. **(C)** Demand for laborers increased in this time period due to the intensification of trade. This intensification of trade increased demand for cash crops (such as sugar, cotton, tobacco, and coffee) and finished products (such as cloth, guns, and rum).

309. **(A)** The contract shows a term of five years, while slavery was typically for life.

310. **(D)** In this era, rulers attempted to centralize power by limiting the power of existing elites. These elites were typically large, landowning families (in this case, the *daimyo*). By implementing these regulations, the ruler was eliminating threats to his power.

311. **(C)** These regulations served to limit the power of the *daimyo*, who ruled locally. These regulations prevented the *daimyo* from forming alliances and displaying their wealth, thus ensuring stability throughout Japan and limiting the possibility of rebellion.

312. **(A)** The Tokugawa shoguns feared rebellion due to the prior period of civil war, in which several leaders claimed to be shogun. During that prior period, wars occurred and the *daimyo* changed their allegiances. The Tokugawa shoguns implemented these regulations to limit threats to their power.

313. **(D)** The unification of Japan under the Tokugawa family began a period of peace and prosperity that lasted over 250 years.

314. **(B)** Western encroachment in the nineteenth century forced Japan to open up trade with Europe and the United States. This led to rebellions against the Tokugawa shoguns and the restoration of the emperor to power, known as the Meiji Restoration.

315. **(C)** The passage explains how Dutch merchants could profit from trade by smuggling goods illegally via their wives, which violated the rules of the

VOC (Dutch East India Company) but earned the company officials much more money.

316. **(A)** The Dutch issued a charter to the Dutch East India Company (VOC) and authorized it to act on behalf of the Dutch government to protect the monopoly. The VOC was a joint-stock company because it was less risky due to multiple investors.

317. **(B)** Powerful female merchants in Indonesia who were described in the passage were a continuity of less patriarchal gender roles that existed in the period 600 to 1450 C.E.

318. **(D)** The portrait of a merchant reflects the rising status of merchants as new elites. This is shown by the servant on the left holding an umbrella for the merchant and his wife.

319. **(A)** Europeans served as intermediaries in the Indian Ocean trade networks. They transported goods among ports, trying to profit by selling goods at higher prices in new areas.

320. **(D)** Governments granted charters to companies like the Dutch East India Company (VOC). The purpose was to promote trade and generate revenue from taxing trade, which would benefit the government.

321. **(a)** An acceptable response must identify a specific agricultural innovation from this era that developed during the Agrarian Revolution that preceded the Industrial Revolution. Examples include the practice of crop rotation, in which all fields would be planted but each year the crops in a particular area would be rotated to prevent soil depletion; the seed drill, which inserted seeds into the ground and prevented seed from being wasted; iron plows that were more efficient than wooden plows; the planting of American food crops to add variety to diets, such as potatoes and beans; and consolidation of farms through the Enclosure Acts, which allowed for larger yields. Keep in mind that answers should be explained thoroughly and in complete sentences, so a response such as "crop rotation" would not earn the point.
(b) An acceptable response discusses a specific factor that led to limited production of food. For example, the Little Ice Age was a period of cooler temperatures, so less land was used for cultivation due to larger glaciers, particularly in Northern Europe. Another possible response could be famines due to poor harvests, floods, or crop failures, which were especially devastating when there were few surpluses. Additionally, wars over religion as a result of the Protestant Reformation disrupted agricultural production, leading to shortages.
(c) An acceptable response explains a specific effect of increased food production. Examples include increased yields that allowed for the growth of cities (urbanization) because less farmers were needed, the rise of the working class (proletariat) that fueled the Industrial Revolution, and population growth because the food supply could support more people and diets were more nutritious.

322. **(a)** An acceptable response includes chattel slavery, in which slaves were owned as property and could be bought and sold and in which their status could be passed down to their children; indentured servitude, in which a person agreed to work for a set amount of time in exchange for passage to the Americas; the *encomienda* system, in which Native Americans were enslaved by Spanish landowners to perform labor; or the *mita* system, in which villages had to send a portion of their population to work in Spanish mines.

(b) An acceptable response explains a change that occurred in the period with regard to farm labor. For example, the creation of plantations in tropical areas of the Americas led to the concentration of slave labor for the production of cash crops, such as sugar, cotton, tobacco, indigo, and coffee. Also, serfdom was weakening in Europe due to greater opportunities in cities, while it was implemented in Russia in order to secure laborers for boyars. Another example could be the intensification of peasant labor due to the introduction of new crops from the Americas and the commercialization of the global economy, which increased demand for manufactured goods (e.g., silk, porcelain, and cotton textiles).

(c) An acceptable response includes a specific continuity in agricultural labor, such as the dependence of most empires on peasant labor to maintain the food supply, the trade of slaves in the Mediterranean and Indian Ocean trade networks, or the dependence of landless peasants on large landowners.

323. The historical reasoning skill being assessed in this question is change and continuity over time. A strong response examines the changes in a labor system, such as slavery or serfdom. Contextualization for changes in slavery could examine the European Age of Exploration, which led to the establishment of plantations in the Americas and the increased demand for slavery. The thesis must clearly identify a major change in slavery in detail. For example, "In the period 1450–1750, slavery became more widespread and the slave trade was redirected across the Atlantic in order to meet the increased demand for labor on plantations." In the body of the essay, evidence must be used to prove your argument. For example, discuss the decline in the population of Native Americans due to diseases that led to the importation of African slaves, the use of slave labor plantations for the production of cash crops, and the expansion of the slave trade over the centuries as a result of mercantilist policies. This caused European governments to use colonies for the benefit of the mother country, and the rise of joint-stock companies decreased the risks to those investing in slave voyages. To add complexity to the argument, continuities in slavery should be discussed, such as slave raiding among African tribes in order to participate in regional trade networks.

324. The historical reasoning skill being assessed in this question is change and continuity over time. A strong response examines changes in ethnic, political, or gender hierarchies due to political and economic changes. You should choose one category to examine to make a more coherent argument. For

example, ethnic hierarchies could include the creation of the *casta* system by the Creoles in Spanish America and the rise of Manchu elites in China. Contextualization could include the expansion of empires due to the use of gunpowder technology and the Age of Exploration that led to the Spanish conquest of the Americas. The thesis statement must explain specific changes that occurred. Examples include the creation of a hierarchy based on the birthplace and ethnicity of those living within the Spanish Empire and the creation of Manchu elites as a result of the conquest of the Ming dynasty. Evidence could describe the need for labor by the Spanish, leading to enslavement of the natives; intermarriage between Spanish men and Native-American women that created mixed-race groups (*mestizos*); the incorporation of African slaves due to the need for plantation laborers; and the use of *peninsulares* as governors. For the Qing dynasty, discussion of the conquest by the Manchu and the desire to adopt Chinese traditions while maintaining a distinct Manchu culture would explain how the Manchu became the new political elites. To address historical complexity, continuities can be addressed. These include the role of rulers in relation to the bureaucrats and the prominence of landowning elites in the social hierarchy.

CHAPTER 12: STATE CONSOLIDATION AND IMPERIAL EXPANSION

325. **(C)** The building of monumental architecture like those shown was financed using money generated from taxing trade and mercantilist policies.

326. **(B)** Throughout history, empires have sponsored the construction of buildings to display their power and wealth.

327. **(D)** The king was justifying his right to rule by stating that kings are God's lieutenants, or representatives, on Earth. This concept is called divine right.

328. **(A)** The Mandate of Heaven claims that a ruler's right to rule is supported by the gods, which is similar to the European concept of divine right.

329. **(C)** Enlightenment ideas rejected absolutism. It was viewed as unnatural for one person to have so much power. Enlightenment ideas also questioned divine right theory because it could not be proven and because the Enlightenment promoted consent of the governed or input of citizens through elections.

330. **(B)** The Ottomans were able to conquer the remains of the Byzantine Empire and the city of Constantinople by using superior gunpowder weapons and siege tactics. The Ottoman Empire expanded in the eastern Mediterranean using its navy.

331. **(D)** The Ottomans used the *devshirme* system of recruitment in which Christian boys from the Balkans were enslaved, converted to Islam, and trained as either bureaucrats or janissaries (soldiers). This enabled the sultans to create a loyal bureaucracy that was merit-based rather than related to family ties.

332. **(A)** The Chinese civil service exam was merit-based. It served to recruit bureaucrats who were capable and to limit the influence of landowning families.

333. **(C)** Native-American tribes and empires, such as the Aztecs and Incas, were conquered by Europeans who used new ships and navigational tools to reach their land. These tribes and empires lacked gunpowder weapons that were used by Europeans to subdue them.

334. **(C)** Mercantilist economic policies were embraced by European monarchs in order to increase revenues. One goal of mercantilism was to have a favorable balance of trade in which the kingdom exported more than it imported. Another goal was for the kingdom to have a monopoly on trade with its colonies. This allowed a kingdom to pay relatively low prices to the colonies for raw materials and to charge high prices for selling finished goods to the colonies.

335. **(A)** As the Spanish conquered Native Americans and colonized much of Latin America, they developed a hierarchy of racial classifications often referred to as the *castas* system. In this system, those of European descent had higher status than mixed-race groups (*mestizos*) and those without European ancestry.

336. **(D)** If Russia had been involved in global trade, the government would have benefited from taxing trade and using the revenue to fund the military, infrastructure, and monumental architecture.

337. **(B)** Edict 2 required nobles to serve in the lower ranks of the military before being promoted based on merit. This was designed to limit the influence of nobles by forcing them to earn their positions rather than inherit them. Nobles were the existing political elites. This decree issued by a monarch demonstrated how the power of the nobles changed as monarchs consolidated power.

338. **(A)** Russia's interest in increased participation in global trade was the result of greater connections among world regions due to the incorporation of the Americas and the rise of the silver trade.

339. **(C)** Increased participation in global trade by Russia and military reforms helped to increase the power of Russian *tsars*.

340. **(B)** The Manchu were able to expand by using gunpowder weapons and strategies adapted from their experiences fighting other nomadic tribes.

341. **(A)** Expansion caused the Manchu to incorporate groups that were not ethnically Chinese, such as Turkish-speaking groups in Central Asia. Additionally, any new government had to demonstrate its right to rule.

342. **(D)** The Qing Empire was land-based. In contrast, most European empires were maritime and spread across the globe, including colonies and trading posts.

343. **(C)** The Ottomans established an enduring and extensive empire because of the use of advanced gunpowder weapons. They administered their empire with the help of an elaborate legal code.

344. **(D)** Ottoman expansion into Eastern Europe was viewed as another wave of aggression by an Islamic empire and caused Western European powers to form alliances against the Ottomans.

345. **(A)** Ethnic nationalist movements by non-Turks within the empire, such as Greeks and Egyptians, led to the loss of territory and thus the contraction of the empire.

346. **(A)** The Tokugawa shoguns sought to limit travel outside of Japan. They wanted to regulate trade closely in order to prevent *daimyo* from forming alliances with Europeans and gaining exposure to ideas that might cause them to overthrow the shoguns.

347. **(D)** These edicts regarding trade gave the shoguns greater control over the Japanese population, thus allowing the shoguns to centralize their power.

348. **(B)** These edicts restricted connections between the Japanese and outsiders, thus limiting Japanese knowledge of foreign technology and culture.

349. **(C)** The elevation of the emperor on the palanquin and the creation of the painting were both ways the Mughal leaders showed their power.

350. **(A)** The sacrifice by the emperor shows the Manchu rulers' willingness to adopt Chinese traditions, so they were seen as legitimate rulers by the Chinese masses they conquered.

351. **(B)** Manchu and Mughal rulers both used artwork to display their power. In fact, Image 2 shows the emperor performing a religious ritual to show the people he had the right to rule.

352. **(D)** The proclamation claimed that the nobles, who were the landholding elites, were "enemies" and "oppressors." The proclamation also stated that peasants should have land without taxation.

353. **(C)** Rebellions similar to the one in the document occurred in many empires. They challenged the central government because the largest groups in those societies, the peasants and serfs, participated in the rebellions.

354. **(A)** Serfs in Russia were emancipated in the mid-nineteenth century as a result of Enlightenment ideas and the continued rebellions that destabilized the empire.

355. **(a)** An acceptable response gives a detailed method that a ruler used to get more power or prove to his subjects that he had the right to rule. Examples include using religion to justify power, such as European rulers claiming divine right or Chinese use of the Mandate of Heaven; the use of monumental architecture, such as France's Palace of Versailles or Mughals' building of the Taj Mahal; limiting the power of landowning elites, such as European nobles,

Japanese *daimyo*, or Russian boyars; and the recruitment of bureaucrats, such as the Ottoman devshirme or Chinese civil service exam.

(b) An acceptable response provides a specific change, beyond stating that the empires were maritime. Examples can include how the empires controlled areas overseas much larger than the original kingdoms; how they conquered areas that had different climates, which enabled them to gain access to new resources, such as cash crops; and how this required them to establish lines of communication. They controlled groups that had very different cultural traditions and languages and also subjugated these groups due to the view that they were inferior.

(c) An acceptable response provides a specific continuity in the way empires were built. Examples include the use of bureaucracies for enforcing laws and collecting taxes; the use of tax revenues to fund the military to enforce its rule; and the use of religion to justify claims to power.

356. **(a)** An acceptable response gives a specific cause of imperial expansion. Examples include navigational innovations, such as improved ship designs and use of the compass. This enabled Europeans to build overseas empires and larger navies allowed European powers to conquer trading posts. Use of gunpowder technology enabled Muslim empires (Ottomans and Mughals) to conquer weaker states; and the Qing and Ottoman Empires took advantage of declining empires (the Ming and Byzantine, respectively).

(b) An acceptable response explains a similarity among these empires that is detailed and goes beyond a simple explanation, such as, "They both expanded/conquered." Examples include the incorporation of diverse ethnic or religious groups (Spanish, Ottoman, Mughal, Russian); the use of a merit-based bureaucracy to administer the empire (Ming/Qing and Ottomans); the conquest of weaker groups (Spanish Conquest of Native Americans, Ottomans Conquest of Byzantine); and decentralized regions (Mughals in India, British in North America).

(c) An acceptable response clearly explains a difference beyond the fact that Asian empires were land-based and European empires were sea-based, because that is already provided by the question. Examples include European Empires having outposts (colonies and trading posts) around the world, whereas Asian land empires only expanded in one region. European empires developed mercantilist policies to benefit from controlling colonies, while Asian land empires imposed taxes on conquered groups. Asian land empires were tolerant of religious beliefs (Ottomans, Mughals, Manchu), while some European empires forced Christianity on the Native Americans (Spanish).

357. The historical reasoning skill being assessed in this question is causation. A strong response includes two to three specific ways that rulers gained more power. Since the question asks for one or more, it is best to choose two or three general methods and then use examples to prove your argument. For example, an acceptable thesis could be, "In the period 1450–1750, rulers consolidated power through the use of religion to justify their right to rule,

limiting the power of landholding elites and recruiting bureaucrats who were trained to be loyal." Evidence could include the use of divine right by European leaders and the Mandate of Heaven by the Chinese as well as the restrictions placed on daimyo by the Tokugawa shoguns and the tsars appointing boyars to their positions rather than inheriting them in Russia. The civil service exam in China and the *devshirme* system in the Ottoman Empire can also be included. To earn 2 points, it is important to explain how each practice enabled rulers to get more power and to use specific evidence to support your argument. For contextualization, you could discuss the European Age of Exploration that enabled European monarchs to increase revenues and the spread of gunpowder technologies were used by Ottomans and Mughals to conquer larger territories. To show complex understanding, the effects of these policies can be examined and connections can be made to the methods used by previous empires.

358. The historical reasoning skill being assessed is comparison. A strong response includes two to three major differences between European empires and the Ottomans. This could include treatment of conquered groups, with the Ottomans showing more tolerance through the millet system while the Spanish forced Native Americans to convert to Christianity. You can also include the different methods of conquest, with the Ottomans using naval power and advanced gunpowder technology and the Europeans benefiting from the Native Americans' lack of access to gunpowder weapons. There were also different economic policies, with the Europeans using coerced labor such as the *encomienda* system, African slavery, and how the Ottomans taxed peasant laborers but did not have extensive use for coerced labor. Contextualization could include how the Ottoman expansion in the Mediterranean caused European merchants to search for alternate routes to Asia, leading to the conquest and colonization of the Americas. It can also include how the Ottomans were able to take advantage of Byzantine weaknesses. In order to earn the complexity point, the argument should include similarities in empire building or make connections between the argument and another historical period, such as European empire building in the period from 1450 to 1750. Thoroughly explaining the differences in detail while identifying a general pattern will get your point across.

359. This question is assessing the historical reasoning skill of causation and is similar to question 357, which is a long essay question. Contextualization could include the rise of European maritime empires due to exploration and increased participation in global trade. It could also include the rise of Asian land empires due to the use of gunpowder weapons and conquering weak empires of previously decentralized regions. The thesis should identify two to three main factors that led to increased control by rulers during this time. These should include the use of religion to justify one's rule (documents 4, 7), taking steps to limit corruption and control bureaucrats (documents 3, 5), and limiting the power of landowning elites (documents 1, 2, 6). To earn

2 points, the essay must go beyond summarizing the documents. Instead, each document cited must be connected back to the argument. In other words, the essay should explain how this enabled rulers to get more power. For three documents, the essay must explain why the document's point of view, purpose, audience, or historical situation matters in understanding the document. For example, in document 7, King James I is addressing Parliament, the law-making body of his kingdom. So he is likely trying to claim he has to answer only to God in order to persuade Parliament that he is not subject to their laws. Appropriate outside evidence can provide an example of what was not in any of the documents, such as the use of the Mandate of Heaven in China when discussing the use of religion to legitimize one's rule or the use of the civil service exam by Chinese emperors to limit the influence of landowning families. To demonstrate complex understanding, the essay should examine distinctions among different factors, such as the reasons for limiting corruption; examine the effects of these policies; or draw connections to other time periods.

CHAPTER 13: INDUSTRIALIZATION AND GLOBAL CAPITALISM

360. **(B)** The image shows a factory where production was concentrated in a single location, which was a major shift from production in homes or small workshops.

361. **(A)** Increased industrial production in Europe fueled the demand for raw materials. For example, the mass production of textiles increased the demand for cotton, and the development of electrical lines and tires fueled the demand for rubber.

362. **(D)** Anger over the exploitation of children by factory owners and managers led people to pressure their governments to pass laws to end child labor, to establish compulsory public elementary schools, and to improve working conditions.

363. **(C)** The factory system, urbanization, wage labor, and mass production contributed most directly to social changes, such as the rise of the working class and division of the family based on jobs.

364. **(B)** Mass production of textiles in Europe led to decreased demand for Indian textiles, which were handwoven and more expensive than machine-made goods.

365. **(D)** The passage claims that canals and railroads allowed for fields to be cultivated for the production of food for humans rather than animals, which supported rising populations.

366. **(D)** Workers were often paid low wages. They could not afford the comforts described by the author and, often, not even the necessities.

367. **(A)** European participation in global trade in the early modern period provided profits that were used to invest in factories and other ventures. In addition, changes in government caused by Enlightenment ideas led to laws protecting private property.

368. **(C)** Industrial centers developed in areas where there was an abundance of coal, iron ore, and timber, so these items did not have to be transported long distances.

369. **(A)** As cities grew quickly, crowded conditions and lack of sewers led to a dirty environment. The emission of smoke from factories led to pollution.

370. **(D)** Urban workers formed unions to address the exploitation by factory owners and to get the government to intervene to improve working conditions.

371. **(A)** Communism developed as a reaction to the inequalities created by the capitalist system. Communism offered the elimination of private property as a solution.

372. **(B)** Laws were passed to address poor working conditions and limit hours. Workers organized themselves into unions in order to push for improved wages. This led to less support for communism as the existing system helped improve conditions.

373. **(D)** *Laissez-faire* capitalism rejected government intervention in the economy, leading to social inequalities due to the desire of factory owners to maximize profits at the expense of the workers.

374. **(A)** Marxist ideas led to the Russian Revolution of 1917, which overthrew tsarist rule and led to the establishment of the communist Soviet Union.

375. **(C)** The trans-Siberian railroad crossed the Russian Empire in Asia in order to connect Russia's western industrial centers with its eastern areas that had natural deposits of coal and iron ore.

376. **(D)** Although industrial technology developed in Western Europe and the United States, it spread around the world. Industrial technology was adopted by Japan's government during the Meiji period when the government actively promoted industrialization.

377. **(A)** The introduction of railroads in Russia and of cars in Japan was mainly an effect of government programs that promoted industrialization, such as the opening of factories.

378. **(B)** Ideologies, such as the White Man's burden and scientific racism caused Europeans to view themselves as superior and native groups of the places they conquered as inferior, so the British felt that conquest was justified.

379. **(C)** Although in the early modern period Indian textiles were in demand, the handmade cloth could not compete with cheap, machine-made European cloth. Instead, India's economy shifted to the production of cash crops for its mother country, which reflects the policy of mercantilism.

380. **(A)** Resistance to British rule and intolerance of Indian cultural traditions led to Indian nationalism and the desire for independence.

381. **(D)** Smiles did not feel that governments should help the poor. Instead, he felt that the poor should help themselves and be invigorated by the process. Discussion over the role of government occurred in the industrial period as politicians and economists debated about the benefits of *laissez-faire* policies over the enactment of laws.

382. **(C)** *Laissez-faire* capitalists believed that the market should be able to function with little to no interference from the government, which is what Smiles advocated for in this passage.

383. **(C)** Factory workers generally supported government regulations to improve working conditions because the factory owners would rarely improve wages or conditions on their own as doing so would be less profitable.

384. **(B)** Europe's share of global manufacturing increased as a result of the invention of coal-powered machines and the factory system, both of which increased the output of finished goods.

385. **(A)** The profits and technology that generated from the process of industrialization in Europe led to the rise of large companies that operated around the world, including banks and shipping companies.

386. **(D)** The governments of Russia and Japan actively tried to promote industrialization by financing factories, railroads, and mines. In contrast, Western European industrialization was mainly due to investments by individuals or private corporations.

387. **(D)** Capitalists invested in new inventions to make production more efficient, and machines were often large and expensive. This all led to the rise of the factory system.

388. **(C)** Innovations in transportation, such as diesel engines and cars, promoted the growth of the economy by making overland transportation more efficient.

389. **(A)** As European economies and empires thrived, the Ottoman and Chinese governments experimented with reforms to help improve their economies.

390. **(a)** An acceptable response identifies one change in global trade as a result of industrialization. Examples include the growth of export economies and demand for raw materials needed for production, such as rubber, oil, cotton, iron, and copper; the increase in the trade of European manufactured goods as a result of mass production; the expansion of mercantilist policies to new areas, such as Asia and Africa, due to European imperialism; and the increased involvement of the United States and Japan in the global economy due to industrialization.
(b) An acceptable response explains why a change occurred and, ideally, explains the reason for the change identified in part (a). Examples include the formation of the working class due to the demand for unskilled labor

in urban factories; the new elites in the upper class, such as factory owners, due to the profits from industrialization; less demand for farmers due to agricultural innovations and machines; and the growth of the middle class due to jobs in management and professional jobs. These were educational opportunities.

(c) An acceptable response identifies a specific continuity, such as the continued domestic role for women after marriage, the privileges of the landholding elites or nobility, and the living conditions of rural farmers. Avoid continuities that are too general, such as the presence of social classes.

391. (a) An acceptable response provides an economic effect of industrialization, or patriarchy. Examples include the rise of multinational corporations, such as HSBC Bank or the United Fruit Company; mass production of consumer goods, such as textiles; lower prices of manufactured goods because labor was less expensive and goods were produced quickly; and new financial instruments, such as the stock market and insurance.

(b) An acceptable response provides a detailed similarity. Examples should include the desire to address living conditions, such as overcrowding and unsanitary cities; the attempt to improve working conditions, such as wages, hours, and safety; and the desire to extend suffrage to all men in society.

(c) An acceptable response provides a clear difference between two groups. For example, the government passed laws to regulate working conditions and improve living conditions, such as child labor laws. At the same time, the workers organized themselves into unions to advocate for themselves. Another example is that workers embraced new ideologies such as Marxism. At the same time, the government continued to support capitalist economic structure and representative government.

392. The historical reasoning skill being assessed is change and continuity over time. A strong response includes a thesis that identifies two to three major changes in the global economy due to industrialization. These could include the increase in Europe's share of manufacturing and the decline of other regions' output, the spread of mercantilist policies as industrialization led to imperialism, and greater interdependence of economies around the world. Each of these aspects will have to be explained in the body paragraphs. Analysis will have to explain the link between industrialization and the changes. For example, to explain mercantilist policies, the essay should describe mercantilist theory, such as the goal of achieving a favorable balance of trade, the desire for colonies as sources of raw materials and markets for finished goods, and the monopoly the mother country has on trade. For contextualization, the factors leading to industrialization and the causes of European imperialism in this period should be explained to illustrate how they contributed to the economic changes. To show complexity, continuities can be examined, such as the use of colonies as sources of commodities despite the change in the location of the colonies. Another continuity is that mercantilist theory was used in the previous time period in the Americas.

393. The historical reasoning skill being assessed is causation. A strong thesis identifies two to three specific causes of industrialization, such as the Agricultural Revolution, the Enlightenment, and European participation in global trade in the early modern period. Contextualization could describe how the Age of Exploration contributed to the growth of European empires as they claimed territories overseas and the growth of European economies. Within the essay, specific pieces of evidence could include how the spread of Enlightenment ideas led to changes in law that protected private property, giving an incentive to business owners to invest in machines; how innovations of the Agricultural Revolution (crop rotation, seed drill, fertilizers, new plows) increased yields that provided food for urban factory workers; and how European economic policies enabled manufacturers to get cheap raw materials from overseas colonies. This included cotton, which made textile production profitable. To show complexity, effects can be shown, such as the impact on social structure and a new wave of imperialism in Africa and Asia.

394. This essay is assessing the skill of comparison. For contextualization, the factors contributing to the Industrial Revolution and the reasons for poor living and working conditions should be explained. The thesis should indicate the various responses to the negative effects of industrialization, such as those who feel that the poor should help themselves (documents 1 and 3), those advocating for political reform (documents 5 and 7), and workers organizing themselves (documents 2, 4, and 6). Each document should be used to further your argument about the differences in the responses. You must analyze the sourcing of at least three documents (historical situation, point of view, purpose, audience) and their significance. For example, the Leeds woolen workers in document 4 felt resentful that machines replaced their jobs, so they were calling for change because they lost their livelihood. Outside evidence can include the additional legislation passed, such as universal male suffrage and compulsory education. This allowed the lower class the opportunity to voice their opinion and improve their jobs.

CHAPTER 14: IMPERIALISM AND NATION-STATE FORMATION

395. **(A)** Europeans benefited from the use of gunpowder weapons and helped them conquer large empires quickly. In contrast, native peoples of the Americas lacked gunpowder and metallurgy.

396. **(D)** Imperialism between 1750 and 1900 was mainly to secure cheap commodities and cash crops needed for industrial production that grew in climates that were warmer than Europe's.

397. **(C)** European empires shifted to control much of Africa and Asia, because Enlightenment ideas led to successful independence movements in the Americas.

398. **(B)** Natives generally fought back violently. They also resisted colonization in nonviolent ways, such as by refusing to pay taxes and cooperate with ruling powers.

399. **(C)** Interactions among Africans and Europeans at this time were the result of the Scramble for Africa and colonization.

400. **(B)** Racial ideologies, such as Social Darwinism and the White Man's burden, contributed to the idea that Europeans were superior to Africans.

401. **(A)** Colonization and European claims of superiority caused rebellions.

402. **(D)** The style of clothing and furnishings shown in the image are Western, such as the style of the uniform and the chair. These Western styles are the result of increased contact with westerners following Matthew Perry's visit and the Treaty of Kanagawa.

403. **(A)** In the late-nineteenth century, Japan rapidly industrialized and attempted to gain more territory to acquire resources. This led to the Sino-Japanese War.

404. **(C)** In the decades leading up to World War II, Japan sought to expand its empire and gain resources, such as oil and iron ore, in order to fuel industrialization.

405. **(B)** Democracy was an Enlightenment idea and private enterprise is another way of describing capitalism.

406. **(A)** European industrialization and the wealth that was generated depended on imports of commodities from outside of Europe.

407. **(D)** Anti-imperialists did not support colonialism or give it "two cheers."

408. **(C)** The images and text depict the British as dominant, with victories in battles and with the most colonies, so these images show nationalist feelings.

409. **(B)** The images are from a children's book designed to promote patriotism for Britain.

410. **(A)** Industrialization resulted in steamships, mass-produced weapons, and the motivation to obtain raw materials cheaply.

411. **(D)** The reforms were an attempt to modernize China in response to Western economic imperialism that occurred following the Opium Wars, namely the creation of European spheres of influence.

412. **(B)** In Japan during the Meiji Restoration, the government actively sought to modernize the country and promote reforms that would improve technology and the economy, which is what China was attempting to do.

413. **(C)** The weak government and failure to modernize led to the overthrow of the Qing and eventually to a civil war between Chinese Communists and Nationalists (also known as the Guomingdang) and the Chinese Communist Revolution.

414. **(A)** The Spanish and Portuguese lost their colonies in the Americas through revolutions, which led to greater American economic and political influence particularly in Latin America.

415. **(C)** Neocolonialism is when a country exerts influence on economic, political, or cultural affairs. That is what characterized the relationship between the United States and Latin America in the nineteenth and twentieth centuries.

416. **(B)** The German emperor was promoting overseas conquest, which was a typical pattern in this period.

417. **(D)** The idea that Germany will be better if more Germans travel overseas shows nationalist feelings. Gaining "new points where we can drive in the nail on which to hang our armor" shows the goal of imperialism.

418. **(C)** As the process of industrialization spread across Europe in the nineteenth century, European powers competed for control of territory, as shown by the Scramble for Africa. They also competed for the resources that could be extracted to support manufacturing, such as cotton, rubber, and copper.

419. **(A)** The cartoon was drawn in response to the Boxer Rebellion. It shows that the European powers subdued the Chinese and were at odds with one another.

420. **(D)** The Qing dynasty survived the Boxer Rebellion. However, the monarchy was overthrown about 10 years later due to economic imperialism by Western powers, a lack of industrialization, and the desire to implement a more stable government.

421. **(B)** The caption refers to the "wake," which is what would happen after the death of China. In the early-twentieth century, World War I broke out. There was a struggle for control of spheres of influence in China, resulting in Germany losing its sphere to Japan.

422. **(A)** The use of the phrase "half devil and half child" and the use of the term "White Man's burden" reflects European racial ideologies that viewed nonwhites as inferior.

423. **(C)** The concept of "White Man's burden" was the idea that Europeans had an obligation to spread their superior medicine, scientific knowledge, and technology to nonwhites, whom they viewed as inferior. However, it was actually more of an excuse or justification for their conquests.

424. **(A)** Conquered groups did not simply accept their fate. In response there were violent and nonviolent resistance movements.

425. **(a)** An acceptable response includes a specific fact that supports the author's claim that the British Empire created strong links among many modern nations. Examples include the use of the English language as a global business language, the popularity of parliamentary forms of government resulting from the mimicking of British government structure by former colonies, and the use of capitalist economic systems and free trade in many former colonies.

(b) An acceptable response discusses a link between countries that is present despite British rule. Examples include the common religion of Islam in South and Southeast Asia despite British attempts at conversion; regional organizations, such as the African Union and ASEAN, which were formed to promote cooperation in the period after British rule; and the persistence of local languages despite the use of English.

(c) An acceptable response explains why much of history was Eurocentric. One example is the idea that Europeans were often those who studied history and dominated the field, so they promoted their dominance. Another example is the economic and political control of European powers until relatively recently. This created instability among non-Europeans and reinforced the idea that Europeans were superior.

426. (a) An acceptable response provides a specific change in Africa that happened because of the Scramble for Africa. Examples include the creation of colonies that were controlled by European powers; the control of African resources, such as gold, diamonds, and oil; the use of African labor on plantations and in mines at low wages or as a labor tax; the creation of borders that disregarded tribal, ethnic, and linguistic patterns; and the building of railroads, telegraphs, and schools.

(b) An acceptable response examines how the taking of African lands and resources continued earlier patterns of history. Examples include how imperialism in Africa was similar to imperialism in the Americas in that the lands were colonized and resources were extracted; the idea that expansion in Africa followed the colonization of India; and the exploitation of African resources that was much like the economic imperialism in China.

(c) An acceptable answer gives a specific response of Africans beyond a general response such as "rebellion." Examples include rebellions that sought to remove Europeans or gain independence, such as the Mau Mau Rebellion in Kenya; cooperation by some African tribal leaders so they could keep their leadership positions; and the rise of nationalist movements that rallied African people to support independence movements.

427. This essay question is assessing the skill of causation. An acceptable thesis identifies two or three specific factors, such as "The establishment of European empires around the world between 1750 and 1900 was due to industrial technology, the demand for resources and markets for European products, and ideologies that justified conquest." Avoid general statements, such as "There were military, economic, and intellectual causes of European imperialism." Contextualization should describe the inventions of the Industrial Revolution and the impact on global capitalism. It could go as far back as the Age of Exploration, which enabled Europeans to begin dominating global trade. Evidence provided in the body paragraphs should be specific and tie back to the argument to support it. Do not just list facts. For example, to prove the argument that industrial technology helped Europeans establish empires, the essay should describe how the invention of the steam

engine used in steamships provided an edge in battles with sail-powered ships, such as in the Opium Wars. The essay should also describe how the use of mass-produced weapons that were increasingly accurate allowed Europeans to put down rebellions by native peoples in the conquered areas. To explain the increased demand for resources, the essay should describe how the process of industrialization led to mass production of manufactured goods, such as textiles, and also increased the demand for raw materials, such as cotton. Ideologies that could be discussed could include the concept of White Man's burden and racism. A complex argument may examine the effects of imperialism on the places conquered. These effects could include the exploitation of resources and people, the loss of native culture, and the treatment of the natives as inferior due to racial ideologies.

428. The skill being assessed is change and continuity over time. An acceptable thesis includes two to three specific changes that occurred as a result of imperialism in one or more regions. If you feel comfortable enough with one region and are able to go into depth when describing the changes for that region, focusing on just one region may be easier. Otherwise, a broader essay works, too, but you have to use specific examples from a variety of regions. An acceptable thesis for a more general essay could be, "In the period between 1750 and 1900, the establishment of overseas empires by Europeans changed Asian and African economies in that they became controlled by Europeans. They also transformed cultural elements by introducing European values." A thesis that would be too broad and would not earn a point would just simply state that there were economic and cultural changes without alluding to what they were. Contextualization could include information about the Industrial Revolution and how the technological changes in Europe provided technology for conquest and the economic motives for imperialism. In the body paragraphs, the essay should include specific evidence that explains the changes and reasons for them. For example, for economic changes, the essay could discuss how the introduction of mass-produced European manufactured goods hurt local economies. One example is the textile industry in India. It could not compete with machine-made British cloth, leading to a decline in opportunities for skilled laborers in India. Cultural changes could include the introduction of Western languages, Christianity, and values such as democracy and Enlightenment ideas. A complex argument could weave in continuities, such as the continued practice of Islam and Animism in sub-Saharan Africa, Hinduism and Islam in South Asia, and Buddhism and Islam in Southeast Asia despite European missionaries' attempts at conversion to Christianity.

429. This DBQ essay is assessing your ability to create an argument about the responses to imperialism by natives. An acceptable thesis makes a claim about the various types of responses, such as a violent rebellion (documents 2, 5, 6), cooperation (1, 3, 4, 7), and curiosity (documents 1, 7). Contextualization discusses European economic changes as a result of industrialization and

resulting technologies that led to the conquest of colonies, or the racial ideologies that Europeans used to justify their actions. Throughout the essay, evidence from six documents must be used to illustrate the types of responses natives had toward European imperialism. The documents should be used to support the stated argument, rather than merely being summarized or quoted from. For three documents, the significance of the historical situation, purpose, point of view, or audience should be explained. For example, the African queen mother in document 5 is likely claiming that the women will fight to make the men in the tribe feel embarrassed and fight back against the British. Outside information that would extend your argument could include information about Indian Brahmins cooperating with the British to obtain positions in the bureaucracy or the rise of nationalist movements in response to European actions.

Note: Full Answers Explained with detailed explanations why the incorrect answers are wrong can be found at *www.barronsbooks.com/ap/docs/h72bdc/QA1125.pdf* or by using the QR code below.

CHAPTER 15: NATIONALISM, REVOLUTION, AND REFORM

430. **(D)** This document includes Enlightenment ideas such as equality under the law, natural rights, popular sovereignty, and liberty, which had been circulating in France and inspired the French Revolution to overthrow the absolute monarchy.

431. **(B)** The source was written during the French Revolution to restructure the government so that citizens' rights would be protected.

432. **(A)** Enlightenment ideas led to a greater participation in government by citizens through representatives.

433. **(C)** European monarchs would lose power if governments that protected rights and encouraged participation by citizens were implemented.

434. **(B)** The poster is celebrating the emancipation and freedom granted to slaves, which was inspired by Enlightenment ideas.

435. **(D)** The slave trade began as a way to supply labor for plantations in tropical climates of the Americas. This labor helped to produce cash crops such as cotton, sugar, indigo, tobacco, and coffee.

436. **(A)** While most were unsuccessful, there were slave rebellions and other resistance movements that contributed to debates about ending the practice.

437. **(C)** Bolivar is explaining the major complaints colonists had that caused them to rebel against the Spanish government.

438. **(B)** Mercantilist policies are described when the author discusses that Spain had exclusive trading privileges and restrictions on crop production and manufacturing.

439. **(A)** The Latin American revolutions were inspired by Enlightenment ideas of freedom.

440. **(D)** Most Latin American colonies achieved independence by 1830 as a result of rebellions inspired by Enlightenment ideas and the resentment of imperial policies.

441. **(A)** The cartoon represents the use of gunpowder by Garibaldi that helped unite the Italian peninsula under the rule of the king.

442. **(C)** Nationalist feelings united Italians and inspired them to form a country. The Italian peninsula had not been unified since the fall of the Roman Empire. Italians were united by a common cultural heritage and a temporary unification under Napoleon that inspired them to form a nation.

443. **(D)** The Seneca Falls Convention was an event of the feminist movement that called for the extension of women's rights.

444. **(B)** The ideas of inalienable rights, equality, and overthrowing unjust governments expressed in the passage were from the Enlightenment. The wording of the declaration is similar to the American Declaration of Independence, a revolutionary document.

445. **(C)** The proposed gender equality is an example of a reform movement in this era, which challenged patriarchal gender roles.

446. **(B)** Latin American colonies achieved independence following rebellions against their mother countries.

447. **(A)** Enlightenment ideas inspired colonists to overthrow oppressive imperial rule.

448. **(D)** Slavery continued in all Latin American nations except Haiti after independence. The *Creoles* who led the revolutions were mainly plantation owners whom did not want to lose their inexpensive labor force.

449. **(C)** The passage describes how Indian princes were afraid of losing power due to British interference, so they joined the rebellion to preserve their power.

450. **(B)** British racial ideologies led to the treatment of natives as inferior while viewing their cultural traditions as barbaric, which caused the Indian soldiers to be angry.

451. **(A)** The British had established trading posts in the period between 1450 to 1750. Following the Seven Years' War and the Sepoy Mutiny the British sought more direct control of India.

452. **(D)** An Indian view of the rebellion would likely be less dismissive of the tensions that existed and would provide a firsthand account if written at the time of the revolt.

453. **(A)** British political and economic policies reinforced their ideas of superiority. This lead to resentment and the rise of nationalist movements seeking independence.

454. **(D)** A settlement of runaway slaves shows that there were resistance movements because they escaped.

455. **(B)** Reform movements called for the abolition of slavery on humanitarian grounds, but also took into consideration that rebellions were disruptive to society and preventing them was costly. This led some to question the economic benefits of coerced labor.

456. **(C)** The caption of the cartoon shows anger toward the slaves by calling it a "horrid massacre" and using the phrase "cruelly murdered." The cartoon was designed to enrage those who viewed it.

457. **(B)** As an abolitionist, the author likely admires Louverture because of his help in ending the practice of slavery in Haiti.

458. **(D)** Abolitionists were inspired by Enlightenment ideas of equality and liberty.

459. **(A)** The Haitian Revolution was inspired by the American Revolution and took place during the French Revolution. This was due to Haiti being a French colony and wanting the Enlightenment ideas of the revolution to apply to the colonists.

460. **(a)** An acceptable response will provide a specific idea about how Enlightenment ideas caused changes in government. Examples could include the questioning of divine right and absolutism, and the support for more representative governments rather than the rule of a single monarch; the idea that governments should protect rights rather than oppress subjects; the questioning of the role of religion in public life and advocating for the separation of religion and government; the idea of natural rights leading to the desire for greater participation in government; and the idea that the people have the right to overthrow oppressive governments, such as France's monarchy, which led to the French Revolution.
    (b) An acceptable response explains continuity in political theory. Examples could include continued views of gender roles that led to the idea that since women should not participate in government, women were not granted the right to vote until the early twentieth century. You can also explain how the continued dominance of nobles in government, since many of the

philosophers were wealthy and looked down upon the masses, led to the lack of universal male suffrage until the end of the period; and the view that colonists were inferior. This meant that most European Enlightenment thinkers did not apply the ideas of freedom to colonial territories.

(c) An acceptable response explains how Enlightenment ideas spread outside Europe and brought change to other regions. Examples could include anticolonial movements that used Enlightenment ideas of representative government, natural rights, and liberty to call for independence from European control, such as those in Africa, India, or Latin America; the push for the extension of rights in Latin American and African societies ruled by oppressive regimes after independence; and the extension of rights to groups such as women, ethnic minorities, and religious minorities.

461. (a) An acceptable response explains major Enlightenment ideas used by Haitian revolutionaries. Examples could include the use of the idea of equality to advocate for the emancipation of slaves held by French colonists; the use of the idea of liberty to justify the overthrow of French rule; and the use of the idea of equality to call for equal status of white plantation owners and free people of color.

(b) An acceptable response will explain a difference in the motivations or causes of the American and Haitian Revolutions. For example, British colonists in North America were most upset with taxation policies imposed by the British, whereas the French colonists in Haiti were advocating for the emancipation of slaves. The leaders of North American revolutions were mainly against emancipation of slaves, whereas most Haitian revolutionaries were slaves themselves. The North American colonists were upset with mercantilist policies which restricted trade, while the Haitians were resentful of the coerced labor system.

(c) An acceptable response will explain the impact of Enlightenment ideas following the revolutions. Examples include the establishment of constitutions that protected natural rights; the implementation of representative governments; and how the abolition of slavery was based on Enlightenment ideas (although delayed in the United States).

462. This question is assessing the skill of causation. A strong thesis would identify at least two Enlightenment ideas that led to revolutions, such as the principles of natural rights and the idea that the people have the power to overthrow an unjust government. Contextualization would discuss the rise of Enlightenment ideas in response to the consolidation of power by European absolute monarchs; the economic situation that led to control of colonies in the Americas; or the role of the Seven Years' War in the American and French Revolutions. Throughout the essay, evidence must be clearly used to support your argument. For example, the American Revolution was caused by the lack of representation in colonial governments that gave them no say in taxation policies by the British, so they embraced the concept of consent of the governed to justify the Declaration of Independence. Another example

could be how the French revolutionaries established the National Assembly and issued the Declaration of the Rights of Man and Citizen based on the use of Enlightenment ideas. These ideas embraced natural rights and increased participation in political life. To show historical complexity, the different situations of the American colonists and French subjects can be compared, or effects of these revolutions and the extent to which Enlightenment ideas were truly incorporated could be discussed. For example, equality only applied to men, rather than women, and liberty did not apply to slaves in most cases.

463. This essay is assessing the skill of comparison. The best approach to this essay is to compare the French Revolution against the absolute monarchy with the American Revolution against British colonial rule, or even compare the Haitian Revolution against the French with the Latin American revolutions against the Spanish. Reform movements can be addressed as well, such as comparing the abolitionist movement with feminist movements. Contextualization would discuss the rise of Enlightenment ideas in response to the consolidation of power by European absolute monarchs; the economic situation that led to control of colonies in the Americas; or the role of the Seven Years' War in the American and French Revolutions. This depends on the examples discussed. An acceptable thesis will address at least two specific similarities in the causes, events, or results of revolutions. This could include comparing the role of Enlightenment ideas resulting in revolutions, as explained in the answers to question 462, or the similar constitutional governments that were established by governments following the revolutions. To show historical complexity, the essay should explain the differences between the motives for revolutions and reasons for the differences, such as the existing governments.

464. This DBQ is assessing the skill of causation. A strong thesis identifies two to three ways Enlightenment ideas were used in the American, French, Haitian, and Spanish American revolutions, collectively referred to as the Atlantic Revolutions. For example, "Enlightenment ideas regarding natural rights, the right to overthrow oppressive governments, and the participation of citizens in government inspired revolutionaries in the Atlantic World to overthrow their imperial rulers and create governments that incorporated these principles into more representative governments." Contextualization should explain how Enlightenment ideas developed in response to the English Civil War and centralization of power by French monarchs, such as Louis XIV. Also included can be how the Scientific Revolution inspired Enlightenment philosophers to embrace the use of reason and examine human relationships. Six documents should be used to support an argument based on the thesis, and analysis of how the ideas from each document inspired revolutions and political change must be included. For example, explaining how the Enlightenment concept that the people have the right to overthrow an oppressive government (document 1) and that citizens should participate in governments (documents 2) was used to justify rebellions such as the

American (documents 3 and 6), French (document 4), and Spanish-American (document 7) revolutions. The concept of natural rights was incorporated into new governments, as shown in the Haitian Constitution (document 5) and the Declaration of the Rights of Man and Citizen (document 4). For three of the documents, an analysis of the point of view, purpose, audience, or historical situation must be explained. For example, in the Declaration of Independence (document 3), colonists were trying to justify their right to rebel by listing complaints against the king of England and the ways he violated their rights, so he is depicted as a tyrant. Relevant outside evidence could include that the Spanish-American Revolutions resulted in the formation of republics based on Enlightenment ideas. To show historical complexity, nuances can be explained, such as how the revolutionaries sought equality and liberty, but yet they did not apply those ideas to women and most newly independent states did not abolish slavery (except in Haiti).

CHAPTER 16: GLOBAL MIGRATION

465. **(C)** Increased agricultural yields led to population growth, which in turn led to migrants seeking better living conditions and job opportunities. New forms of transportation, such as steamships and railroads, made long-distance travel more accessible.

466. **(D)** When migrants arrived in new lands, they brought cultural traditions, such as languages, foods, and religions, to areas where they settled. Migrants tended to form enclaves of people from the same country so they could provide assistance to one another and continue traditions.

467. **(A)** Most migrants tended to leave their home countries to go to areas with economic opportunities—jobs that required unskilled labor or specialized professions.

468. **(B)** The image was taken in Chinatown in New York City in the United States, which is an example of an ethnic enclave.

469. **(D)** In some regions, laws were passed to restrict immigrants from coming into the country. For example, the United States had the Chinese Exclusion Act and placed quotas on migrants from southern Europe.

470. **(C)** The document describes Chinese laborers working in mines, which was due to an increased demand for coal. This was due to the result of the development of steam engines and railroads. Also, many Chinese migrants worked laying tracks for the railroads.

471. **(D)** Indentured labor resulted from an increased demand for plantation workers due to industrialization.

472. **(A)** Labor migrants were typically men due to the physical labor that was required.

473. **(B)** These areas are tropical climates and mostly consisted of plantations.

474. **(C)** Railroads facilitated travel to and from cities and steamships accelerated overseas travel.

475. **(C)** English was used in India as a result of British conquest and colonization in the nineteenth century.

476. **(D)** Migrations of Indians, Chinese, and Japanese in this era were most often for agricultural work that was coerced or semicoerced in that it often took the form of indentured servitude. In this arrangement, a migrant's passage to the new land would be paid for and in exchange the migrant would work until the debt was paid; however, low wages and high costs of housing and food made this difficult.

477. **(A)** Migrants transplanted their cultural elements to their receiving societies, so East Asian belief systems, such as Buddhism, spread along with Chinese and Japanese migrants.

478. **(B)** The White Australia policy was designed to limit nonwhites from migrating to Australia.

479. **(D)** The cover has national symbols and a map, and touts the song as "The Great National Policy Song."

480. **(C)** Italian migrants were able to travel long distances thanks to the development of steamships.

481. **(A)** Most Italian migrants ended up in the Americas or other parts of Europe due to the availability of jobs, since Italy was late to industrialize.

482. **(B)** Migrants tended to bring their cultural traditions to their new homelands, and often settled in small areas where previous migrants settled, such as Little Italy or Chinatown in New York City.

483. **(D)** The abolition of the slave trade led to labor shortages since new laborers were not brought in, and industrialization increased the demand for commodities.

484. **(B)** The language used makes the editorial sound like an urgent labor shortage in order to persuade the colonial governor, to whom it is addressed.

485. **(A)** After the abolition of slavery, indentured servants or contract laborers from parts of Asia often filled labor shortages.

486. **(C)** Scientific advances led to longer life spans, and innovations in food production led to better diets and larger populations.

487. **(D)** Population pressures led to movements from Europe to the Americas and from China to the United States.

488. **(B)** The cartoonist labeled immigrants in a negative light, as demonstrated by the labels used, reflecting prejudice.

489. **(A)** The artist is clearly opposed to immigrants and most likely feels that they must be limited.

490. **(C)** Many migrants arrived in the Americas with the idea that they could achieve the "American Dream" if they worked hard enough.

491. **(B)** Negative views of immigrants led to laws, such as the Chinese Exclusion Act in the United States, limiting immigrants from certain countries.

492. **(D)** Enlightenment ideas led to the end of slavery, which was the main source of labor on plantations.

493. **(D)** Steamships made oceanic travel cheaper and faster, which opened up opportunities for migrants.

494. **(D)** Migrants tended to help people of similar ethnic background in the face of prejudice by receiving societies and continuing cultural traditions.

495. **(a)** An acceptable response indentifies a continuity from previous eras, especially 1450 to 1750. Examples could include the continued movement of Europeans to the Americas for economic opportunities, coerced labor migrations that continued previous patterns of the trans-Atlantic slave trade, the movement from rural areas to cities, and continued patterns of urbanization that were occurring in the early modern period. Specific examples must be discussed.
(b) An acceptable response identifies one major change in patterns. Examples can include migrants from Europe to the Americas being unskilled laborers seeking industrial employment rather than escaping religious persecution or wanting to establish farms, or how coerced labor migrations went from mainly West Africa to the Americas previously to Indian and Chinese contract laborers to the Americas in this period. Another example could include migrants going to Latin America were from all parts of Europe and Asia, as opposed to Spain and Portugal.
(c) An acceptable response identifies a cultural change as a result of migration. Examples include: the introduction of religions such as Buddhism and Hinduism to new areas as a result of the migration of Chinese and Indian laborers to the Caribbean, Africa, and the United States; the introduction of new languages that migrants carried with them to new areas, such as Chinese to North America or Italian to Brazil; or the introduction of new cuisines as immigrants retained their traditional diets, such as Italian food in the United States.

496. **(a)** An acceptable response explains a change in patterns of migrations to the United States. Examples include: the shift in migrations from Western Europe, such as England, France, and Germany, to migrations from Southern Europe, such as Italy; the shift in labor migrations from Africa to labor migrations from Europe and Asia; and the shift in migrations for the opportunity to buy land and build farms as well as opportunities to work in factories in urban areas.
(b) An acceptable response includes a specific continuity in views of immigrants through the present. Examples can include the negative attitudes

toward new minority groups that led to restrictions and quotas that limited migrants from certain European countries; the idea that immigrants are less loyal to the government than natives, such as suspicions of foreigners being communists during the Cold War; and the questioning of voting rights and citizenship process for migrants. This includes the increased requirements to naturalize.

(c) An acceptable response includes economic reasons for changes in migrations to the United States. Examples include how the Industrial Revolution led to poor working and living conditions in European cities, resulting in migrations to the Americas; the idea that the United States was a land of opportunity leading to movements for jobs; and the mechanization of farming in Europe resulting in more unskilled laborers who were seeking jobs.

497. This question assesses the skill of causation. A strong thesis identifies two to three major effects, and should identify broader patterns. For example, "Overseas migration in the period 1750–1900 led to diffusion of cultural elements, such as foods, religious beliefs, and traditions, and increasingly hostile reactions to incoming migrants in receiving societies, such as the Americas." Contextualization can include the economic changes resulting from the Industrial Revolution and the transportation changes that occurred facilitating long-distance travel, such as railroads and steamships. Throughout the essay, effects must be explained with specific examples of evidence to back your claims. For example, religious beliefs such as Hinduism and Buddhism spread to Africa and the Caribbean with Indian and Chinese laborers, respectively. An analysis of the reasons why these changes occurred should be included. For historical complexity, long-term effects in the twentieth century can be discussed, as well as comparisons of effects on two different regions.

498. This question addresses the skill of causation. A strong thesis identifies two to three factors that caused overseas migration, such as new transportation technologies and economic opportunities. Contextualization could include a discussion of the Industrial Revolution and shifting patterns of work, such as an increase in demand for unskilled labor, or the Agricultural Revolution that led to less demand for farmers and more food production. In the essay, causes of migration must be clearly explained with specific examples. For example, migrations occurred from Europe and the United States because European population growth and *laissez-faire* capitalist economies led to poor living and working conditions, resulting in the desire to achieve the "American Dream." This was motivated by the stories that the streets were paved with gold. For historical complexity, effects can be discussed (see explanation for question 497).

CHAPTER 17: SCIENCE AND THE ENVIRONMENT

499. **(B)** Agricultural innovations resulting from advances in science and the mechanization of farming were able to increase yields to support a growing population.

500. **(C)** Medical advances, such as vaccines and antibiotics, increased longevity rates since diseases that were once deadly could be cured.

501. **(A)** As global population expanded in the twentieth and early twenty-first centuries, resources such as clean air and fresh water become strained due to the large demand for these necessities.

502. **(C)** The technologies referred to in the passage led to the production of more food per acre.

503. **(A)** The clearing of land for plantations in the Caribbean caused ecological destruction and less diversity in crops because mainly single cash crops were produced on plantations.

504. **(B)** The author is arguing that the Green Revolution negatively impacted the environment by decreasing plant diversity, so she would likely not agree that the environment should suffer at the hands of technology.

505. **(A)** "Total war" is a strategy that views civilians as targets for military attacks, which is why over 60% of deaths in World War II were civilians.

506. **(C)** Many civilian victims in Eastern Europe and the Soviet Union were targets for Hitler's campaign to annihilate the Jews of Europe and kill political prisoners.

507. **(B)** Genetically modified crops developed beginning in the 1970s during the Green Revolution, aimed at increasing agricultural yields.

508. **(D)** As an environmental organization, Greenpeace would be concerned with the impact of human activity, such as the release of greenhouse gases, on climate change.

509. **(A)** Nongovernmental organizations, like Greenpeace, developed to bring attention to environmental issues that have arisen due to globalization and population growth.

510. **(C)** The title shows that Greenpeace is attempting to argue that GM crops have failed to produce results that supporters of commercial agriculture claim have occurred.

511. **(D)** Malaria is treatable, which is why it has declined globally, but in many places in Africa it is deadly because of lack of access to antibiotics due to poverty.

512. **(C)** Medical innovations and antibiotics led to a significant decline in global malaria cases.

513. **(A)** The production of cash crops leads to soil depletion, and the clearing of land for agriculture leads to deforestation.

514. **(C)** Intensive production of food crops depletes the available supply of fresh water and clean water.

515. **(B)** The authors would likely agree that ecological devastation has occurred due to pollutants that contributed to climate change since they are ecological economists.

516. **(D)** The trend shown on the graph is longer life spans, due to medical advances such as vaccines and antibiotics.

517. **(B)** As humans live longer, there are higher incidences of diseases associated with old age, such as Alzheimer's and heart disease.

518. **(A)** In the period 1750–1900, global population increased greatly due to longer life spans.

519. **(C)** The global economy became more integrated in the twentieth century due to policies that reduced trade barriers and supported private enterprise.

520. **(D)** The expansion of the global economy and increased production of manufactured goods contributed to pollution and debates about causes of global warming.

521. **(B)** Movements have arisen to protest the inequalities associated with rapid economic growth.

522. **(A)** Economic organizations have helped provide loans for development and promoted international trade.

523. **(B)** The Green Revolution led to the use of chemical fertilizers and experiments with crop strains to make plants more resistant to fungi and weather patterns. These factors have contributed to higher wheat yields.

524. **(D)** As food production increases, population generally tends to increase as well, leading to greater competition for resources such as clean air, fresh water, and oil.

525. **(C)** Between 600 and 1450 C.E., China was introduced to a new rice strain, referred to as champa rice or fast-ripening rice, which doubled yields because there could be two harvests per year.

526. **(A)** Rates of diabetes have increased due to the prevalence of fatty foods, such as fast food, and more processed foods including sugar.

527. **(B)** The World Health Organization (WHO) is an arm of the United Nations, and is an example of an institution that promotes cooperation—in this case, for improvement of health.

528. **(D)** Despite medical advances and the decline of other infectious diseases, AIDS and Ebola were prevalent in the late twentieth and early twenty-first centuries.

529. **(a)** An acceptable response will discuss a specific factor that led to population growth between 1750 and 1900. Examples include advances in agricultural production, such as the use of fertilizers and new tools like the seed drill, that increased yields; medical advances, such as germ theory, that led to longer life spans; and lower infant mortality rates due to availability of food and improved diets.

(b) An acceptable response will discuss how increased population led to changes in the environment. Examples include the depletion of resources such as fossil fuels, clean water, and fresh air due to more people using limited resources; and the increased release of greenhouse gases due to increased industrial production resulting from greater demand for consumer goods.

(c) An acceptable response will include a continuity in human-environment interaction since 1000 C.E. Examples include the desire to increase agricultural yields to meet increased demands; the disparity between large landowners and small farmers due to the ability to purchase tools for production; and the influence of climate on production and yields, such as the Little Ice Age and global warming.

530. **(a)** An acceptable response will examine one reason why the institute was making a judgment as to whether the Green Revolution was positive or negative. Examples include the rise of organizations that protested environmental changes, such as the impact of chemicals; and debates about the causes of climate change as a result of greenhouse gases.

(b) An acceptable response will compare the causes or impact of increased agricultural yields with the Agricultural Revolution between 1750 and 1900. Examples include both resulted from improvements in farming techniques as a result of scientific advances, such as crop rotation in Western Europe and chemical fertilizers during the Green Revolution; and the growth in population as a result of greater availability of food.

(c) An acceptable response would explain a difference between the Neolithic and Green Revolutions. Examples include how the Green Revolution did not change lifestyles to the extent that the Neolithic Revolution did, in that the Neolithic led to the shift to a sedentary lifestyle whereas the Green Revolution increased yields; and how the Green Revolution led to diversified diets while the Neolithic Revolution led to poorer diets in the short run.

531. This question assess the skill of causation. An acceptable thesis would identify at least two scientific advances that led to population changes, such as medical innovations and the Green Revolution. For contextualization, the broader trend of population growth stemming from the Agricultural Revolution and the continued advances in biology and chemistry of the nineteenth century could be explained. Specific evidence for medical advances could include the development of vaccines, such as the polio vaccine, which made communicable diseases less common; antibiotics which improved treatment for communicable diseases and made them less deadly; and innovations such as the artificial heart. Evidence for the Green Revolution could include

the use of chemical fertilizers and pesticides to improve agricultural yields; experimentation with genetically modified crops to make them more drought and pest resistant; and experimentation with new plant strains. To demonstrate historical reasoning, the essay must explain the relationship between these developments and increased population. To demonstrate historical complexity, the essay may compare the pattern population growth due to increased food production that occurred in the early eighteenth century or explain effects of increased population, such as the strain on natural resources and increased population density.

CHAPTER 18: GLOBAL CONFLICTS AND THEIR CONSEQUENCES

532. **(B)** The caption explains how the Germans sunk a Red Cross ship, which was not a military vessel, but one providing humanitarian aid. This illustrates the concept of "total war," in which civilians mobilize in the war effort, but are also considered as potential targets.

533. **(C)** Hitler rose to power in the aftermath of World War I partly due to the economic crisis in Germany that was caused by the Treaty of Versailles and worsened by the Great Depression. Also, the Great Depression contributed to World War II because Western powers were more focused on their economic situation than international affairs and responding to German aggression.

534. **(A)** Both posters served to encourage civilians to support the war by buying war bonds (Image 1) and carpooling (Image 2).

535. **(D)** After World War I and World War II, international organizations such as the League of Nations and the United Nations were created in order to resolve conflict diplomatically.

536. **(A)** In this document, Ho Chi Minh is declaring independence, thus challenging French colonial rule.

537. **(D)** The passage states that the French "violated our fatherland and oppressed our fellow citizens."

538. **(B)** In this document, the Vietnamese are explaining that they are seeking freedom because the French are hypocritical in that they declared rights for themselves but those rights did not apply to the colonies.

539. **(C)** When India received independence from Great Britain, the region was partitioned into mostly Hindu India and mostly Muslim Pakistan. Migrations happened and violence broke out because of tensions between the groups that were fueled by British rule and because the Hindus in Pakistan and the Muslims in India feared being a minority in the new countries.

540. **(D)** These migrations occurred due to the partition of India, which split the British colony into two states.

541. **(A)** The creation of Israel led to mainly Palestinian Arab refugees to flee to neighboring countries due to border changes.

542. **(B)** The Mexican Revolution was partly a reaction to economic imperialism by Western powers who dominated Mexico's resources and industries while the majority of the population was landless and poor.

543. **(C)** This plan explains how Zapata wanted to return land to the *pueblos* and citizens who owned it before it was taken by landlords.

544. **(D)** The Russian Revolution was a communist revolution that promised "peace, land, and bread" while the Mexican Revolution promised "land and liberty." Both sought to redistribute land.

545. **(A)** The speeches reflect tensions between Western powers and the Soviet Union after World War II. These tensions were over the fate of Eastern Europe and the Soviet failure to hold elections in occupied countries.

546. **(C)** Churchill states that the "difficulties and dangers will not be removed by waiting to see what happens," showing that he feels the issue needs to be addressed.

547. **(D)** The European powers dominated much of Asia and Africa in the nineteenth and early-twentieth centuries. Because of this, the leaders of independence movements in those regions would likely also feel that the West looked down upon non-Western peoples.

548. **(B)** Tensions over Eastern Europe led to the Cold War, which was not a direct military conflict between the U.S. and the Soviet Union, but included proxy wars in which the powers supported those with the same ideology; these include the Korean War, the Vietnam War, and the Soviet invasion of Afghanistan.

549. **(C)** NATO and the Warsaw Pact were alliances during the Cold War that developed due to tensions between the United States and its capitalist allies and the Soviet Union and its communist allies. Non-Aligned Members wished to remain neutral in the conflict between the United States and the Soviet Union.

550. **(B)** The Non-Aligned Movement was meant to reject the polarization of the world into communist and capitalist spheres.

551. **(D)** There never was a direct outbreak of war between the United States and the Soviet Union, but there was indirect fighting in proxy wars, such as Korea and Vietnam. The Soviet Union provided weapons and intelligence for the communist groups while the United States provided aid to those fighting communism.

552. **(B)** The statement about Europeans robbing the continent and inflicting suffering refers to the period of colonial rule. Nkrumah, as an African nationalist, would naturally be against imperialism.

553. **(A)** Nkrumah was calling for unity of all Africans as a continent, called Pan-Africanism. Since it is a regional movement it would be considered transnational, or across nations.

554. **(D)** European imperialism was justified by ideologies such as the White Man's burden, which claimed that whites had an obligation to spread their superior civilization with groups they deemed inferior.

555. **(C)** When the European imperialists carved up Africa during the Berlin Conference in the late-nineteenth century, they disregarded tribal and ethnic groups. This led to some groups being divided and rival tribes forced into one colony. Civil war and border disputes broke out after independence because the new nations generally kept the European borders, and often minority groups were suppressed. Wars over control of the government broke out and some tribes wished to be united across borders.

556. **(A)** This poster was created by the United States government for distribution in Asia encouraging women to vote so that democratic institutions would strengthen in Asia. This would prevent communism from spreading. United States' policy during the Cold War was containment, or preventing the spread of communism.

557. **(C)** It was designed to empower women by stating that it makes them better than men, in order to encourage women to exercise their newly granted right to vote. Many Asian societies were highly patriarchal so the women's rights movements in these countries were not as dominant as in the West.

558. **(B)** In the twentieth century, due to the United Nations' Declaration on Human Rights and spread of Enlightenment ideas, many societies extended the right to vote to women and expanded rights to minority groups that were previously suppressed.

559. **(D)** In the Cold War era, instead of direct fighting with the Soviet Union, the United States engaged in indirect struggles in proxy wars. This took place overseas in order to stop the spread of communism and end the nuclear arms race to discourage the Soviet Union from attacking for fear of nuclear war.

560. **(A)** During the Cold War, the United States and the Soviet Union tried to avoid direct conflict by relaxing tensions and attempted to connect through exchanges of people, exhibitions, and performances.

561. **(B)** The Soviet Union was spending on industry and the arms race in order to compete with the United States. Since businesses were state-run, they suffered, and there were shortages of consumer goods and even food. Also, the invasion of Afghanistan led to a long, costly war.

562. **(a)** An acceptable response explains a process of the twentieth century. Examples include the use of propaganda by governments to support a cause, such as war, or to disparage a cause or group; the mobilization of all citizens

in supporting the war effort, such as encouraging men to enlist; and the development of global conflict, which was considered "total war" because of civilian involvement. The images must be specifically referred to in the response.

(b) An acceptable response explains a difference in the groups the message of the poster was directed toward. Examples include the following: The first image is directed toward women and encouraging them to support their husbands' enlistment in the war, while the second image is directed toward Britain's colonies to get them to participate in the war effort; or that the first image is designed for British citizens in Britain proper, while the second image is directed toward colonists overseas.

(c) An acceptable response explains a larger pattern of the use of propaganda. Examples include the use of propaganda during times of war, such as the world wars to engage civilians in the war effort; and the use of art for political purposes by governments in order to promote nationalist feelings.

563. **(a)** An acceptable response discusses population changes as a result of military conflicts, but must go beyond a vague response, such as population decline. Examples can include the loss of a large segment of the male population of Europe, especially aged 18–30, due to the world wars; the death of 11 million as a result of the Holocaust during World War II, 6 million of which were Jewish victims; the movement of colonists, such as Indians, to fight in World War I in Europe for their mother country, Great Britain; the deaths of Japanese civilians due to Allied firebombing campaigns and the use of atomic bombs against Japan in World War II; the death of European civilians as a result of bombing campaigns in Great Britain and Germany in World War II; and the relocation of Jews to Israel in the aftermath of World War II.

(b) An acceptable response discusses a specific continuity in either war or relationships between countries. Examples include how World War I was partly due to competition over colonies, such as those in Africa, and similar to the Seven Years' War that was fought in the 1750s and also the Napoleonic Wars that were fought to counter French expansion in Western Europe in the early nineteenth century. This was similar to World War II's attempt to stop Germany's expansion in the 1930s.

(c) An acceptable response discusses an impact of wars on world politics. For example, in the aftermath of World War II, European powers were declining due to the physical and financial devastation of the war and the loss of overseas colonies, so the United States and the Soviet Union emerged as superpowers. This led to the polarization of the world with the struggle between capitalist nations aligned with the United States against communist nations aligned with the Soviet Union. Another example is how World War I led to the loss of Germany's overseas territories and gave Japan more territory. This paved the way for Japanese aggression in the 1930s as a result of the tensions from the end of World War II.

564. This question is assessing the skill of causation. A strong thesis will discuss how a specific challenge led to global conflict, such as the rise of fascist governments in the decade before World War II; the rise of anticolonial or nationalist movements in Africa and Asia; or the development of the Cold War between the United States and the Soviet Union. For this topic it is best to focus on one military conflict to ensure that the essay is coherent. Contextualization could include an explanation of ideologies which were spreading at this time, such as communism, nationalism, and fascism, and how the First World War contributed to the Great Depression and the rise of extremist groups in Germany and Italy. For two points, evidence must be specific and clearly linked back to the thesis or claim. For example, the Indian independence movement could be used as an example of a nationalist movement that used passive forms of resistance against the British government. This eventually led to a negotiated independence and the partition of India and inspired other nationalist movements in Africa and Asia. To show historical reasoning, the essay should compare various types of challenges, such as military, ideological, and economic, or examine long term effects of the changing global order. To demonstrate historical complexity, a discussion of the proxy wars in the Cold War should demonstrate the idea that the ideological tensions between the superpowers also led to traditional fighting. Another aspect that could be discussed to show historical complexity is the idea that challenges could be addressed in a variety of ways. This could be both violent and nonviolent methods by nationalist leaders attempting to win independence.

565. This question assesses the skill of change and continuity over time. A strong thesis will discuss at least two specific changes in empires across the twentieth century. For example, "European empires, such as Britain, gradually lost their overseas territories through war or negotiation and their economies were weakened as a result of anti-imperialist ideologies." Contextualization could include a discussion of the role the world wars played in creating resentment on the part of colonists who fought and died for their mother countries; and the spread of Western values, such as democracy, and technology, such as weapons. Specific evidence includes several examples of independence movements, and could focus on more than one empire. For example, a discussion of how India's mainly nonviolent nationalist movements against Great Britain led to the loss of a cash crop producing territory and hurt British industrial production, while the independence of South Africa after World War II resulted in the implementation of apartheid by the white settler population. Historical reasoning should clearly discuss the cause of the anti-imperialist movement and how that led to independence and the change in relationship with the mother country. To demonstrate historical complexity, the essay could compare different anticolonial movements. These can include violent versus nonviolent movements, or British reactions of negotiation in India and Ghana compared to French responses of war in Algeria and Vietnam.

566. The DBQ question is assessing the skill of causation. A strong thesis will examine two to three issues resulting from the end of World War I and make a judgment as to whether those were the primary causes of World War II. For example, "World War II developed mainly as a result of treaties ending World War I that were deemed unfair, especially to Germany, which led to the rise of extremist groups that were allowed to pursue aggressive policies by major world powers." Contextualization could examine the factors leading to World War I, or the ways the war itself impacted the writing of the peace agreements. For example, the United States' desire to avoid getting pulled into another war or France's desire for revenge due to the fighting on French soil led to the U.S. proposal of self-determination, while France pushed for reparations from Germany. The essay should use evidence from the documents to demonstrate each claim and should show analysis of how the information presented in each document used demonstrates a cause of World War II. For example, documents 1, 2, 5, and 7 all relate to the treaties following World War I, so discussing the components that were viewed as unfair and the responses by Germany could help support the claim that flawed peace agreements were the main cause of WWII. Documents 3 and 5 show that extremist groups arose in Italy and Germany and attempted to claim land, while other powers did not respond to aggression firmly. This led to continued invasions, as shown in documents 4 and 6. For three documents, an analysis of the significance of each author's point of view, audience, purpose, or historical situation should be included. For example, in document 3 it could be pointed out that Mussolini was the founder of Fascist ideology, so it is natural that he would promote it over democratic liberalism and advocate for war. Outside evidence could include information about the Great Depression which was a main reason why Western powers did not react strongly to German and Italian aggression. They were focused on their domestic economies which were in crisis. To show complexity, the argument should discuss how the Western powers sought to avoid war with Stalin and the Soviet Union following World War II, but realized that appeasement or signs of weakness would not be a sufficient response, since it failed in the prewar years.

CHAPTER 19: NEW CONCEPTUALIZATIONS OF GLOBAL ECONOMY, SOCIETY, AND CULTURE

567. **(C)** Industrialization increased demand for products such as raw materials from colonies in Africa and Asia due to the climate in which certain plants grew, such as cotton or rubber.

568. **(A)** The author is Marxist and is writing during the Cold War, when tensions between communist and capitalist nations were high. This was due to the ideological competition between them, so it makes sense that the author disparages capitalism.

569. **(D)** Even after political independence, many former colonies relied on their mother country for manufactured goods due to slow industrial growth. In many cases, European companies or individuals continued to own mines and land in former colonies.

570. **(A)** International organizations, such as the United Nations, were designed to give every member nation a voice in international affairs and promote cooperation, which would refute his claim that the global order is dominated by a few strong powers.

571. **(D)** The Russian Revolution led to the establishment of the Soviet Union, and was caused by unhappiness with the tsar and economic troubles due to the war.

572. **(C)** Marxist ideology arose in the midst of the Industrial Revolution in Europe due to the economic inequalities caused by the capitalist system.

573. **(A)** The governments in Russia and China seized control of the means of production, such as lands and businesses.

574. **(B)** Both posters are propaganda aiming to convince the masses that the programs, namely industrialization in the Soviet Union and collective farms in China, were beneficial.

575. **(A)** The communist nations were in an ideological struggle with Western capitalist nations and would not encourage the adoption of Western culture.

576. **(B)** Inalienable rights, freedom, and justice were ideas of the Enlightenment that were gradually incorporated into governments.

577. **(C)** This document was written in the aftermath of World War II and the Holocaust, during which Jews and other minority groups were systematically murdered.

578. **(D)** A rights-based discourse led to new ideas about groups that were previously marginalized.

579. **(A)** The protection of the rights of ethnic, religious, social, or political groups led to greater participation in government.

580. **(C)** As the United States and Western Europe moved toward knowledge-based jobs and service industries, manufacturing shifted away from the West toward Asia and the Pacific Rim. This was aided by faster shipping.

581. **(B)** Economic institutions, such as the World Bank and International Monetary Fund, as well as regional agreements, such as the European Union, have facilitated economic growth.

582. **(D)** The rapid economic growth among Asian Tigers mimics the growth of Europe's economy during the Industrial Revolution.

583. **(A)** The creation of a global economy has been aided by improvements in communication, such as the Internet, and transportation, such as air travel. Those technological developments have led to stronger ties between nations that are separated by geographic distance.

584. **(C)** The passage discusses how opponents of globalization complain that it has led to the shifting of jobs overseas since companies are subject to less stringent labor and environmental regulations. This has led to the rise of manufacturing facilities in the developing world, particularly the Pacific Rim and Latin America.

585. **(D)** Movements have occurred to demonstrate the negative effects of global integration, including pollution in developing nations due to looser regulations.

586. **(B)** As companies spread their products, consumer and popular culture spread and became more globalized, including movies, music, and sports.

587. **(B)** The celebration of Earth Day arose from environmental groups that wished to bring attention to environmental issues.

588. **(D)** New technologies, such as cars, air planes, and freight trains, contributed to increased release of greenhouse gases.

589. **(C)** The cartoon is designed to point out the contradiction between human behavior on Earth Day versus every other day when we contribute to environmental damage.

590. **(A)** The European Union (EU) reduced economic barriers to trade, such as tariffs, in order to promote economic growth.

591. **(B)** After revolutions occurred in Eastern Europe, and the Soviet Union collapsed, Eastern European nations could liberalize their economies and participate in trade agreements.

592. **(A)** The United Nations is considered an organization of "global governance" because it promotes cooperation and the use of diplomacy among member nations.

593. **(D)** The United Nations was created in the aftermath of World War II due to the failure of the League of Nations in preserving peace and the desire to prevent such a devastating war.

594. **(C)** Conflicts have broken out between nations despite the charter's goal of avoiding military conflict, such as Iraq's invasion of Kuwait.

595. **(A)** Participation in the Olympics encouraged international cooperation and healthy competition among nations.

596. **(B)** As athletes from around the world have participated in the Olympic games every two years (Summer and Winter), popular culture such as movies, cuisine, and fashion spread.

597. **(a)** An acceptable response identifies a challenge or issue that governments were attempting to address. Examples include the Great Depression, which led to unemployment and a decline in production that devastated national economies; the world wars, which required the mobilization of resources and the investment of capital into the war effort; or the need of newly independent countries to industrialize in the aftermath of independence.

(b) An acceptable response will explain a difference in policies of communist and newly independent states in the twentieth century. For example, communist states, such as the Soviet Union and China, controlled all aspects of the national policies through policies such as the Five Year Plans to promote industrialization and the Great Leap Forward in China to promote increased agricultural yields to support industrial workers; whereas newly independent states often promoted industrialization through government investment in business, such as the government-run factories in India following independence.

(c) An acceptable response explains how, in the last few decades following the end of the Cold War in 1991, the global economic trend has been that governments reduce trade barriers, such as tariffs, and promote participation in regional trade agreements, such as the European Union.

598. (a) An acceptable response explains why economies have become more reliant on one another. Examples include technologies such as faster ships and airplanes that have reduced the cost of shipping; communication technologies such as radios, cell phones, and the Internet that have made it easier to do business overseas; and the promotion of international organizations for economic cooperation, such as the World Bank.

(b) An acceptable response explains an example of how governments changed their economic policies. Examples include the control of the economies of communist states, such as the Soviet Union and China, in order to promote rapid industrialization and the implementation of communist ideology; and the increased role of governments in the economy during the Great Depression, such as the New Deal in the United States, which used tax revenues to create jobs.

(c) An acceptable response will include a continuity throughout the twentieth century. Examples include capitalist economies in the Western European industrialized states and the United States has been the consistent economic system despite periods when government regulation increased or the extraction of nonrenewable resources, such as oil and coal, due to the demands of industrial production.

599. This essay question assesses the skill of causation because it looks at how challenges led to new policies. An acceptable thesis identifies at least one state or one challenge that led to government responses. For example, the essay may focus on responses to the Great Depression, such as the New Deal in the United States and the directive nature of fascist governments. It could examine one or more examples of policies designed to initialize the process of industrialization in newly independent countries, such as government control of manufacturing in India and Egypt. Contextualization could include the general causes of economic changes in this period, such as the world wars and the mobilization they entailed, or the Great Depression that devastated global economies. To show historical reasoning, an explanation of how these events led to the reaction discussed should be included. To demonstrate historical

complexity, a comparison of the effectiveness of differing responses to the same challenge can be addressed.

600. This essay question is assessing the skill of causation since it requires an explanation of how new ideas about rights led to political changes. An acceptable thesis would look at factors leading to new attitudes toward a particular group to be discussed, such as women's rights and feminism or the end of apartheid. Contextualization should discuss Enlightenment ideas and how those were incorporated into the United Nations' Declaration on Human Rights in the mid-twentieth century; or how feminist movements in the twentieth century were an extension of movements that first developed in the nineteenth century. To support the argument, specific evidence should be used. This should be a description of the policies of apartheid and the factors that contributed to the end of the laws promoting separation between the races of South Africa, or how the right to vote was extended to women around the world after World War I. Increased economic opportunities, especially for middle- and upper-class women, can also be discussed. To show historical reasoning, an explanation of the specific reasons why these responses brought change can be included. To show historical complexity, an evaluation of the extent to which rights-based discourses brought change for all members of society, such as homosexuals, could be discussed.

ACKNOWLEDGMENTS

Pages 8–9: From Joseph E. Pluta (2014) Technology vs. Institutions in Prehistory, *Journal of Economic Issues*, 46: 1,209–226, DOI: 10.2753/JEI0021-3624460109. Reprinted by permission of the publisher Taylor & Francis Ltd, *http://www.tandfonline.com* and The Association for Evolutionary Economics (AFEE), *http://afee.net/*

Page 15: Republished with permission of Sage Publications, Inc., from *The Underside of History: A View of Women Through Time*, Elise Boulding, First edition, 1976; permission conveyed through Copyright Clearance Center, Inc.

Page 90, page 120, page 126: Republished with permission of *Journal of World History*, from Southernization, Lynda Shaffer, *Journal of World History*, Volume 5, no. 1, 1994: permission conveyed through Copyright Clearance Center, Inc.

Page 70: From Jerry H. Bentley, *Traditions & Encounters: A Global Perspective on the Past*, 4th ed., Vol. I. (New York: McGraw-Hill, 2008), p. 300

Page 123: Jerry H. Bentley, *Traditions & Encounters: A Global Perspective on the Past*, 4th ed., Vol. I. (New York: McGraw-Hill, 2008), p. 384

Pages 133–134 and page 145: Republished with permission of *Journal of World History*, from *Born with a "Silver Spoon": The Origin of World Trade in 1571*, Dennis O. Flynn and Arturo Giraldez, *Journal of World History*, Volume 6, no. 2, 1995: permission conveyed through Copyright Clearance Center, Inc.

Page 141: From Jerry H. Bentley, *Traditions & Encounters: A Global Perspective on the Past*, 4th ed. (New York: McGraw-Hill, 2008), pp. 705, 733–734, 765

Page 157: Statistics from H. H. Lamb, *Climate, History, and the Modern World*, 1995, p. 189

Page 222: Republished with permission of *Journal of World History*, from "Is Humpty Dumpty Back Together Again?: the Revival of Imperial History and the Oxford History of the British Empire," Douglas M. Peers, *Journal of World History*, Volume 13, no. 2, 2002: permission conveyed through Copyright Clearance Center, Inc.

Page 249: Adapted from David Northrup, *Indentured Labor in the Age of Imperialism, 1834–1922*, 1995

Page 271: Reprinted with permission from *World Health*, May–June 1991, Hilary King, "WHO and Diabetes," Copyright © 1991, World Health Organization

Page 288: Republished with permission of Sage Publications, from "Militarism, the United States, and the Cold War," Hubert P. van Tuyll, *Armed Forces and Society: An Interdisciplinary Journal*, Volume 20, no. 4, 1994: permission conveyed through Copyright Clearance Center, Inc.

Page 304: Reprinted with permission of Cagle Cartoons. "Earth Day!" by R. J. Matson, 2009

The tools you need to succeed on your AP World History exam

Barron's AP World History with Online Tests
With Bonus Online Tests, 8th Edition
John McCannon
This fully updated manual includes: two full-length practice tests with answer explanations reflecting the most recent exam; a review of world history, from the foundations of civilization circa 600 B.C.E. to world cultures of the twenty-first century; revised test strategies, unit short cut charts, key concepts, and more. Also includes FREE access to three additional full-length online tests with all questions answered and explained. The online exams can be easily accessed by computer, tablet, and smartphone.
ISBN 978-1-4380-1109-7, $23.99, Can$29.99

Barron's AP World History Flash Cards
3rd Edition
Lorraine Lupinsky-Huvane and Kate Caporusso
These thoroughly revised and updated flash cards present a history topic on the front of each card, with key information listed on the reverse side. Includes FREE access to one full-length online AP World History test with all questions answered and explained. Also includes FREE access to one additional full-length online AP World History test with all questions answered and explained.
ISBN 978-1-4380-7630-0, $18.99, Can$22.99

Barron's AP Q&A World History
600 Questions and Answers
Christina Giangrandi
This all-new, handy AP test prep guide features 600 questions and thoroughly explained answers. Learn why your answer is correct—and the rationale behind why each other answer choice is incorrect, thereby reinforcing the facts you need to know in order to answer each question correctly on your AP exam. Practice questions and answers help you review history from the foundations of civilization circa 600 B.C.E. to world cultures of the twenty-first century.
ISBN 978-1-4380-1125-7, $16.99, Can$21.50

Ultimate AP World History
Find everything you need to score a 5 on your AP World History exam—and **save over 20% OFF** items when purchased separately! Includes *Barron's AP World History*, *Barron's AP World History Flash Cards*, and *Barron's AP Q&A World History*.
ISBN 978-1-4380-7922-6, $47.99, Can$59.99

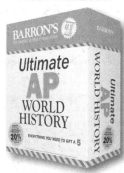

Available at your local bookstore or visit **www.barronseduc.com**

Prices subject to change without notice.

Barron's Educational Series, Inc.
250 Wireless Blvd.
Hauppauge, N.Y. 11788
Order toll-free: 1-800-645-3476

In Canada:
Georgetown Book Warehouse
34 Armstrong Ave.
Georgetown, Ontario L7G 4R9
Canadian Orders: 1-800-247-7160

#320 R 6/18

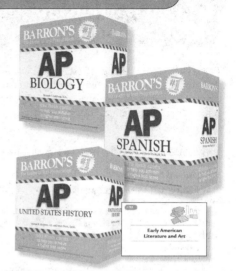